Total Quality Management as a Holistic Management Concept

The European Model
for Business Excellence

Springer
Berlin
Heidelberg
New York
Barcelona
Budapest
Hong Kong
London
Milan
Paris
Santa Clara
Singapore
Tokyo

Klaus J. Zink

Total Quality Management as a Holistic Management Concept

The European Model for Business Excellence

With 165 Figures

 Springer

Prof. Dr. Klaus J. Zink
University of Kaiserslautern
Chair for Industrial Management and Human Factors
Postfach 3049
67663 Kaiserslautern
Germany

All rights reserved. Authorized translation of the German edition
"TQM als integratives Managementkonzept"
published by Carl Hanser Verlag Munich Vienna, 1995

ISBN 3-540-63958-6 Springer-Verlag Berlin Heidelberg New York

Die Deutsche Bibliothek – CIP-Einheitsaufnahme
Zink, Klaus J.: Total quality management as a holistic management concept: the European
model for business excellence / Klaus J. Zink. – Berlin; Heidelberg; New York; Barcelona;
Budapest; Hong Kong; London; Milan; Paris; Santa Clara; Singapore; Tokyo: Springer, 1997
  ISBN 3-540-63958-6

© Springer-Verlag Berlin · Heidelberg 1998
Printed in Germany

Hardcover-Design: Erich Kirchner, Heidelberg

SPIN 10662870   42/2202-5 4 3 2 1 0 – Printed on acid-free paper
JK

Preface

Even after years of dealing with Total Quality it is still a challenge to achieve Business Excellence by applying this management approach.

Total Quality Management is now established in Europe. This was supported by the European Model for Business Excellence and the many national quality awards derived from it. It is for this reason that the European Model is the focus of the following chapters. In addition, there are two further objectives:

1. to show that TQM is not a short-term oriented rationalisation programme, but a holistic management concept;

2. to describe how such a management concept can be implemented in practice as an organisational development process.

In order to emphasise the practical relevance various examples from different industries will be shown, which have been taken from a collection of case studies (Zink, K.J. (Ed.): Successful TQM - Inside Stories from European Quality Award Winners, Gower Publishing House, London 1997). In the third part of the book relevant management tools will be explained. Since every tool will be described separately there might be some repetitions e.g. of figures.

In addition to the people that helped to work out the examples shown in the book I would particularly like to thank those who assisted in the translation of the German text: Mrs. S. Broschart, Mrs. C. Cannon, Mrs. C. Özdemir and Mrs. C. Vickers as well as Mr. Dipl.-Wirtsch.-Ing. T. Bäuerle, Mr. Dipl.-Wirtsch.-Ing. U. Klein, Mr. Dipl.-Wirtsch.-Ing. A. Schmidt, Mr. Dipl.-Wirtsch.-Ing. W. Voß and Mr. cand.-Wirtsch.-Ing. T. Wunder. Moreover, my thanks to Mr. Dipl.-Wirtsch.-Ing. M. Egger who was responsible for coordination and layout and for Mr. cand.-Wirtsch.-Ing. S. Athanasiadis, Mr. cand.-Wirtsch.-Ing. H. Köhler, Mr. cand.-Wirtsch.-Ing. T. Schütz and Mr. cand.-Wirtsch.-Ing. S. Steck who supported Mr. Egger in fulfilling his task.

Finally, I would like to thank Springer Publishing House and in particular Dr. W. A. Müller for publishing this book.

Kaiserslautern, Summer 1997   Prof. Dr. Klaus J. Zink

Table of Contents

Part III: Selected Managerial Methods in Context of Total Quality

Comments and Registers

Part I:
Business Excellence through Total Quality

1 Present situation

The final years of the 20th century which is now drawing to a close have led to a new line-up within international competition. Significant changes have occurred within the triad of Southeast Asia (in particular Japan, but also the "Four Small Tigers"), the USA and Europe. In the post war period, Japan has discovered how to successfully conquer the economic dominance of Europe and the USA. Certainly, this was favoured by changing external conditions regarding economic policy (e.g. the role of the Ministry of International Trade and Industry (MITI) in Japan), the money markets (better availability of capital at low interest rates) and a favourable cultural environment (for participation and group work). Nevertheless, this success cannot be traced back only to these conditions.

The growing market share of Japanese car manufacturers in the USA demonstrated Japan's new economic power. It shows what international competitiveness means today: outstanding customer orientation based on flexible reaction to marketplace needs. This requires systematic recording of customer needs - or better, customer problems - and the offer of adequate solutions within a reasonable time frame. The latter aspect can be termed "Time to Market" and applies particularly to the problem of drawn-out development periods.

Furthermore, costs have to be in proportion to the benefits reaped from products or services. Here again, the Japanese automotive industry has demonstrated that they have achieved equal or even superior quality standards compared to Western competitors. This is illustrated by long warranty periods of approximately three years by most Japanese manufacturers. In Japan, outstanding quality is mostly achieved through robust production processes while in Europe, the vision is often restricted to quality assurance in the sense of testing. This strategy requires extensive investments in test facilities, it cannot, however, prevent high fractions defective. A study by Germany's "Arbeitsgemeinschaft Industrieller Forschungsvereinigungen" (AIF, Association of Industrial Research Organisations) shows that the expenses for securing product quality in absolute figures equal the total investment per year, and as a percentage, exceed the net operating margin in industry.[1] This leads to considerable problems for international competitiveness.

Inspired by the Japanese success story, European companies thoroughly discussed management concepts coming from the Far East and tried to do what the Japanese had done after Word War II: They intended to copy and take over the concepts of those who were successful. This can be seen especially in times of a weak economy with sell-by dates of latest management concepts becoming shorter and shorter and impressive headwords superseding each other. Quality Circles, Kanban, Just-In-Time, Time-Based-Management, Total Productive Maintenance, Total Quality Control, Quality Function Deployment, Simultaneous Engineering, Kaizen and - in the recent past - Lean Production, Lean Management, or Business Reengineering are just a few randomly selected examples. Have these concepts maintained or restored economic competitiveness, either on a national or on a worldwide level?

This question is answered by the fact that currently several key European industries find themselves in a structural crisis. So, none of the concepts mentioned before has turned the tide of events. However, a hopeful perspective comes from the USA where the automotive industry has gained ground again after a severe economic crisis. Since the beginning of 1993, the Big Three[2] have won back market shares from Japanese manufacturers. Although this success is, of course, at least partly based on a favourable exchange rate between the US-Dollar and the Japanese Yen, it is also bound to the better quality of American cars, improved production methods reducing production costs, and visibly shortened development times. Therefore, with careful optimism, the conclusion can be drawn that America's automotive industry has learned some of their lessons. Nevertheless, considerable differences can be recognised within this industry and even within single companies as far as their success in regaining competitiveness through enhanced quality is concerned.

A similar situation can be found in the European automotive industry, where initially Japanese manufacturers were controlled by import quotas rather than competition via better products and improved concepts. It was the MIT world-wide study on the automotive industry which first led to a more detailed analysis of Japanese production concepts, in particular the concept of Lean Management. However, there are of course some manufacturers in this industry (e.g. Renault) who improved their market position even earlier through holistic concepts.

Before analysing differences between successful and less successful approaches, changed external conditions have to be taken into consideration. The Japanese companies' ability to better adapt to these shifting demands has contributed considerably to their outstanding success.

The following aspects illustrate some of the present and future challenges all competitors have to face:

- ❑ Globalisation has intensified competition because customers can compare products or problem solutions worldwide according to their cost-benefit-ratio.

- ❑ Cost structures also become comparable world-wide, whereby labour, always being pushed to the fore in some West-European countries, is only *one* element.

- ❑ The interdependence of organisation and cost structures becomes apparent.

- ❑ The role of human resources is an increasingly important factor.

- ❑ Ecological effects of industrial production are critically analysed.

- ❑ Qualified industrial workers show increased demands on their work. This development is supported because many of them come from the "generation of heirs" with interests being shifted from merely financial aspects to facets like interesting and satisfying tasks.

- ❑ Because more and more assets are in private hands today, the customer's market power will steadily rise.

All these trends directly or indirectly contribute to an increase in the influence of customers in all economic sectors. That is why companies have to remember the truism that the customer pays the wages. This awareness must be reflected by outstanding customer orientation which certainly has different facets: Products and services have to contribute in order to solve a customer's problem. Their costs have to be in proportion with the benefits whereby the latter are determined by time (quick solution) and adequacy (appropriate solution).

However, these are not new insights. Numerous management conferences have discussed topics such as "Market-Driven Company Management". Countless seminars have been held on "Time-Based-Management". It is impossible to tell the number of cost-cutting programmes propagated over the years. If all the "homework" in this context has been done, then why are there still problems?

The core of these problems can be found in the word "Programme"!

We have never had a lack of programmes - every day, new ideas are crowding our letter-box. The problem of most, if not of all these programmes is that they are often one-sided and mostly implemented without creating a suitable environment. Predominant fixation on short-term success and cost-cutting causes further problems, supported by the traditional industrial management concept of accountancy.

Nowadays, achieving quality and quantity simultaneously requires a radical change in the methods of thinking, organisation, information and payment within the framework of a customer-oriented company structure. Here, partial concepts have to be replaced by integrative management concepts.

2 The necessity of integrative management concepts

A long-term solution for the problems described in the introduction requires an integrative approach that can only be found within a corresponding management concept. Therefore, it is necessary to examine how "traditional" concepts fit in with these demands.

2.1 Demands on integrative management concepts

Management as a function in principle comprises all processes and functions resulting from the division of labour in an organisation (such as planning, organisation, leadership and supervision). However, many different interpretations have emerged since the term first evolved in the trail of industrialisation. The understanding not only depends on the individual conception of the world and the vision of man, but also on the (scientific or practical) perspective.[3]

Some concepts focus on personnel topics, others are restricted to methods and tools. However, all of them show a model structure based on explicit or, more usually, implicit premises (e.g. many management theories are based on the "economic man" conception whose behaviour is absolutely rational). That is why they simplify reality or disregard external factors that can be observed in practice. Thus, these models are often unable to adequately reflect and explain reality. Furthermore, in times when the economy is booming and when there is only limited competition, there is no vigorous drive to analyse in detail the success factors of management.

However, competitive pressure is currently rising and most markets and market segments are more dynamic and complex than ever before. These trends have altered traditional prerequisites and require a corresponding change of paradigms. Bleicher and the St. Galler School have developed the concept of Integrative Management as an answer to these developments.[4] It is based on the assumption that only holistic thinking can contribute to solving complex problems. An integral, systematic approach is characterised by the following aspects:[5]

- ❑ Companies as open systems closely connected with the environment

- ❑ The approach based on both analytical and synthetic thinking and on the notion of network structures

❏ Linear thinking in simple cause and effect schemes replaced by sytems thinking (e.g. leadership as a feedback loop for continuous improvement)

❏ Thinking and cooperation across functional and departmental lines

❏ Structures and processes to cope with the increasing significance of information

According to Ulrich[6], three management dimensions are differentiated: normative, strategic and operative tasks. However, their interdependence is explicitly emphasised. They are integrated via a management philosophy clarifying the theoretical basis of everyone's actions.[7] It determines the vision, or final objective, and supports commitment of all participants.[8]

Starting from the vision, general normative targets can be derived. The corporate constitution (e.g. allocation of competence and responsibility at management level) can be found within the structural dimension. The latter also refers to how the organisation pays attention to various (internal and external) interests, and solves conflicts. The personnel dimension of *normative management* is reflected in the corporate culture and realised via corporate policy, putting the vision through missions in concrete terms.

Strategic management translates these normative premises into organisation structures, management systems, and certain behaviour patterns. These are determined through a suitable management concept. Strategic management is implemented through corporate planning.[9]

Operative management is the implementation of standards and strategies. This requires systematic implementation processes leading to definite results and supporting cooperation. In a dynamic environment the management process must adapt to changes in external conditions.

The following figure shows these correlations:

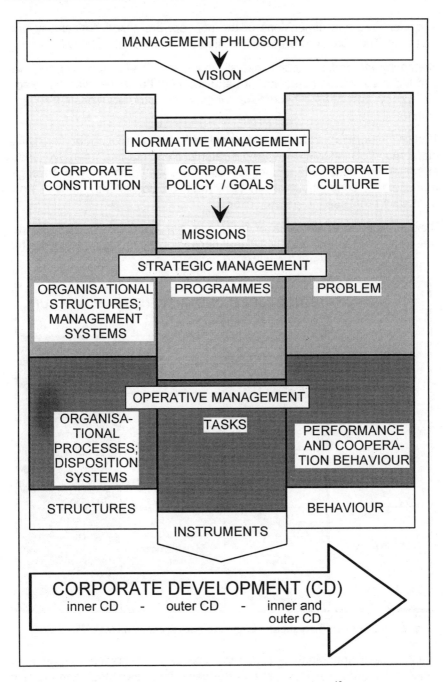

Fig. 1: Normative, strategic and operative management[10]

The elements and dimensions of the concept are linked horizontally and vertically. They are combined by the integrative power of a joint vision.

Horizontal integration means that all "instruments" and activities are embedded in structural, personnel or behavioural patterns, i.e. that, for example, policy and targets become a function of corporate constitution and culture.

Vertical integration includes the consistent transformation of normative elements into strategic ones, and strategic elements into operative ones. Management behaviour and cooperation are determined by a strategic management concept, which, in turn, must be consistently derived from normative premises (corporate culture).

Bleicher introduces the idea of "harmonisation" through interdimensional "fit". This requires that each individual dimension is consistent in itself. This is called "basic fit"[11] (see the following figure):

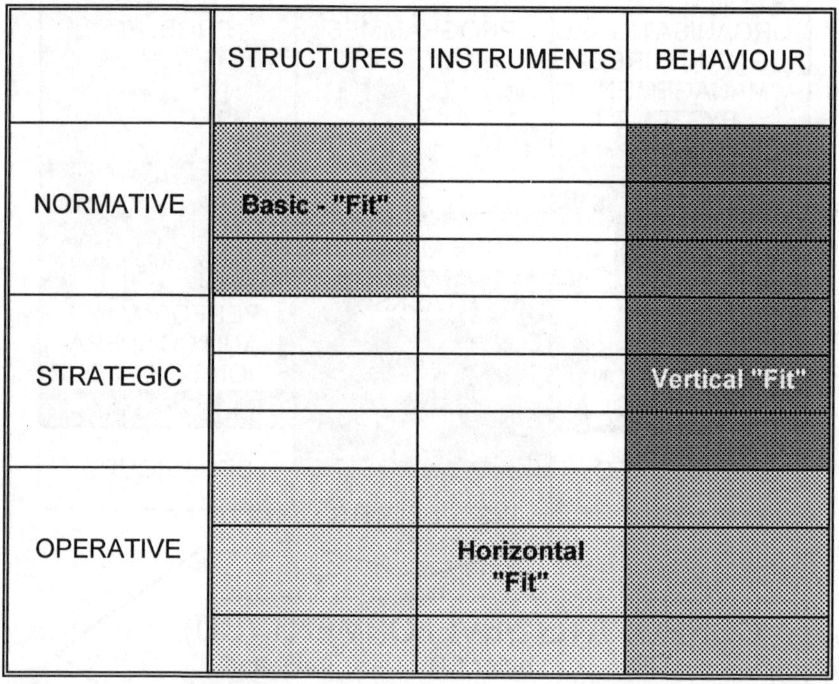

	STRUCTURES	INSTRUMENTS	BEHAVIOUR
NORMATIVE	Basic - "Fit"		
STRATEGIC			Vertical "Fit"
OPERATIVE		Horizontal "Fit"	

Fig. 2:   Harmonising separate management dimensions (see: Bleicher)[12]

These general statements describe the idea of an integrative management concept[13] in principle. They provide the basis for understanding the recent "management concepts" which will now be discussed.

2.2 Other concepts and their assessment

In times of economic decline, numerous management concepts are offered as "canned solutions". They are vigorously promoted by consultants and are emerging together with an intense discussion of Total Quality Management. Due to this development, some recent concepts are briefly outlined in the following discussion, in order to analyse their strengths and weaknesses.

2.2.1 Lean Production (Lean Management)

Few books on economic and organisation sciences have been more popular in Germany than the study by Womack, Jones and Roos[14] on the "International Motor Vehicle Program" of the Massachussetts Institute of Technology (MIT). In this publication, John Krafcik has created the term Lean Production. In earlier publications, "lean" and "fragile" (as opposed to "robust"/"buffered") had been used synonymously.[15]

Daum and Piepel have discussed the concept of Lean Production.[16] They differentiate between the following elements:

a) Lean sales:

   The idea was born in Japan, where manufacturers and car dealers aggressively sell cars by regularly visiting customers, thus creating household profiles in order to improve product development. In return for the customer's cooperation, the car dealer offers a wide range of additional services, such as car registration, delivery of the new car, picking up the old car, and other gestures of good will, which strengthens customer loyalty. The sales channel is lean in so far as there are considerably less car dealers on the first sales level (compared to western nations).

b) Lean product development:

   Lean product development requires up-to-date information on customer demands. It is characterised by the following four aspects:

   - interdisciplinary teams with clearly assigned members

   - team leader with extensive responsibilities (authoritative project leader)

- comprehensive information provided as soon as possible (to determine and solve problems, such as allocation of resources)

- simultaneous development of automotive parts, production processes, and equipment (simultaneous engineering)

c) Lean procurement:

This aspect refers to the cooperation with suppliers. Supply chains are organised hierarchically with few key suppliers on the first level. The latter join the production planning team and take part in a mutual exchange of experiences in order to improve production processes. They in turn cooperate in the same way on the next level, i.e. with indirect suppliers. This relationship affects various issues: manufacturers and suppliers jointly work on cost reduction. They agree on target costs under the premise of reasonable profits for each partner. This is achieved through value engineering and analysis allowing a decrease in procurement costs.

d) Lean production:

Here, parts manufacture (e.g. forging and moulding) and assembly must be separated:

In *parts manufacture,* reducing change-over times from several hours to a few minutes allows the cost-effective production of smaller batches, and thereby a considerable inventory reduction. A further advantage can be found in shorter feedback loops for employees, which may lead to quality improvements.

In *assembly,* Kanban-control and Just-In-Time production have led to a dramatic inventory reduction. According to the vision of "Zero Defects", there is no need for rework. Thereby less floor space is needed. Eventually, space between work benches is kept to a minimum in order to improve communication and further personal contact. Semi-autonomous work groups integrating manifold indirect tasks are another element. If an error occurs, the conveyor belt stops, the cause is determined and systematically eliminated in order to avoid reoccurrence.

These new structures require both qualified and motivated employees.

Precisely these last elements of Lean Production are based on the Toyota Production System (TPS) with the prevention of any kind of waste as its major aim ("Muda").[17] Many of these ideas are 20 years old or more. They focus on production and thus mainly contribute to improving the production system. However, this also applies to supplier and customer relationships and those functions within the company which support the production process in the narrow sense.

Discussing the term "lean", we have, on the one hand, to remember where these ideas come from and, on the other hand, watch the further developments taking place in the country of its origin:

Initially, one could argue that the term "lean" is hardly suitable to describe everything that is labelled as such. Is "lean" really sufficient as the only strategic target? What does "lean" really mean? Referring to TPS, it means avoiding every kind of waste (Japan.: "Muda"), whereby there are different types of Muda: e.g. overproduction (inventory buildup), excessive transportation, manufacturing nonconforming items, unnecessary procedures within processes, or waiting time - in other words, anything which fails to add value.[18]

Referring to the concept of Daum and Piepel mentioned above, we have to discuss "lean sales" first. Womack et al. believe that "the system makes no sense unless cars are built to order and delivered almost immediately."[19] This means that sales replace expensive and often inaccurate market research on the one hand, and, on the other hand, require smooth production flow resulting in dramatic reduction of storage costs.[20] Better customer orientation based on a systematic use of customer feedback increases customer loyalty.

Nowadays, it is generally accepted that "lean product development" is necessary to optimise processes and to reduce "Time to Market". However, recent studies show further possibilities for improvement even with suppliers in the automotive industries, who are traditionally at the leading edge.[21] In this context, the idea of simultaneous engineering plays a decisive role, however, it often fails in practice due to a lack of communication between different functions and departments (e.g. marketing and development).[22]

"Lean purchasing channel" is another buzzword that has attracted much attention in recent years. Many organisations have reduced the number of suppliers and boosted cooperation with them. When transferring this strategy to the Western hemisphere, however, the particular economic situation of Japanese suppliers has to be taken into consideration. Furthermore, the question of how profits from joint improvement projects are distributed among the partners has to be answered.

"Lean Production" will be discussed under the following three aspects:

a) Customer-oriented production:

TPS is based on considerably reduced change-over times, i.e. more flexibility and less inventories, leading to great advantages even for mass production. Kanban or Just-In-Time and other tools necessary for control and planning have been used in Germany for years.[23] The storage reduction is, however, generally only possible if potential fluctuations in quality and capacity are counter-balanced by time buffers between the shifts, or through workers' overtime.

b) Reduction in the need for space:

Robust production processes allow smaller rework areas. However, one should not try to copy the concept completely: if machinery is placed so closely together that operation, maintenance, and repair become difficult for the average European, one has to keep in mind that real estate costs are not comparable to those in Japan.

c) Focus on people:

In recent literature on Lean Production, those who proclaimed the vision of an automated plant without human operators have now changed their mind and placed people at the center of their concepts. Again, one should remember the Toyota Production System. Although workers receive additional indirect tasks (such as maintenance or quality checks), the work itself contains practically no leeway (e.g. also by Poka-yoke), and is part of a steady assembly-line system. The following figure shows the differences between various forms of group work.

Division of Labour according to Taylor/Ford	Lean Production Group concepts	Self-managing work groups
high division of labour	high division of labour	division of labour determinable
high standardisation	high standardisation	goal instead of path orientation (separate assignment of activities and work scheduling)
assembly line production	assembly line production	work stations, work on a stationary object
responsibility for and payment according to quantity	responsibility for quantity, quality and costs	responsibility for quantity, quality and costs
no involvement in improvement process	continuous improvement (KAIZEN) as integrated element	continuous improvement through Quality Circles (e.g. to solve interface problems)
"direct" (execution) tasks only	integration of "indirect" tasks, especially Quality Management, failure correction (e.g. inspection, set up, maintenance)	integration of "indirect" tasks, especially Quality Management, failure correction (e.g. inspection, set up, maintenance)
continuity ensured through material buffer, but no time buffering between shifts	no material buffer: Jjust-Iin-Ttime or Zzero Ddefects production, but buffer between shifts for reworking and loss of output (Management by Stress)	material buffer for de-chaining of subsystems (individual handling)

Fig. 3:   Taylorism, Lean Production and Self-managing work groups

The additional implementation of the Andon principle (i.e. when errors occur, stopping the process until the cause has been determined and eliminated) contributes to eliminating the definitive source of defects. Nevertheless, it creates considerable strain for all involved. This fact, and the need to make up for these interruptions at the end of the regular shift may have led to Japanese car manufacturers to experiment with alternative forms of group work (e.g. Toyota in the new part of the Tahara plant or Honda in the new factory for the NSX). The results of a survey carried out in a Mazda plant in the USA also report about the employees` (dis)satisfaction with this system.[24] We must therefore seriously ask ourselves whether we are preaching something here, which they are at least considering abolishing in Japan.

In summary we see that it is once more better to concentrate on the most important issues and to replace complexity with simplicity. This motto gives a simple but adequate description of the term "lean". Lean concepts have led to rediscovering people and putting them at the centre. However, the above-mentioned Mazda survey shows that this aspect tends to get lost in practice.

One deficit of the concept is its lack of visionary power ("What is the vision for the future of 'lean'?"). Another problem refers to its image as a cost-reduction programme, which is predominant at least in practice ("What potential is there for motivation - rather than fear?"). These are parallels to earlier programmes, like Zero-Base Budgeting. Furthermore, the concept is focused exclusively to microeconomics. Macroeconomic effects or impacts on society such as lay-offs are neglected.

Lean Production - or Lean Management - is primarily a concept designed to erase past mistakes. All in all, it is a partial concept with its focal point on processes and resources. It is not yet a holistic approach.

2.2.2   KAIZEN

KAIZEN, and the Continuous Improvement Process (CIP) are further terms taken from discussions in the recent past. Staying close to Imai, the inventor of KAIZEN, and his book now being sold in the nth edition, the first thing that can be found is an umbrella:

Fig. 4:   The KAIZEN umbrella[25]

On observation, it appears that the author has done little more than pack all the currently fashionable terms under an umbrella, label it KAIZEN, give it the subtitle "The key to Japanese success in competition", and use this to start a new "doctrine".

Apart from this complicated figure, the following issues are characteristics of KAIZEN:

a) KAIZEN as process-oriented management (in contrast to being exclusively result-oriented) as shown in the following figure:

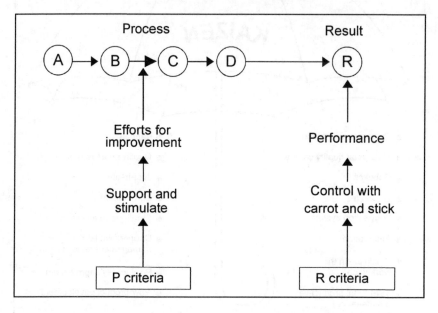

Fig. 5:   Process-oriented criteria (P) vs. result-oriented criteria (R) [26]

b) KAIZEN and innovation

Here, particular emphasis is placed on the fact that innovations in the West can be distinguished by their aim for a breakthrough. In contrast, KAIZEN means innovation in small stages. Figure 6 shows these differences.[27]

Stabilising minor changes is certainly easier than innovative leaps, however both cases require adequate structural conditions. Otherwise, even small improvements will not stand the long run, which is confirmed in our experiences with quality Circles.[28]

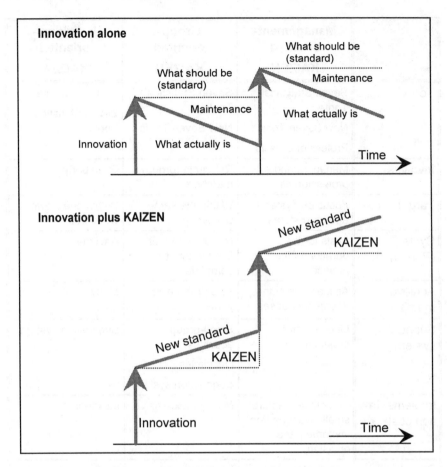

Fig. 6:   Innovation and KAIZEN[29]

c) KAIZEN as a change process:

The three aspects of KAIZEN refer to management, groups, and individuals. The following figure goes into further detail:

	Management-oriented KAIZEN	Group-oriented KAIZEN	Individual-oriented KAIZEN
Tools	Seven Statistical Tools New Seven Tools Professional skills	Seven Statistical Tools New Seven Tools	Common sense Seven Statistical Tools
Involves	Managers and professionals	QC-circle (group) members	Everybody
Target	Focus on systems and procedures	Within the same workshop	Within one's own work area
Cycle (Period)	Lasts for the duration of the project	Requires four or five months to complete	Anytime
Achieve-ments	As many as man-agement chooses	Two or three per year	Many
Supporting system	Line and staff project team	Small-group activities QC circles Suggestion system	Suggestion system
Implementa-tion cost	Sometimes requires small investment to implement the decision	Mostly inexpensive	Inexpensive
Result	New system and facility improvement	Improved work procedure Revision of standard	On-the-spot improvement
Booster	Improvement in managerial performance	Morale improvement Participation Learning experience	Morale improvement KAIZEN awareness Self-development
Direction	Gradual and visible improvement Marked upgrading of current status	Gradual and visible improvement	Gradual and visible improvement

Fig. 7:   The three aspects of KAIZEN[30]

It is obvious that the company must create basic conditions for a permanent review. Everyone's involvement will later be described as a people-centered approach. When trying to pinpoint the core of KAIZEN, one encounters the problem that in many cases the relation between KAIZEN and Total Quality Control (TQC) is not clearly defined. On the one hand, TQC is interpreted as one element of KAIZEN, but on the other hand, described as the "motorway" to KAIZEN. These statements contradict not only countless publications where these terms are used as synonyms, but also Imai's statement "Within the framework of TQC, profit and KAIZEN are closely linked". Does TQC therefore include KAIZEN? In favour of this view are the instruments suggested (the "seven statistical tools" and the "new seven") and the organisational structures intended to provide the basis for continuous improvement (e.g. quality circles).[31]

Furthermore, other technical elements of the Toyota Production Systems[32] turn up again, giving an impression of KAIZEN as a "general store" of more or less up-to-date tools. Due to this development, issues such as cross functional management, policy audit, customer orientation and the relationship with suppliers are discussed. As the idea of KAIZEN is rather old and originated in Japan under the specific social conditions of that time, environmental and social issues barely play a role. People orientation - as far as Toyota or the lean concept are concerned - should be analysed critically. However, it would be desirable and helpful for many companies if they were able to achieve an atmosphere of continuous improvement in their organisation (including all employees!). This, however, requires the creation of structural conditions[33], including, for example, new reward systems - an aspect Imai only deals with briefly.

In this respect, KAIZEN is more a philosophy or an attitude of mind rather than a self-contained concept. Many statements only make sense in connection with Total Quality Control - and continuous improvement is one more indispensable requirement for promoting total quality.

KAIZEN cannot suffice as an holistic management concept, or even merely as an innovation concept, because improvements carried out exclusively in small steps run the risk of adhering to the present state.

As mentioned before, "group-centered" KAIZEN has been practised for years in Germany in the form of quality circles. Here too, experience has shown that it has to be incorporated within integral concepts, along with appropriate structural conditions.[34]

2.2.3   Business Reengineering

"Business Reengineering" by Hammer and Champy has caused quite a stir in the United States as well as in Germany. The authors promise a radical cure for the company.[35] The process of reengineering begins with the question "Why do we do the things we do?"[36] It aims at basically restructuring the company,[37] in order to achieve improvements which by far exceed benefits from traditional rationalisation measures.[38]

Business reengineering - according to Hammer and Champy - is looking for new models of work organisation while throwing overboard the paradigms of industrialisation, such as division of labour, economies of scale, supervision, etc.[39]

Analysing the constituents of business reengineering,[40] some vaguely familiar aspects, such as (re-)integration concepts combining fragmented tasks (horizontal integration) or employee empowerment (vertical integration) can be found. This subject has been discussed under the heading "structuring of labour" since the 1970's[41] and has been taken up again in more recent years as "semi-autonomous work groups" (referred to in Hammer and Champy as "case groups").

Integrating different functions in the workplace through electronic data processing (EDP) was discussed relatively early in Scheer.[42] The theory that work should be carried out in the most logical location is part of Höhn's "Harzburger Führungsmodell".[43]

Hammer and Champy's book is innovative as it combines these already existing ideas. Furthermore, information technology plays an important role - in contrast to most of the above-mentioned older sources. In other words, new technologies create a basis for radically questioning existing organisational concepts.[44] Reengineering means not being satisfied with average results. The concept, however, recognises that this can only be achieved through a far-reaching change in corporate culture: new corporate values are necessary.[45] Thus, the prerequisites for successful implementation or the reasons for failure are mostly identical to those of other concepts of change.[46]

When comparing business reengineering with, for example, lean management, Hammer and Champy's statements on customer orientation or corporate culture are considerably clearer. However, the attempt to distinguish these from "quality programmes" also highlights the limits of business reengineering:[47] The current quality movement is blamed for only referring to existing company processes, and for pursuing solely the aim of continuous improvement in the sense of KAIZEN. Although this misunderstanding can be disproved by a number of sources,[48] the statement shows that business reengineering is mainly a methodical restructuring concept which nevertheless also includes the goals of change. Continuous improvement, which is intentionally left out of this comparison (e.g. using survey and feedback methods) is, however, an essential requirement for rendering a tool to change a holistic management concept. Nevertheless, this does not reduce the significance of implementing change in a specific company situation.

2.2.4   Organisational intelligence or learning organisation

Like the previously mentioned concepts of Lean Production and KAIZEN, "Organisational Intelligence" (O.I.) also has Japanese origins - at least in its present form of implementation.[49] For many years, Japan experts[50] have announced that the next step of the "Japanese challenge" would be a new way of dealing with knowledge. While knowledge, intelligence, and problem solving ability in general used to be treated mainly as implicit productive factors, organisational intelligence as a product and process is now put at the center. O.I. processes (perception, storing, learning, communication and decision-making) lead to O.I. products (data, information, knowledge).

Information and communication technologies play an important role as they do in Hammer and Champy. They are not supposed to replace human intelligence, but rather to supplement it. The strength of O.I. lies on the one hand in its holistic approach, and on the other hand in its general applicability in the sense that it is independent of specific external conditions. O.I. is often discussed together with Organisational Design. It aims at increasing an organisation's ability to solve problems by transforming it into a learning organisation[51]. The main focus is particularly on people-centered aspects such as perception, learning, communication and decision-making as a management task. Although until now the concept has generally shown little interest in information technologies, the use of CBT (Computer-Based Training) has been discussed within concepts aimed at self-controlled learning.[52] Team learning and learning networks once more play an important role, particularly in modern vocational training.[53]

Those few publications on O.I. not written in Japanese show that it is a meta-concept which can improve competitiveness. The emphasis is put - here even more than in business reengineering - on the methodical approach.

2.2.5   Summary

The concepts mentioned above have been thoroughly discussed in recent years, both in science and in consultancy. They are to be compared with the demands on a holistic management concept. This is particularly necessary, because Lean Production, KAIZEN and Business Reengineering claim to be able to solve the current economic problems.

A holistic management concept should have a normative, strategic and an operative dimension. These dimensions must fit to become a holistic approach. From this point of view the concepts presented here are only fragmented visions.

The first element is a shared vision with integrating power, which has something to offer for all members of the organisation. "Being lean" as such is just as inadequate as KAIZEN (continuous improvement). Neither determine the final destination - which is the purpose of the vision. Business Reengineering only contains some general statements (e.g. under the label "the new working world"[54]). On the contrary, there is already an (implicit) vision in the definition of O.I, it is however unclear what this means for the members of the organisation.

While most concepts (Lean Production, KAIZEN, Business Reengineering) ask for the corporate culture to change, little is said concerning transformation in strategies or operative goals regarding vertical integration. With O.I., this vertical integration becomes visible on an abstract level in the hierarchic structure of the "O.I.-products".

Statements on horizontal integration can only rarely be found in all concepts. They refer to the links between corporate culture, policy, and objectives (e.g. how a culture characterised by people orientation can be aligned with corporate policy, and, most importantly, translated into concrete targets).

All in all, these approaches are, in reality, fragmented concepts. They must be embedded in a comprehensive context, including continuous improvement, process optimisation, customer orientation, and economic success, along with aspects such as environmental protection and people satisfaction.

3 Business Excellence through integrative management concepts

Before Total Quality Management can be properly assessed as an integrative management concept, it is necessary to define some basic terms. The aim is to show how TQM differs from traditional quality management or quality assurance. Therefore, in a first step, various quality terms will be described.

3.1 Business Excellence as a new quality understanding

The discussion about a new quality understanding starts as a traditional notion of Quality as found, for example, in DIN 55 350, part 11. This standard defines quality as the composition of a unit (i.e. product or service) with regard to its suitability to fulfil quality requirements. Accordingly, quality is understood as the compliance with requirements or agreed characteristics. This definition illustrates two aspects:

a) The customer's requirements are the decisive factor. Hereby the understanding of "customer" is not restricted to external organisations or individuals who purchase products or services but also includes internal customers, i.e. departments that receive benefits. Suppliers, recipients of benefits and the process of tendering performance can therefore be presented as a system of customer-supplier relationships (see Fig. 8).

Besides this network of internal customer-supplier relationships, there are diverse relationships with external customers. Fig. 9 shows how complex a network between customers and suppliers can be: It becomes clear that it is no trivial matter to define who the actual customer is and, correspondingly, what quality standards are required.

A company's customer orientation can be assessed in two dimensions. On the one hand, there is the way complaints are handled . Are they considered to be an annoying interruption by the customer - turned away by a subordinate employee whenever possible? Or are they understood as an opportunity for improvement and therefore receive the attention of senior management, too? On the other hand, customer orientation becomes visible when employees or departments are confronted with diverging demands from customers and the management. Can they really act on behalf of the customer or are they strictly bound to company interests? Therefore, the relation between customers and the established organisation structures gives decisive clues on customer orientation.

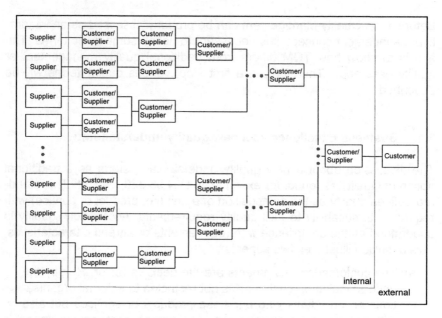

Fig. 8:   Customer-supplier relationships

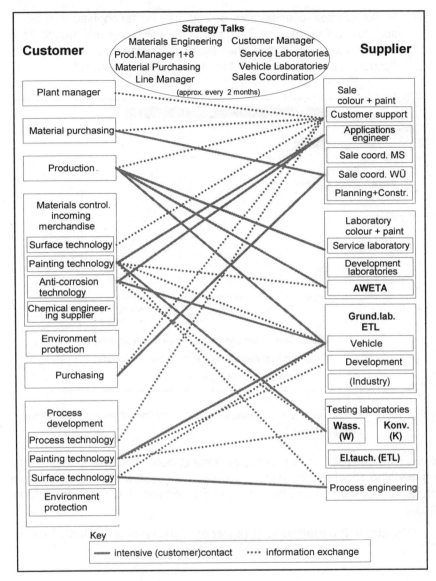

Fig. 9:   Customer-Supplier Relationship between a car and a paint manufacturer"

b) Customer orientation is crucial for a new quality understanding. However, it is only possible to efficiently fulfil customer demands if they are specified and agreed upon by both partners. This in turn means further tasks for those departments that are in close contact with external customers.

In this context, considerable deficits can be recognised in practice. An earlier study by Tavolato et al. which has maintained its
topical relevance, shows that systems engineering in order to
support cooperation with customers can still be improved.

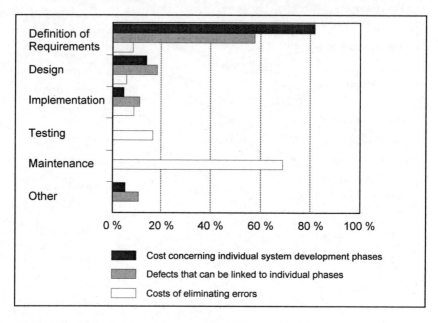

Fig. 10:   Efforts, errors and costs for the elimination of errors in different
             design stages[55]

Even fulfilling specified requirements is not enough, because it does not tell
us anything about further aspects such as the cost-benefit-ratio. Therefore,
customer satisfaction has to be taken as an additional criterion for defining
quality:

**"Quality is the fulfilment of (agreed) requirements for long-term
·customer satisfaction."**

Two further aspects must be dealt with regarding a result-oriented definition of quality:

a) The differentiation between product and service quality, because
   many studies have shown that shortcomings in service are the
   main reason for customers turning to competitors.

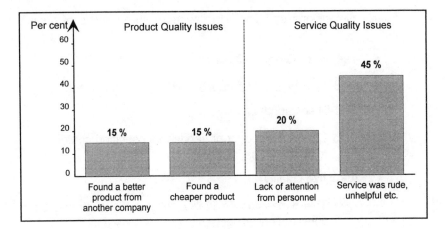

Fig. 11:   Reasons for turning to a competitor [56]

The following quality grid shows how both aspects are linked:

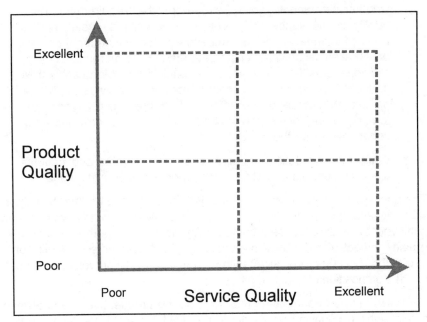

Fig. 12:   The quality grid[57]

b) The question of whether fulfilling agreed requirements contributes
   to long-term customer satisfaction or not. In this context, there
   are two different positions. One of them becomes visible in the

quality dimensions by Kano. He describes three levels of quality:[58]

- "Take-it-for-Granted-Quality"

  ↳ Quality is only perceived when it is insufficient.

- "One-Dimensional-Quality"

  ↳ Quality of product or service as specified contributes to customer satisfaction.

- "Attractive Quality"

  ↳ This dimension of quality delights the customer because it is unexpected.

  ↳ This understanding of quality can barely be evaluated by traditional customer surveys.

The view of "delighting the customer" leads to the discussion whether permanently going beyond specified requirements (best quality in the sense of "happy engineering") is useful, or if it means the same as failing to meet them. Exceeding requirements only makes sense when customers are offered more solutions for their problems than they actually expect: "I am able to solve their problems better than my competitors, or I provide additional benefits that others do not offer." Therefore, going beyond customers' requirements only makes sense when it provides additional benefits for them.

While meeting defined requirements, added value and benefits are to be secured for both *the customer* and *your own company*.

The understanding of quality has changed in the course of time. Initially, it was focused on the quality of product and service, which was mainly achieved by testing. Consequently, quality used to be both input-oriented (quality impact of purchased materials) and output-oriented ("quality products" through comprehensive testing). This idea is still prevalent as shown by the composition of quality costs.

Naturally, quality of purchased materials (in the broadest sense) is always a relevant topic. Saving potentials in this field are even greater because, due to reduced manufacturing penetration, material costs make up 60 % of the total manufacturing costs. Savings in purchased materials are, however, rarely made without a loss of quality. Therefore, (more) intensive cooperation with suppliers is required in order to assure quality in early manufacturing stages. In contrast to former opinions, this must also lead to a reduced number of suppliers. (Keyword: "Single Sourcing"). Such cooperations have been built up, for example, in the automotive industry (e.g. Ford has introduced quality assurance guidelines Q 101 and the concept of "self-affirming suppliers").[59] With the reservation of periodic site visits by the customer, the supplier takes over complete responsibility for:[60]

❑ Testing product quality using statistical process control

❑ Confirming test results on sample reports

❑ Testing the first batches

❑ Maintaining process capability

A survey carried out amongst car manufacturers in Germany showed that these trends will increase in the future:

Question Supplier	How many suppliers are you working with at present?	How will this develop in medium-term? (Goal)	With how many of your suppliers do you have on-line data-connection?	How will the period of validity of contracts change in the next few years?
VW	900 Suppliers	100 Suppliers	permanent on-line contact via logistic headquater	permanent contract
AUDI	900 Suppliers	400 Suppliers	direct on-line contact with 410 suppliers expansion to 90 % of suppliers planned	lifetime and over several years
BMW	1700 Suppliers	450 Suppliers	direct data-link with 45 % of suppliers medium-term expansion to all suppliers	long standing contracts over 2-5 years
Mercedes-Benz	1400 Suppliers	Reduction	data-link with 750 suppliers	long standing contracts
FORD	900 Suppliers	600 Suppliers	1175 (including branches)	long standing contracts
OPEL	1400 Suppliers	1120 Suppliers	on-line contact with 86 % of suppliers medium-term goal: expansion to 99 % of suppliers	long standing contracts

Fig. 13:   What car manufacturers expect from their suppliers in the future[61]

An altered quality understanding also affects the evaluation of suppliers, which is no longer limited to questions about product quality. Figure 14 on the one hand shows the demands of a customer (light grey line) and on the other hand how they were met by the supplier (black line).

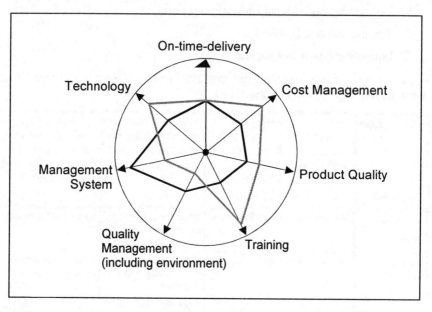

Fig. 14:   Supplier evaluation system of the company KOMATSU[62]

Quality can only be achieved directly in production, making extensive testing obsolete. This truism has increased interest in processes and techniques, and has therefore lead to process orientation. Considerations of this nature result in a "quality loop", i.e. a phase concept for quality assurance, whereby customer-supplier relationships play a particular role (see Fig. 15).

This quality loop starts with market research (defining customer demands) and ends with customer service (after-sales quality), which makes clear that all areas have to be included. In production, robust processes must be implemented, whereas in previous stages (e.g. development), preventive measures (e.g. FMEA - failure mode and effects analysis or design review) have to be enforced. In order to promote customer-supplier relationships, it is vital to establish responsibilities for these measures so that quality can be produced at all. Practical experiences in various companies show the relevance of preventive measures at the planning level, where the majority of errors are caused. They have to be eliminated in production, through end-of-the-line testing, or even after they have been delivered to the customer, leading to great expense (see Fig. 16).

Due to these aspects, costs have to be observed very closely over the whole product life cycle. Naturally, errors discovered in the design stage will cost significantly less than those which are disclosed in the pilot phase or full-scale production (see Fig. 17).

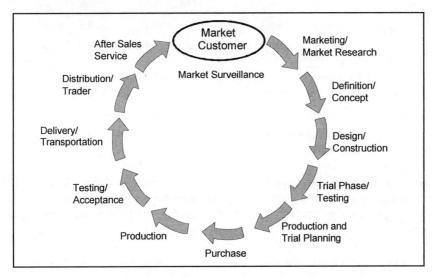

Fig. 15:   Quality circle as a phase concept for quality assurance[63]

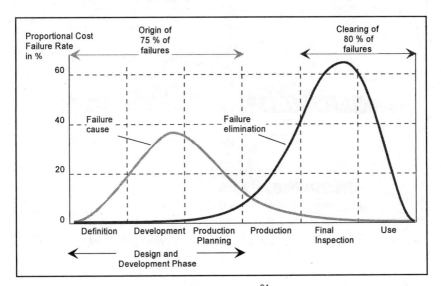

Fig. 16:   Significance of the planning phase[64]

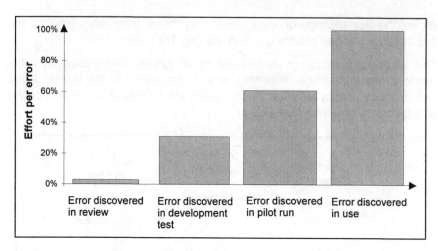

Fig. 17:   Expenditure of time and energy per error in relation to the time of
             discovery of the error[65]

Similarly, a precise description of customer demands and their "translation"
into the company's language - using, for example, Quality Function Deployment - has a very positive effect on the starting costs of a production process.

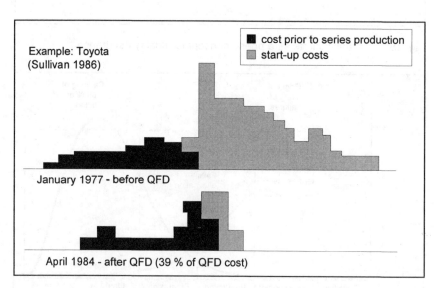

Fig. 18:   Effect of QFD (Quality Function Deployment) on cost structure[66]

Furthermore, up to 60 % of all errors in systems engineering can be traced back to the requirement definition. They determine over 80 % of the total costs for eliminating defects.[67]

With regard to after-sales quality, all turnover-related market reactions should be taken into consideration. In the capital goods industry, this includes not only minimal defect rates, but also expert repairs, availability of spare parts, capacity of the service net, an emergency service and efficient warranty and goodwill services. Turnover-related market reactions can also be the result of an interdependence between warranty costs and periods.

Linking up quality with normative aspects, working conditions must be addressed as a further element of a comprehensive quality understanding. This includes participation, technical, methodical or social training on the job, cooperation within and across departments, and providing adequate operating resources. Such a task centredness of quality has been known for a long time as "Quality of Working Life".

A comprehensive quality understanding also includes an organisation's relationship towards the environment. Therefore, a quality of external relationships can be defined, which refers to social responsibilities - e.g. environmental protection or an active role in the community. Environmental protection has an impact on products (waste management), processes (emissions and consumption of resources) and working conditions (work-related diseases). The social dimension of quality (e.g. social responsibilities) has become obvious in recent years since the issue has been discussed increasingly in non-profit industries including, for example, hospitals. They have to maintain service quality on an increasingly narrow budget and therefore recognise their patients as customers. The demand for quality also appears in the new edition of the German Bundessozialhilfegesetz (BSHG, i.e. Federal Law on Social Welfare).[68] Organisations will be evaluated and receive funds according to the quality of their services - whereby quality is understood in a comprehensive sense.

Obviously, the elements presented here are not independent. While the links between product (or service) and process quality are generally accepted, some still find it difficult to integrate the quality of working life or of external relationships into this concept.

The development of quality understanding, which is, incidentally, by no means common property in Germany, has gone through similar phases in Japan or in the United States. This can be seen in the criteria for national or international quality awards. The Malcolm Baldrige National Quality Award, for example, places strong emphasis on customer orientation,[69] but also regards public responsibility and human resources (see Fig. 19). A corresponding list of criteria for the European Quality Award can be seen in figure 20.

Malcolm Baldrige National Quality Award
Examination Categories, Items and Point Values
1997

Examination Categories / Items	Point Values
1.0 Leadership	**110**
1.1 Leadership System	80
1.2 Public Responsibility and Corporate Citizenship	30
2.0 Strategic Planning	**80**
2.1 Strategy Development Process	40
2.2 Company Strategy	40
3.0 Customer and Market Focus	**80**
3.1 Customer and Market Knowledge	40
3.2 Customer Satisfaction and Relationship Enhancement	40
4.0 Information and Analysis	**80**
4.1 Selection and Use of Information and Data	25
4.2 Selection and Use of Comparative Information and Data	15
4.3 Analysis and Review of Company Performance	40
5.0 Human Resource Development and Management	**100**
5.1 Work Systems	40
5.2 Employee Education, Training and Development	30
5.3 Employee Well-Being and Satisfaction	30
6.0 Process Management	**100**
6.1 Management of Product and Service Processes	60
6.2 Management of Support Processes	20
6.3 Management of Supplier and Partnering Processes	20
7.0 Business Results	**450**
7.1 Customer Satisfaction Results	130
7.2 Financial and Market Results	130
7.3 Human Resource Results	35
7.4 Supplier and Partner Results	25
7.5 Company-Specific Results	130
Total Points:	**1000**

Fig. 19:   Malcolm Baldrige National Quality Award 1997: Examination Categories and Items[70]

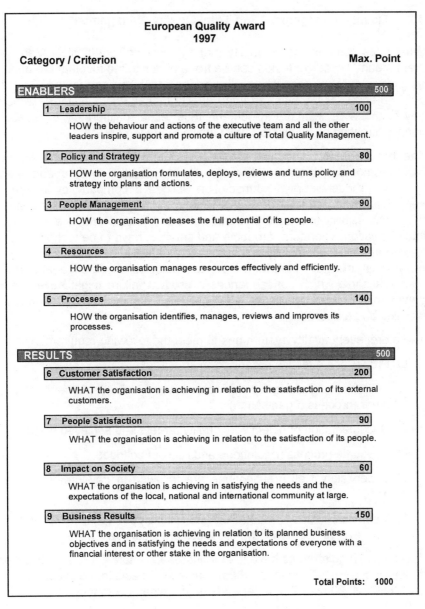

European Quality Award
1997

Category / Criterion   **Max. Point**

ENABLERS   500

1 Leadership   100

HOW the behaviour and actions of the executive team and all the other
leaders inspire, support and promote a culture of Total Quality Management.

2 Policy and Strategy   80

HOW the organisation formulates, deploys, reviews and turns policy and
strategy into plans and actions.

3 People Management   90

HOW the organisation releases the full potential of its people.

4 Resources   90

HOW the organisation manages resources effectively and efficiently.

5 Processes   140

HOW the organisation identifies, manages, reviews and improves its
processes.

RESULTS   500

6 Customer Satisfaction   200

WHAT the organisation is achieving in relation to the satisfaction of its external
customers.

7 People Satisfaction   90

WHAT the organisation is achieving in relation to the satisfaction of its people.

8 Impact on Society   60

WHAT the organisation is achieving in satisfying the needs and the
expectations of the local, national and international community at large.

9 Business Results   150

WHAT the organisation is achieving in relation to its planned business
objectives and in satisfying the needs and expectations of everyone with a
financial interest or other stake in the organisation.

Total Points: 1000

Fig. 20:   The criteria of the European Quality Award[71]

3.2   Quality management and Total Quality Management

What does comprehensive quality management or Total Quality Management mean? Some confusion can be traced back to the fact that the quality assurance system, described in the series of international standards DIN EN ISO 9000 - 9004, was renamed quality management system - without any changes being made in content, thus, either deliberately or unintentionally, creating an affinity to Total Quality Management.[72]

The idea of creating a quality assurance system that can be certified has been promoted by the adaptation of national legislation to European directives on product liability:[73] Jurisdiction obliges a company or its representative (owner, director or board) to take all necessary measures within their responsibility to ensure that only sufficiently safe products are brought into circulation. Therefore, products and services have to be technically up-to-date and all economically viable measures have to be taken. So, a company must maintain state-of-the-art technological knowledge and thoroughly analyse which consequences a product failure might have. Companies are obliged to realise all legal requirements through adequate facilities and processes.

Therefore, every quality system has to meet the following requirements:

❑ Proper and effective organisation structures

❑ Systematically designed work processes which supplement each other (process organisation)

❑ Documentation of objectives, quality targets and achieved results

❑ Adequate process regulations and rules of conduct

❑ Supervision if all prescriptions are followed in day-to-day business

❑ Meaningful testing procedures with results corresponding to long-term experiences from the product's practical use

These legal requirements have lead to increased interest in the certification of quality systems. The standard applicable as a basis for certification (DIN EN ISO 9001, 9002 or 9003) depends on the type of company.

A systematic structure and, even more, a detailed documentation of the quality system ensure robust and reproducible production processes, which in turn are supposed to allow a consistent quality of product or service.

While the standards presume that quality is achieved by *doing things right,* a total quality concept focuses on the question whether *the right things* are done. Customer orientation is the focus of attention, which means that TQM is outwardly bound while the DIN EN ISO 9000 - 9004 are mainly focused on the in-house perspective.

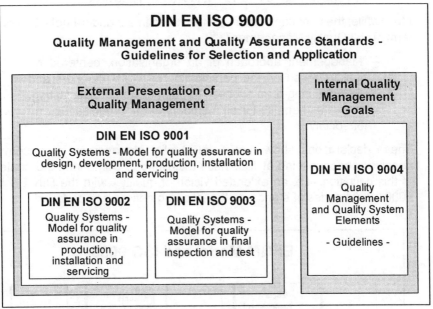

Fig. 21:   The DIN EN ISO 9000 series of standards[74]

Total Quality - as opposed to traditional quality assurance - can be described as follows:[75]

❑ Quality is concerned not only with products and services, but also with (value adding) processes, working conditions and the environment.

❑ Quality is not a purely technical function or department, but rather a systematic process which penetrates the whole organisation.

❑ Total Quality requires an organisational structure which focuses on quality not only on the level of individual work places, but also regarding cooperation between departments and beyond company limits.

❑ The idea of continuous quality improvement must not be limited to production, but should cover all areas of an organisation.

❑ The needs of the customer are the only measure for quality - not
the interests of marketing or production departments.

❑ Comprehensive quality improvements can only be achieved if
everyone is involved - and not just a few specialists.

Meanwhile, these notions have been included in a standard definition of the
term "Total Quality Management":[76]

> "Management approach of an organisation, centered on
> quality, based on the participation of all its members and
> aiming at long-term success through customer satisfaction,
> as well as benefits for all members of the organisation and
> for society."

These declarations show that Total Quality Management is a comprehensive concept aiming at "Business Excellence". Comparing the contents
of this definition - i.e. an extended vision of quality - with the DIN EN ISO
9000 - 9004 series of standards the following deficits can be found:

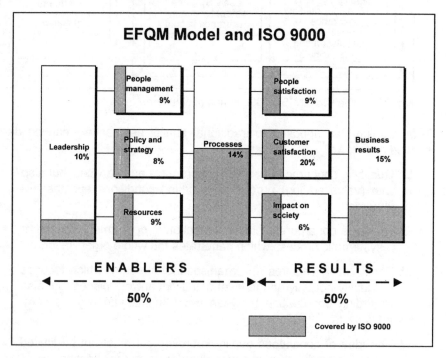

Fig. 22:   Differences in content between Total Quality Management and
            DIN EN ISO 9000[77]

In contrast to the standards, the international evaluation concepts for Total Quality Management were developed on the basis of a comprehensive quality understanding. This can be seen particularly well in the criteria of the Malcolm Baldrige National Quality Award. While the first versions more or less clearly referred to quality in the narrow sense, the award documents for 1997 demonstrate an understanding based on company quality in its widest sense. The following figure contrasts the two sets of criteria from 1989 and 1997.

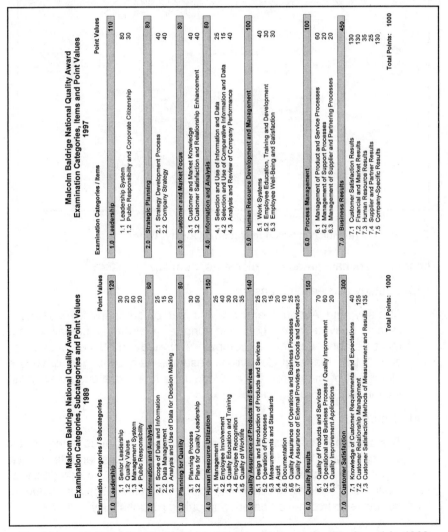

Malcom Baldrige National Quality Award
Examination Categories, Subcategories and Point Values 1989

Examination Categories / Subcategories	Point Values
1.0 Leadership	**120**
1.1 Senior Leadership	30
1.2 Quality Values	20
1.3 Management System	50
1.4 Public Responsibility	20
2.0 Information and Analysis	**60**
2.1 Scope of Data and Information	25
2.2 Data Management	15
2.3 Analysis and Use of Data for Decision Making	20
3.0 Planning for Quality	**80**
3.1 Planning Process	30
3.2 Plans for Quality Leadership	50
4.0 Human Resource Utilization	**150**
4.1 Management	25
4.2 Employee Involvement	40
4.3 Quality Education and Training	30
4.4 Employee Recognition	20
4.5 Quality of Worklife	35
5.0 Quality Assurance of Products and Services	**140**
5.1 Design and Introduction of Products and Services	25
5.2 Operation of Processes	20
5.3 Measurements and Standards	15
5.4 Audit	20
5.5 Documentation	10
5.6 Quality Assurance of Operations and Business Processes	25
5.7 Quality Assurance of External Providers of Goods and Services	25
6.0 Quality Results	**150**
6.1 Quality of Products and Services	70
6.2 Operational and Business Process / Quality Improvement	60
6.3 Quality Improvement Applications	20
7.0 Customer Satisfaction	**300**
7.1 Knowledge of Customer Requirements and Expectations	40
7.2 Customer Relationship Management	125
7.3 Customer Satisfaction Methods of Measurement and Results	135
Total Points:	**1000**

Malcolm Baldrige National Quality Award
Examination Categories, Items and Point Values 1997

Examination Categories / Items	Point Values
1.0 Leadership	**110**
1.1 Leadership System	80
1.2 Public Responsibility and Corporate Citizenship	30
2.0 Strategic Planning	**80**
2.1 Strategy Development Process	40
2.2 Company Strategy	40
3.0 Customer and Market Focus	**80**
3.1 Customer and Market Knowledge	40
3.2 Customer Satisfaction and Relationship Enhancement	40
4.0 Information and Analysis	**80**
4.1 Selection and Use of Information and Data	25
4.2 Selection and Use of Comparative Information and Data	15
4.3 Analysis and Review of Company Performance	40
5.0 Human Resource Development and Management	**100**
5.1 Work Systems	40
5.2 Employee Education, Training and Development	30
5.3 Employee Well-Being and Satisfaction	30
6.0 Process Management	**100**
6.1 Management of Product and Service Processes	60
6.2 Management of Support Processes	20
6.3 Management of Supplier and Partnering Processes	20
7.0 Business Results	**450**
7.1 Customer Satisfaction Results	130
7.2 Financial and Market Results	130
7.3 Human Resource Results	35
7.4 Supplier and Partner Results	25
7.5 Company-Specific Results	130
Total Points:	**1000**

Fig. 23: Criteria for the Malcolm Baldrige National Quality Award in 1989 and 1997[78]

The principle conceptual framework for the Malcolm Baldrige National Quality Award is shown in Fig. 24:

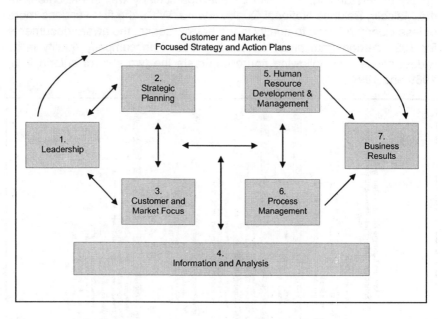

Fig. 24:   The Malcolm Baldrige National Quality Award[79]

The framework has three basic elements, from top to bottom:[80]

❑ Strategy and Action Plans:

Strategy and Action Plans are the set of company-level require-ments, derived from short and long-term strategic planning, that must be done well for the company's strategy to succeed. Strategy and Action Plans guide overall resource decisions and drive the alignment of measures for all work units to ensure customer satis-faction and market success.

❑ System:

The system is comprised of the six Baldrige Categories in the center of the figure defining the organisation, its operations, and its results. All company actions point toward Business Results - a composite of customer, financial, and non-financial performance results, including human resource development and public responsibility.

❑ Information and Analysis:

Information and Analysis (Category 4) are crucial for the effective management of the company and for a fact-based system to improve company performance and competitiveness.

In 1987, President Reagan signed the Malcolm Baldrige National Quality Improvement Act, thus introducing a national quality award. The aim was to react to the increasing competitive pressures from Japan. The European Union (EU) followed this trend in 1988. Supported by the then President of the European Commission, Jaques Delors, CEOs of 14 European companies founded the "European Foundation for Quality Management (EFQM)". The aim of the EFQM is to promote comprehensive quality management concepts in Europe, as well as to support companies when implementing TQM.

The European Quality Award (EQA), which was created and first presented in 1992, plays a key role in EFQM's activities. The award is bestowed to those companies that have achieved excellence by implementing TQM, and can therefore serve as role-models for other companies. The underlying "European Model for Business Excellence" describes the elements of TQM for a model organisation and thus covers the requirements for an integral approach - i.e. involving the whole company.[81]

3.3 From partial concepts to a comprehensive approach

The concepts presented earlier - and the many left undiscussed (such as Time Based Management or Total Productive Maintenance) - are considered as suitable only for particular questions, and therefore labelled as partial concepts. Consequently, the question for alternatives arises. Not surprisingly, Total Quality Management is to be presented here as an integrative management concept. This point of view is based on the integrative management model presented in section 2.1. with a decisive aspect concerning vertical and horizontal harmonisation or fit of different elements.

The model was developed by Bleicher[82]. Its elements are linked through a management philosophy which comes together in a vision. A (quality) management philosophy as an indispensable part of a TQM concept generally contains the following elements:

❑ A multi-dimensional definition of quality:

The starting point for a comprehensive quality policy aiming at "Business Excellence" has to be an extended and multi-dimensional definition of quality. It must integrate the quality of processes, working conditions and external relationships as well as the quality of product and service.

❑ Quality as a company-wide task:

Interesting everyone in quality issues requires the involvement of all departments - whereby planning and administrative functions must not be forgotten. Furthermore, all employees should actively take part in the TQM concept. This refers to those in management positions who understand quality as a leadership task and have to take on the function of a role-model. However, all other employees also have to get involved, which can be achieved by small group concepts taking different attitudes towards cooperation as well as various tasks into account.

❑ Prevention:

Corporate quality policy must aim at prevention. The essential prerequisites for this can be seen in customer and process orientation:

Customer orientation means that long-term satisfaction of external customers is the only goal against which quality can be measured. Therefore, requirements must be clarified and correspondingly applied to internal customer-supplier relationships. This is an elementary prerequisite for quality.

For *process orientation,* turning away from result-oriented quality assurance is particularly significant. Early intervention is only possible if processes and procedures are thoroughly observed. However, this is not restricted to technical processes and their efficiency. Process Management[83] is the systematic analysis of core or key processes within the company aiming at both improving these processes and creating corresponding standards. The starting point is comprehensive, cross-departmental business processes, leading to single processes in specific work stations.

The corporate philosophy is summarised in a finely tuned vision, containing perspectives for the future and providing an idea of identification for all members of the organisation.

Philosophy and vision should be transformed to the level of *normative management* and have to be translated into *missions* and *targets* within the framework of corporate policy. In the case of TQM, this could mean that corporate policy emphasises customer orientation, linking up other aspects such as process and people management as well as the environment.

Implementing vision and corporate policy requires an appropriate *corporate culture* reflecting both in shared values (e.g. concerning customers, employees, the environment). Corporate culture becomes visible in the way complaints are dealt with, suggestions for improvement are treated ("guilt-free atmosphere"), and especially in long-term improvement concepts.

The third element of normative management is *corporate constitution*, which completes the horizontal fit. It contains the structural aspect of organisation - e.g. the standardised basic guidelines for setting targets and matching interests of the organisation, its members, and its environment.[84] Quality management can affect basic conditions of participation and therefore also the target agreeing process and people empowerment. Even the introduction of self-assessment (measuring progress in implementing TQM, in environmental protection, and employee satisfaction) can serve as an example for this kind of basic decision.

Dividing the company into small, legally independent units aiming at improvement in customer orientation (and similarly affecting employee satisfaction) could be another decision made to define corporate constitution. Furthermore, the way in which the works council can be involved in the TQM concept[85] is another constitutional issue, as it reflects corporate culture and policy and thus contributes to horizontal fit.

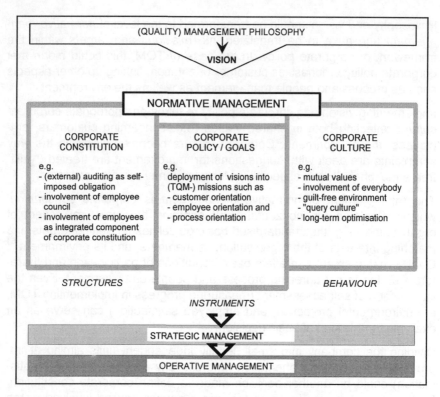

Fig. 25 :   Examples of normative management issues

The next step in an integrative management concept is the translation of normative aspects into *strategic management*. At first, *corporate planning* has to be based on missions or targets, whereby partial plans must be deduced from overall corporate planning in order to guarantee vertical fit. They must always be matched with partial targets. Corporate policy and related targets aimed at strengthening customer orientation can be found for example in the medium-term plans for determining customer satisfaction. Increased participation and identification lead to the strategic alignment of planning. Enhanced customer-orientation requires the designing of an appropriate information system, along with a programme for its implementation.

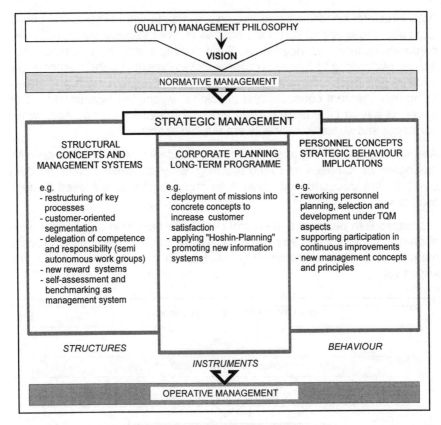

Fig. 26:   Examples of strategic management issues

Strategic corporate planning requires adequate *structural and staff concepts* as well as corresponding management systems. Necessary structural conditions include the knowledge and systematic analysis of key processes underlying the company's critical success factors. In this context, the question of corporate reasoning has to be taken into consideration: Why do we exist? This often leads to a fundamental redesign - which can be a customer-oriented segmentation. Process orientation and participation require reassigning responsibilities and empowering people. Furthermore, compensation systems have to be modified in order to achieve mutual goals within a corporate culture.

Total Quality Management must be understood as Management by Facts, aiming at continuous improvement. Therefore, appropriate management systems are required to ensure that a company is not merely self-centered. Self-Assessment and Benchmarking[86] help to overcome this inward orientation.

Both structural conditions and strategic concepts with behavioural impact must adapt to changed corporate policies in order to generate an adequate corporate culture and vice versa. Such concepts are, for example, personnel planning and human resource development. Further aspects are encouraging people to participate in continuous improvement and developing management concepts and principles. Again, the horizontal fit of all elements has to be ensured. Their practical relevance can be seen when normative and strategic concepts are put into action.

As planning always means "replacing coincidence with error", *operative management* is based on rolling planning, whereby definite plans for daily business are deduced and continuous improvement is achieved through project work.

Processes with decision and control cycles are based on self-control, self-appraisal, statistical process control, KANBAN or other methods of process management. Control parameters must focus on customer benefit and added value.

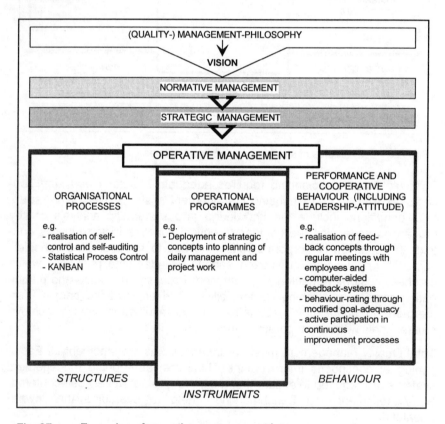

Fig. 27:   Examples of operative management issues

Behavioural impact (performance/cooperation or leadership) can be seen in the way the system is applied. It refers to the method of how feedback systems are designed or used (regular staff meetings and computer-aided systems). Further aspects are how leadership ratings are adequately employed and how participation in the continuous improvement process develops.

A management system is competitive and able to survive if it is continuously improved. Two methodical concepts which ensure this on-going development process have already been mentioned: Self-Assessment and Benchmarking.

Although these few examples can only show some highlights it is obvious that Total Quality Management, if properly understood, is an integrative management concept. The following chapters will describe its practical implementation.

The next figure is a summary of this chapter:

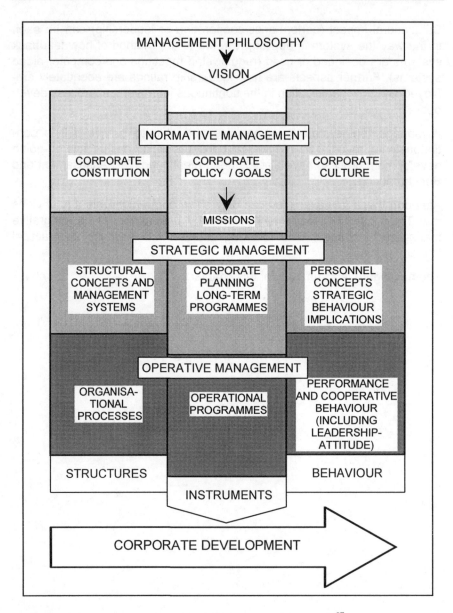

Fig. 28:   Normative, strategic and operative management[87]

4 The introduction of comprehensive quality concepts as organisational development process

Implementing comprehensive quality concepts as described in the European Model for Business Excellence usually requires basic changes in many areas. The basis is a new and comprehensive interpretation of corporate quality which is illustrated in the assessment guidelines of international quality awards. Such a new understanding of quality can only be developed and established under adequate conditions - in particular with the help of an organisational development process.[88]

4.1 Staff and structural approaches for organisational development

Organisational development comprises all approaches aimed at increasing an organisation's competitiveness, enhancing cooperation between teams and work groups, and making work conditions more satisfying for individuals. These objectives are achieved through a change in attitude and behaviour of individuals and groups, as well as a redesign of organisational structures and technology. The ability of a company and its staff to adapt to dynamic changes can be taken as a further aim. Organisational development does not only refer to technology, people or organisational structure, but rather understands an organisation as a complex system with manifold mutual dependencies.

This description of organisational development challenges the conviction that a planned change can be implemented

- **either** by a change in attitudes and behaviour of employees **or**
- by a change in organisation(al structure).

The following figure shows an integral understanding of change regarding quality as a combination of people-centered, structural, and situation-specific factors.

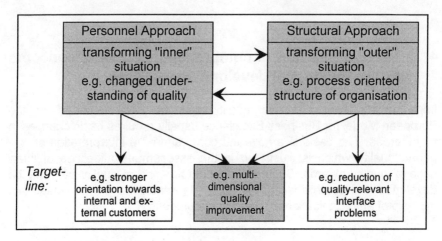

Fig. 29:   Personnel and structural approach to organisational development[89]

In order to show that introducing Total Quality Management (TQM) or Business Excellence is an organisational development process, respective staff and structural approaches will be presented in the following.

4.2   Personnel components for the realisation of Total Quality concepts

Personnel components mainly refer to the way people's attitudes and behaviour can be changed.

Which *attitudes* should be changed?

- ❑ "Customers are an annoying interruption to my work!"
- ❑ "My salary is paid by the company, so it is most important that my boss is satisfied with me!"
- ❑ "When errors occur, it is most important to find out whose fault it was!"
- ❑ "Quality only concerns the production department!"
- ❑ "Quality is restricted exclusively to product and work results. Therefore it is possible to achieve quality through extensive testing!"
- ❑ "There's a quality check after me anyway!"

❑ "The quality department is ultimately responsible for quality. What's it there for otherwise?"

❑ "Planning, implementation and supervision or surveillance must be separated as a matter of principle!"

❑ "If it has worked for the last ten years, it will work tomorrow!"

From these attitudes, it is simple to draw out corresponding behaviour, which is in no way compatible with comprehensive quality understanding. It is definitely no basis for introducing comprehensive quality concepts.

In contrast to these attitudes, the following exemplary behaviour should be supported:

❑ Give the customer the highest priority

❑ Thinking in processes instead of focussing on departments

❑ Teamwork instead of individual competition

❑ Assigning quality as a line function

❑ Encourage criticism - and correspondingly create a guilt-free atmosphere, which supports problem-solving groups

❑ Understand continuous learning as a part of daily business

❑ Accept quality as an issue also for administration

❑ Recognise the quality department as an internal consultant for achieving individual quality goals

How can people's attitudes and behaviour be changed in this way? Will they change at all? Certainly not with mere lip-service! Instead, an organisation has to create appropriate conditions regarding personnel (people management) and structural aspects (focus on quality). Therefore, qualification (in its widest sense) is crucial for successfully implementing TQM. It has to include the following elements:

❑ Information - i.e. communicating topical quality philosophies

❑ Training for various forms of team-work (quality meetings, project groups, quality circles)

❑ Training for specific target groups

All these measures are described in more detail as follows:

❑ Information - e.g. communicating topical quality philosophies

If, after thorough consideration, a company decides to realise a comprehensive quality concept in the sense of TQM, it has to involve all employees in this process and pass on the vision of TQM to them. Practical experiences show that people identify best with these ideas if training is carried out by the management themselves. This does not rule out necessary external support, such as start-up seminars for top management or providing expertise and external knowledge for internal trainers, which is particularly important for superiors who have not been trained to facilitate such processes. Internal training is mostly based on a handbook or a set of overhead slides.

TQM-Manual

Contents

   1. Why TQM?

   2. What does TQM mean for us?

   3. Basic elements of our TQM concept

   4. Implementation

   5. Our TQM organisation

     • steering committee

     • coordinator(s)

     • quality teams

     • feedback workshop

   6. Methods and tools (optional)

Fig. 30:   Exemplary structure of a company-specific TQM manual (also as basis for a set of overhead slides)

When defining the quality philosophy and determining concrete measures, attention must be paid to not restricting people's leeway in bringing in interests and problems of their function or hierarchic level. This ensures that the concept is not prescribed, but rather developed step by step and therefore accepted.

As TQM is an integrative management concept, it has to make its mark on the corporate vision. The vision determines the future state an organisation strives to attain, thus describing the final "destination of the journey". From the vision, missions (or messages) must be deduced showing the planned "path" of the "journey". So, different missions could be derived from the aim "improving business results under the premise of an optimum allocation of (internal and external) resources". These missions would specify more precisely how to increase customer, process and employee orientation.

The following figure shows a vastly simplified train-the-trainer concept.

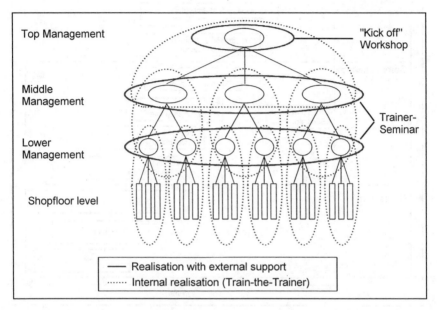

Fig. 31:   Top-down training concept (Train-the-trainer)

An analysis of the company's present state shows which issues the training concept should concentrate on. It is advisable to carry it out as self-assessment based on, for example, the European Model for Business Excellence. This facilitates aligning the efforts, and regularly measuring improvements. Furthermore, interests and problems of the respective functions or departments can be considered. Consequently, training is particularly effective, if the overall idea is deployed into functional or departmental targets, using them to draw up concrete improvement projects. The following figure presents the step-by-step implementation of a comprehensive quality concept:

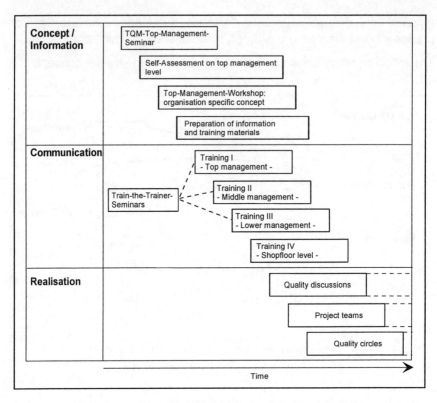

Fig. 32:   Step-by-step implementation of a comprehensive quality concept

❏ **Training for various forms of team-work (quality meetings, project groups, quality circles)**[90]

As cooperation and team work belong to the most important elements of a comprehensive quality concept, all participants must be trained accordingly. Customer orientation - referring both to internal and external customers - should be supported by process analysis and redesign. These methods can be implemented at least as pilot projects within quality meetings. Experience has shown that training and information alone are not sufficient to change attitudes and behaviour. The following figure shows an example of a three-day facilitated training course:

Seminar schedule (amendments reserved)	

Day 1	O Introduction:
	   - expectations
	   - short presentation and discussion of the concept
	
	O role and tasks of the facilitators:
	   - creating a task catalogue
	   - training with the aid of role play and videotaping
	
	O working in and with groups (I)
	   (creativity techniques and group dynamic exercises)
	
	O dinner
	
	O discussion of first day

Day 2	O working in and with groups (II) O problem solving and presentation techniques (I) O problem solving and presentation techniques (II) O dinner O discussion of second day
Day 3	O simulation of a problem solving task O supporting check lists O final discussion

Fig. 33:   A training example for facilitators

Training should cover the following subjects:

- Techniques for facilitating group work for all those in leadership positions and other facilitators

- Problem analysis and problem solving techniques, particularly for members of project groups and quality circles

- Process analysis/examination of customer-supplier relationships for all employees as a basis for regular quality talks

❏ Training for specific target groups

Training for specific target groups is intended for all those employees who need detailed knowledge for specific methods (e.g. QFD[91] in design, FMEA[92] in construction, or SPC[93] in production).

Training plays a decisive role in the introduction of self-appraisal (particularly in production). Here, it is necessary to go step-by-step from supervision and end-of-the-line testing to self-appraisal, which supports quick feedback loops and learning processes.

The participants' positive response to and acceptance of information and training (e.g. in methods to analyse customer-supplier relationships) is dependent on several factors. Firstly, it is important that individuals can recognise benefits for themselves and for the company. As mentioned before, it is therefore helpful to leave sufficient leeway in order to fit training to the individual employees' interests and problems. There is a better chance of acceptance when people are involved in the introduction of the training concept. Additional benefits can be achieved through integration in a target agreement at management level and in regular counselling sessions. On the shopfloor level, there are many possibilities for bonuses and other forms of recognition.[94]

As practical experience shows, middle management should be thoroughly trained and informed in order to enable them to take over structural and coordinational tasks.

Finally, the roles of the quality department and line managers must be redefined. They have to change from supervisors to process advisors. Quality must become the responsibility of middle management and of workers on the shopfloor level, which is achieved by the following measures and attitudes:

❏ Assigning responsibilities for quality to line functions (e.g., with a computer-aided documentation system)

❏ Training and seminars (e.g., in the basics of statistical quality assurance)

❏ Short-term motivation programmes

This demonstrates that there are new demands which directors and all employees of the quality department have to face in their jobs.

4.3   Structural aspects of comprehensive quality concepts

Implementing the measures of people management mentioned before in the organisational development process requires appropriate structural conditions. Amongst those to be considered are:

❑ Integrating quality goals into corporate targets

❑ Assessing management and employees with regard to multi-dimensional targets

❑ Modifying the company's compensation and recognition systems

❑ Realising process-oriented organisation structures

❑ Redesigning the organisation structure in order to facilitate customer and employee orientation

❑ Structural support in the introductory phase

❑ Restructuring information and reporting

These structural conditions can be roughly outlined as follows:

❑ Integrating quality goals into corporate targets

Total Quality Management understood as an integrative management concept is an integral part of corporate targets and planning. This connection is shown in the following matrix:

Corporate goals / TQM missions	A extending market share	B securing revenues	C ...	D ...
I customer orientation	X	X		
II process orientation		X	X	
III ...	X			X

Fig. 34:   Connection between TQM missions and corporate goals

This means, for example, that the first TQM mission (here: customer orientation) contributes to corporate targets A (here: extending market share) and B (here: ensuring revenues). Such a matrix shows the rele-

vance of the pursued approach (or possibly the following of the wrong concept).

Corporate goals and planning are linked through regular (self)-assess-
ments, which supplement traditional business data. Furthermore, benchmark data can be used.[95]

❑ **Assessing management and employees with regard to multi-
dimensional targets**

People in general tend to change their behaviour only in return for the
promise of some personal benefits. Therefore, assessments of superiors
should be adapted in content: Achieving quality targets, enthusiasm for or
initiative to quality projects, and support for problem-solving groups can all
be part of a quality-oriented assessment. The same applies for employee
counselling and hiring.

❑ **Modifying the company's compensation and recognition systems**

Changes in behaviour can be a result of intrinsic or extrinsic "rewards".
While intrinsic motivation comes from the experience of personal success
at work - which can be achieved as side effects of increased process orientation - extrinsic motivation concepts depend on compensation and recognition.

If all employees are supposed to cooperate on the way towards Business
Excellence, the recognition system must be adapted accordingly. Unfortu-
nately, recognition systems are counterproductive in many organisations:
Employees receive, for example, a bonus for every sales contract - regardless of whether agreements on time and quality can be fulfilled. The employees in the purchasing department often receive a bonus for buying at
the most reasonable rates. Though they should pay attention to the quality
of the product, they only receive a bonus for savings made. Furthermore, in
many companies, the performance of the production department is only
measured in the number of units. Recognition for managers is hardly more
encouraging, as it is often bound to short-term successes.

An exemplary recognition system can be found at Rank Xerox. A variable
proportion of management compensation is directly related to the company
targets of

❑ customer satisfaction,

❑ employee motivation and satisfaction,

❑ market share and

❑ return on investment

and their improvement. This, of course, requires respective targets, which are individually put into concrete terms.

❏ **Realising process-oriented organisation structures**

Firstly, organisational structures have to be modified in the sense of process orientation. This is based on the assumption that many quality deficits are caused by interface problems due to a dominating functional division of labour. Basic goals such as customer orientation cannot be achieved without fundamentally redesigning the organisation.

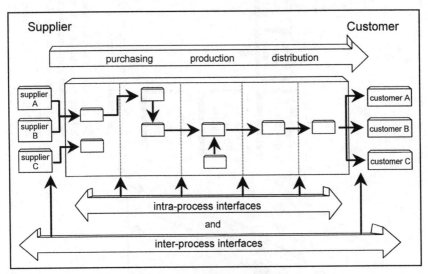

Fig. 35:   Interfaces within or between processes[96]

Process-oriented structures can be achieved in the following steps:

❏ Identifying key processes

❏ Redesigning processes

❏ Stabilising processes

These steps can be described as follows:

a) Identifying key processes

Process orientation requires the definition of key processes, underlying the company's critical success factors. This task can only be carried out by (top) management. The following figure shows how to determine critical success factors from customer expectations (in this example: concerning support services of a computer manufacturer).

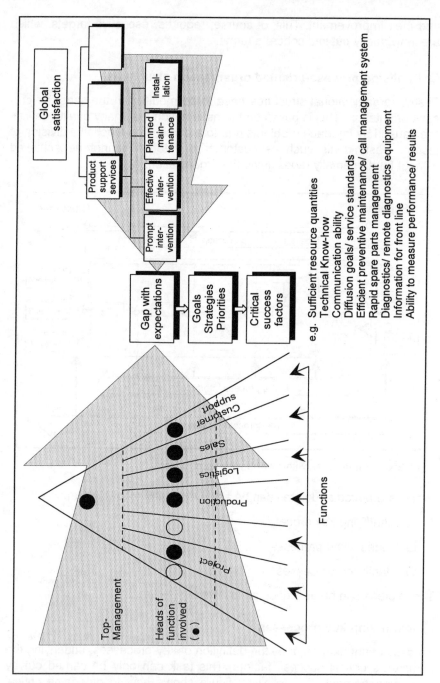

Fig. 36:   Identification of critical success factors[97]

In the next step, these critical success factors are assigned to the corresponding processes:

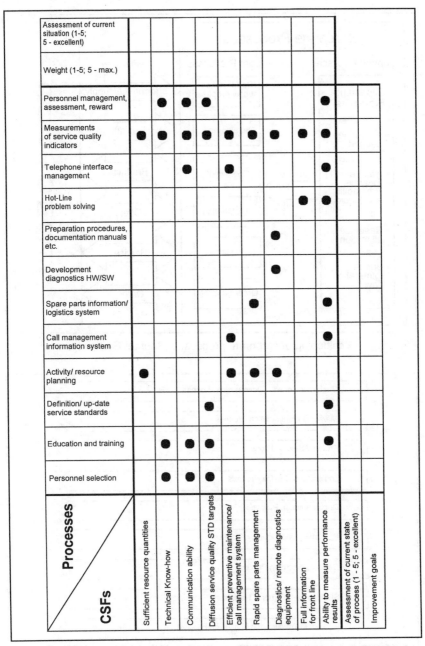

Fig. 37: The transition from critical success factors (CSFs) to processes[98]

Key processes can be identified according to Gaitanides et al. and Sommerlatte and Wedekind.

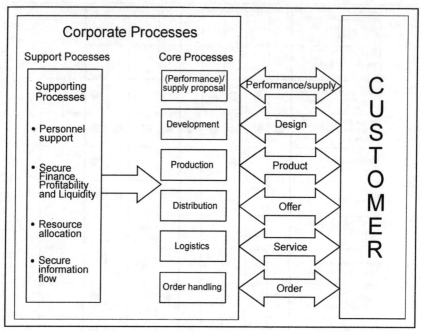

Fig. 38:   Positioning of corporate processes (Source: Gaitanides et al.)[99]

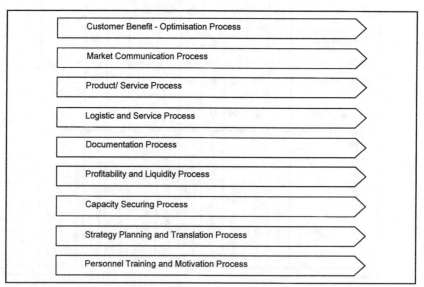

Fig. 39:   The critical performance processes of a company[100]

These key processes can, however, only be defined individually for each company.

b) Redesigning of processes

Process-oriented organisational structures can be developed on many different levels, thus affecting existing structures to varying degrees. With reference to key processes, this could mean a fundamental redesign. One of the concepts currently being discussed in this context is the "Dynamic company".[101]

☐ All resources for routine tasks are combined in the management function "process management", which has to deliver all continuously recurring services and the necessary administrative functions.[102]

☐ Data integration and computer-aided techniques play an essential role in this issue. They support the objectives efficiency, minimal costs and consistent quality.

☐ Innovative and creative tasks are assigned to the "systems management". This is responsible for designing and implementing all systems, procedures and processes which are handed over to the process-management after starting operations.[103]

☐ All innovative tasks in product design and finance are assigned to another management function known as "programme-management", making it responsible for the development of markets and the company's performance both on a strategic and operative level.[104]

All these functions are, of course, aligned by a superior function called "coordination management". This structure is illustrated in the following figure.

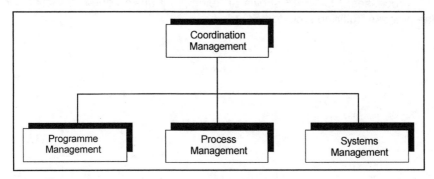

Fig. 40:   Model of an alternative organisational structure[105]

The following matrix gives an example of how far tasks and staff are transferred from the old departments to the new functions.

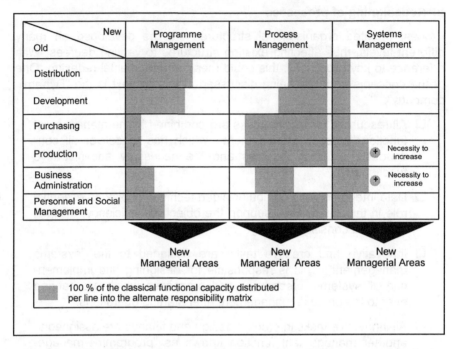

Fig. 41:   Transfer matrix for reassigning personnel based on a practical
            example[106]

These changes basically alter existing structures and responsibilities, thus
inducing many companies to hold back from such a radical approach and
try to compromise instead. The "process owner" concept is an example of
this kind of solution aimed at increased process orientation (at least) for
key processes. Figure 42 shows an exemplary basic course of action for
the process "fulfilling a customer order".

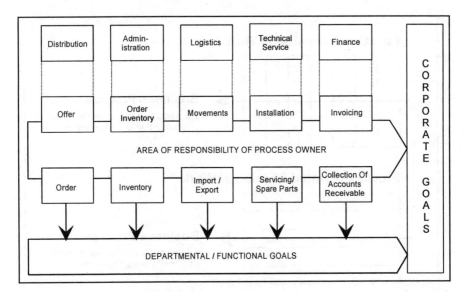

Fig. 42:   Cross-department process: Fulfilment of a customer order[107]

The prevalent functional structure continues to exist. Nevertheless, additional units or responsibilities are introduced for key processes. In order to underline their relevance they should be assigned to higher hierarchical levels.

Another compromise solution is the establishment of process-oriented project teams for simultaneous engineering.[108] During the design process, representatives of all relevant departments and, where necessary, suppliers and customers (e.g. in the case of rapid prototyping) join a project team, whereby efficiency of cooperation heavily depends on the capabilities of the project leader.

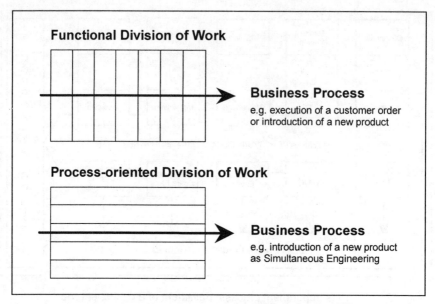

Fig. 43:   Functional and process-oriented division of labour[109]

Process orientation, however, can also be achieved on the shopfloor level through team-work concepts, such as semi-autonomous work groups. They are responsible for a complete process (e.g. order processing) or a self-contained part of a process (e.g. manufacturing packages).

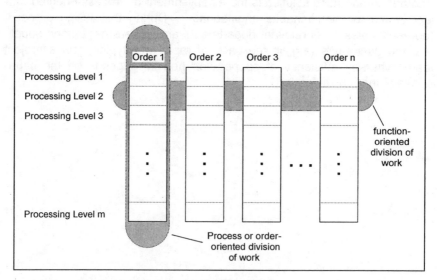

Fig. 44:   Division of labour or group formation for n orders in a working
            system with m processing levels[110]

These concepts had already been discussed at the end of the '70's. They attempt to (re)integrate tasks in order to overcome an excessive division of labour.

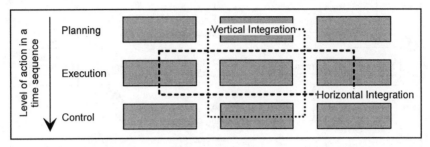

Fig. 45:   Vertical and horizontal integration

Integration in this context means the combination of tasks, either at work stations or in work groups, which were previously carried out separately. This reduces interfaces, thus eliminating quality problems - along with a considerable cut in processing times.[111] Functional integration can be supported by intelligent EDP systems and software packages.

Before redesigning processes, their current state should be thoroughly analysed with regard to their value-adding function. Interfaces between those processes (which might also include external customers) must be defined in detail, which can be achieved through agreements between (internal or external) customers and suppliers affected.

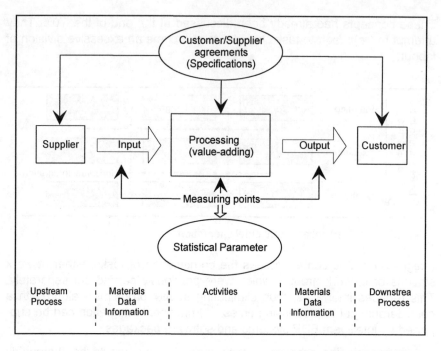

Fig. 46:   Increased added value through a system-oriented approach[112]

c) Stabilising processes

Process stabilisation demands the definition of requirements, supplemented by detailed measures and performance ratios. Depending on the type of process and the defined system bounds, various concepts can be employed. QFD, for example, can be used in order to support the cross-company process of fulfilling customer requirements.

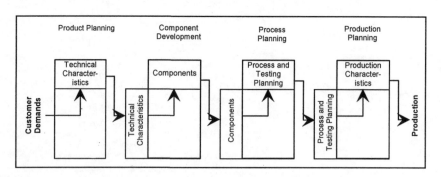

Fig. 47:   QFD as a method to stabilise processes[113]

Processes within the company or organisation can be stabilised through description and assessment within business process management. It is based on the fact that all major processes can be divided into sub-processes, thus creating a "process hierarchy". If sub-processes in turn are broken down into sub-sub-processes, process elements and ratios can be defined in job instructions.

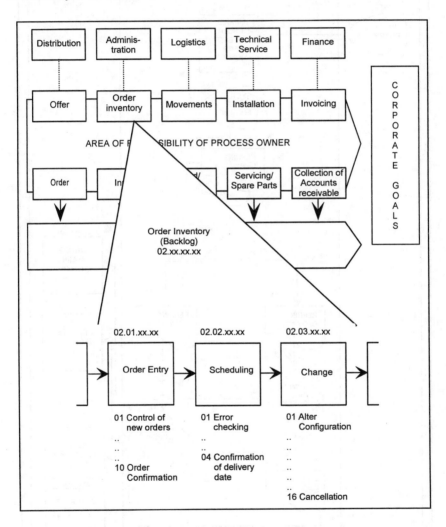

Fig. 48:   Principle outline of the decomposition of the process "Fulfilment of a customer order"[114]

Furthermore, the organisation has to establish continuous review and improvement cycles.

The following figure shows how the process element "order entry and surveillance" is broken down on the lowest level.

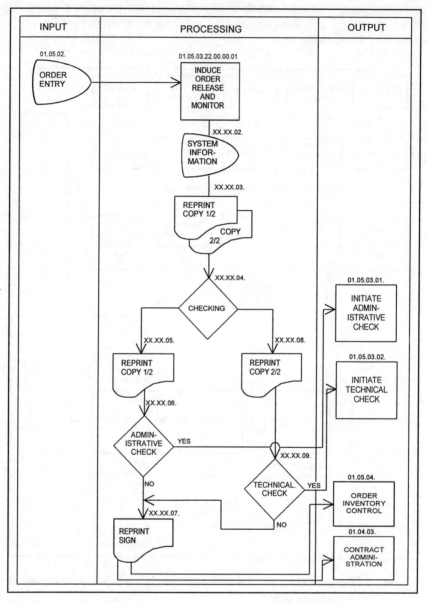

Fig. 49:   Process flow diagram (detail)[115]

The following figure suggests a project plan to introduce process-oriented organisational structures.

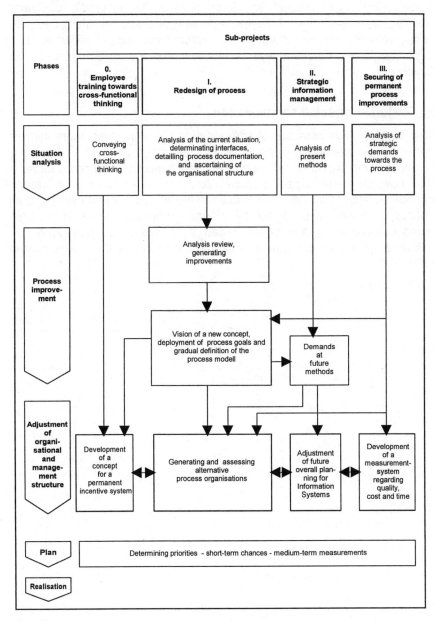

Fig. 50:   Exemplary project plan for introducing process-oriented structures[116]

❏ Redesigning organisational structures in order to facilitate customer and employee orientation[117]

Redesigning organisational structures means, for example, customer-oriented segmentation and the reassignment of responsibilities. The latter aspect requires the redefinition of hierarchical structures, modified tasks for departments and functions and various opportunities for employee participation.

a) Customer-oriented segmentation

The idea of segmentation, divisionalisation, or - in even more general terms - decentralisation, is not new. This becomes clear when looking at "product group organisation" - a concept which has been common for some time now. One new aspect, however, is the stronger focus on customer-orientation and the introduction of customer-oriented, cross-functional team concepts. These are supported by information technology allowing advantages of centralised and decentralised structures to be combined. The following figure shows the idea of segmentation in a Just-In-Time-concept (JIT).

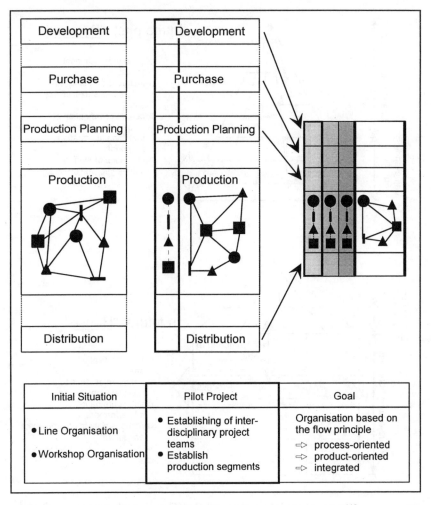

Fig. 51:   Customer-oriented segmentation on the basis of JIT[118]

b) Reassigning responsibilities through the redefinition of hierarchy and the tasks of departments

Nowadays, redefining hierarchy means leaner structures with increased added value. This can be seen in the following figure.

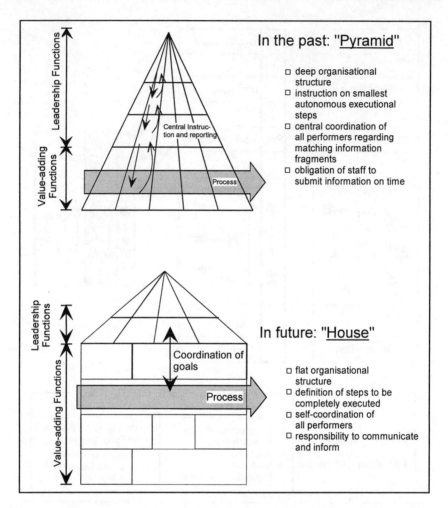

Fig. 52:   Organisation, information and creation of products and services[119]

When realising customer or process orientation, department managers should be replaced - at least in the customer-oriented segments - by process owners. In practice, however, companies still tend to compromise, as mentioned earlier.

A redefinition of the tasks can be seen for example in the quality department. Quality will only become a company-wide line function if there is self-appraisal. In this way, the quality department delegates testing and simultaneously takes over counselling, not only for in-house but also for external suppliers. Medium to long-term people management (as discussed before) helps to provide directors and employees with appropriate qualifications for this new role. The following figure shows how the role understanding of the quality department has to change.

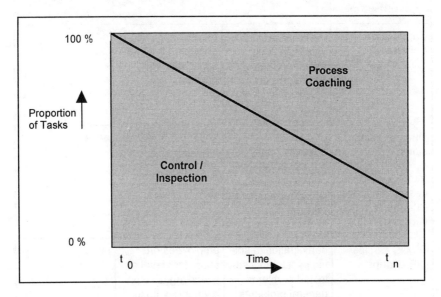

Fig. 53:   Role of the quality department in organisational development

c) Employee participation[120]

Comprehensive quality concepts focus on involving as many employees as possible. This can be achieved in regular meetings between superiors and employees or empowering individuals to make their own decisions. Regarding the individual employee, participation can be improved by reforming the company suggestion scheme. A further aspect is group work resulting from horizontal and vertical integration, as discussed above.[121]

Some group concepts permanently change the organisational structure, others are based on temporary cooperation. The following table gives a rough overview:

Kinds of employee involvement	Tasks	Members/ Combination	Time Restriction
Suggestion Scheme	participation in sol-ving voluntarily se-lected problems (probably only out-side own work area)	for all employees possible (in some cases also for groups)	none
Quality-Discus-sions (possibly also as Learning Groups ("Learning in the Group"))	discussion of relevant quality questions, analysis of exemplary customer-supplier-relationships	superiors and their direct subordinates	none
Quality Circles/ CIP Groups	participation in sol-ving voluntarily se-lected problems (in general problems of own work area)	employees on shop floor level of a working area on a voluntary basis	none
Task Force Groups/ Project Groups	finding solutions for defined problems, analysis of cross-departmental processes	employees from different work areas and hierarchy levels, formed from a professional point of view	disbanding of the group after conclusion of task
Semi-autono-mous work groups	cooperation in a defined task, influence on assign-ment of activities and work content	formed from a professional point of view, in some cases participation regarding selection	none

Fig. 54:   Different kinds of employee involvement

❑ Structural support in the introductory phase

Organisational development can only be successful if it is controlled by a process owner and promoted by people in powerful positions. This is the reason why the introduction of a comprehensive quality concept has to be safeguarded by the following institutional mechanisms:

- Integration of all people in powerful positions into a steering committee, which includes not only top managers but also the works council and its chairman. All fundamental decisions are made in this committee. A coordinator maintains close contact to employees.

- Appointing one or more quality managers or TQM-coordinators, who support awareness of TQM and the implementation of definite measures during the initial phase. Their tasks include the following:

  - Implementing suggestions of the steering committee

  - Designing and supporting TQM-training

  - Coordinating quality groups

  - Counselling on TQM questions

  - Internal auditing (Self-Assessments)

  - Presenting results

After the initial phase, all further organisational units must be integrated into the line functions, otherwise parallel responsibilities will occur. The following figure shows an exemplary organisational structure.

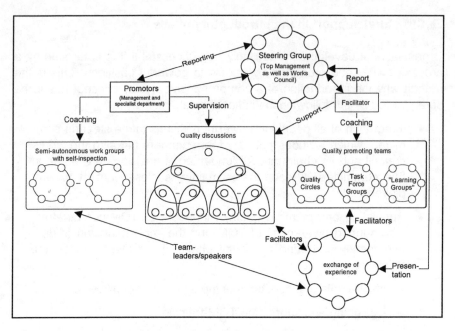

Fig. 55:   Basic form of the organisational structure of a comprehensive, integrated quality management[122]

❑ Restructuring of information and reporting

Traditional accountancy and reporting do not usually fit the requirements described above[123], which can be seen in the following examples:

- Data are exclusively available for management.

- Planning, control, and supervision are based solely on costs.

- Data collection supports the functional division of labour (Cost centre accounting).

- Employees are mainly seen as cost drivers (Cost type accounting).

- Customer satisfaction and process orientation are disregarded issues. In contrast to this, planned targets such as number of manufactured items are often achieved even at the expense of these goals.

A comprehensive quality concept mainly aims at customer and employee satisfaction as well as process orientation. These have to be supported by a reporting and control system providing more than just cost data. Such a quality information system should comprise the following elements:

a) Customer orientation:

- Results of satisfaction surveys referring to the contributions made for solving customer problems

- Customer loyalty over a certain period of time

b) Process orientation:

- Added value from the customer's perspective

- Process flexibility and stability

- Efficiency regarding time and resources

All these aspects must be combined in a comprehensive information system.

4.4 Customer orientation through permanent feedback loops

Current quality concepts strongly emphasise (internal and external) customer orientation. Due to constantly changing demands altering quality requirements, permanent feedback loops are necessary in order to react quickly. They can be realised in traditional survey-and-feedback procedures taken from organisational development: interviewing various target groups as a basis for the introduction of process changes.

Regarding organisational development, this refers first and foremost to all members of the organisation (internal customers). Employee surveys should include quality related questions. The use of such methods only makes sense if the results lead to considerable changes afterwards, which applies equally to external customer surveys. As such measures tend to be expensive, they should be supplemented by further methods to systematically record customer feedback.[124] Corresponding information can be gained from reactions to advertising, the contact with customers when answering requests, carrying out projects, and in order processing. Further contacts are sales, installation or assembly, after-sales services, and, of course, the reaction to complaints. In addition to the above-mentioned customer surveys, all personal contacts should also be systematically evaluated. Furthermore, problem-solving groups on the shopfloor level should contribute to the establishment of quick feedback loops.

4.5   TQM support

TQM as an integrative management concept must be introduced through various methods and tools. Traditional methods of target-finding, planning and control have to be supplemented or modified appropriately. Some of the tools are:[125]

❑ Self-Assessments combined with benchmarking in order to determine the current state and to measure progress

❑ Policy Deployment to deduce targets for individual employees (based on priorities from assessment results)

❑ Quality standards in the form of ratios and costs as a basis for process management

❑ Quality standards in the form of quality manuals (e.g. for certification)

❑ Quality tools for those departments directly operating in the market (e.g. Quality Function Deployment to translate customer demands into production parameters; systematic feedback loops to obtain more information about the customer)

❑ Analysis and problem-solving techniques (e.g. brainstorming, Pareto-analysis, cause and effect diagrams, multivariate analysis, Taguchi-methods, failure modes and effects analysis (FMEA), statistical process control (SPC), part-count-method (PCM))

❑ Methods aimed at improving process quality in individual sections of the quality loop (e.g. Simultaneous Engineering)

❑ Group work or team concepts

❑ Methods for determining customer and employee satisfaction

❑ Computer support (e.g. computer based quality information system) in order to integrate all data relevant to a total quality concept (such as customer and employee satisfaction) and knowledge-based systems to ensure product quality

❑ Motivation programmes

In order to avoid the impression of a temporary programme, these aspects should be part of the regular training scheme.

5 Practical experiences

Initially, TQM was generally overlooked. However, in the meantime it has become a topical issue, and some experience has now been gained in this area. The following empirical knowledge was taken from consultancy and from research work.[126]

5.1 Current problems

A survey on self-assessment and the introduction of TQM has revealed the following problems:[127]

- Customer orientation and satisfaction
- Process orientation
- Employee orientation and satisfaction
- Result orientation

As far as *customer orientation* is concerned, companies claim to attach great significance to customers and to take them seriously. However, there is a lack of data on *customer satisfaction*, showing that they really achieve customer orientation. Mostly, companies only keep some statistics on complaints. A systematic customer survey or workshops with key customers are missing in most cases. The same applies for all other methods systematically dealing with customer feedback.

Relying on the broader vision of the customer and analysing *internal customer-supplier relationships*, severe deficits can be encountered. Although this issue is occasionally addressed within training courses, no practical implementation follows.

Process orientation is at the centre of numerous recent restructuring concepts. Nevertheless, this issue is often overlooked in practice.[128] For many companies, it is relevant only in production where more ratios and measures are available to monitor, e.g. process or machine capability. Aligning these processes with continuous improvement is, however, not necessarily common property.

The main deficits occur when dealing systematically with cross-departmental processes (also key processes). Practice shows that where strong emphasis is placed on process orientation, cooperation improves greatly between individuals and departments - even beyond hierarchical levels. Furthermore, customer orientation also benefits.

Similar observations can be made regarding *employee orientation.* However, companies' awareness in this category is even worse. On the one hand, all companies consider satisfaction and motivation to be important. On the other hand, however, less significance is attached to motivation through group work or empowerment using self-assessment. The survey reveals the negative consequences of "half-hearted" employee participation: Although employees have the opportunity to think about possibilities for improvement at their work stations within problem-solving groups, their solutions are not implemented consistently. Similar demotivation occurs if it takes too long to implement them within the company suggestion scheme.

Positive prerequisites for cross-departmental, process-oriented thinking can be found in those companies where team work is established in quality circles, "Lernstatt" projects[129], or similar concepts concerned with employee participation. The professional and social capabilities acquired there are helpful in dealing with TQM. Experience shows that in many companies qualification needs are not systematically determined. Training is randomly distributed leading to frustration rather than acceptance.

Surveys aimed at ascertaining *employee satisfaction* take place as rarely as customer surveys. However, in some companies the benefits of employee surveys are denied. In companies with a traditionally good environment, where problems are normally dealt with on a personal level, the necessity for anonymous surveys is often doubted. When employee surveys are carried out, great significance should be attached to informing the interviewees about the results. In particular, the data gathered must lead to definite changes, which is often overlooked in practice, thus leading to considerable frustration.

Most companies take statistical data such as absenteeism or staff turnover as indications of employee satisfaction, whereby it is widely recognised that these figures are also influenced by other factors, such as overmanning in the observed departments. However, as other figures are rarely available for assessment, this data at least provides a starting point.

Two further problems can be seen in this context:

❑ There are no suitable feedback systems giving employees a basis for working continuously on improvement.

❑ There is no compensation and recognition system reflecting the aims of TQM and rewarding corresponding behaviour.

A further deficit is result orientation, which means measuring an organisation's performance via figures and ratios. These can be employed to manage and control the TQM process and to assess Business Excellence in the sense of corporate quality. Only 29 % of the companies studied in our survey could even provide such figures. Those who had some attached the greatest significance to quality costs.

These results can be confirmed with several case studies: Although quality-related costs are ascertained in the companies questioned, these costs are partly calculated and partly estimated. In most cases, this information is subdivided into error, error-prevention and checking costs. A particular deficiency in this context is, however, that employees are not adequately informed. Although figures are often published on notice-boards, they are not assigned directly to the individual work station and therefore cannot be used as a managerial tool. Only a minority of companies analyse quality costs on a weekly basis and subdivide them into different components (e.g. per production unit). This procedure enables employees to trace the quality of their work.

5.2   Implementation problems

Introducing TQM generally begins with formulating a quality philosophy and disseminating it within the company. Many companies believe that once this process has been carried out, TQM has been introduced. This often proves to be a mistake! Translating the quality policy into targets for each employee usually proves to be particularly difficult. Therefore, implementing a quality philosophy or policy in practice usually leads to more problems than the process of its formulation.

Experience shows in this context that management support is crucial for the successful introduction and implementation of the process. Employees have to be informed as early as possible and involved in the process. Furthermore, the TQM process must not be labelled as "just another programme".

Support for the quality concept by top and middle management considerably promotes acceptance within the company. A lack of support can, on the other hand, delay or even foil introduction and implementation. Providing resources alone (e.g. funds or time) is not enough. Management must take on the quality philosophy, and act as role model. This could mean that managers train the employees and are therefore actively involved in disseminating the notion of quality. In some companies, this train-the-trainer approach has been extremely successful.

When developing a quality policy, it has to be ensured that it fits with the overall corporate policy (quality policy should be based on and integrated into corporate policy).

In addition to management support, the works council has to be involved from the very beginning (beyond legal requirements on participation and codetermination), because their support can boost acceptance by the employees. This is particularly valid on shopfloor level. Once more, management has to make sure that employees are informed and involved at the earliest possible stage.

Often, day-to-day tasks impede important quality planning and control functions. Management and leadership tasks are pushed aside by organisational tasks (red tape). As management generally does not devote enough time to quality activities, there is often only time left for trouble-shooting.

If a quality promotion concept is only understood as "just another programme", the employees' acceptance will also be damaged. The programme character, described by one of the companies surveyed as "Flavour of the Month", can be caused by a variety of factors: If a lot of independent programmes without any coherence have been started in the company in the past, or if there are several parallel activities, the company runs the risk of TQM also being regarded as another programme, with its strategic significance remaining unrecognised.

It is crucial for the TQM process to set quality-related objectives and to regularly assess whether the actual performance meets these targets. Here, the stages of setting aims, implementing corresponding measures, monitoring results, and (renewed) improvement have to be consistently kept to. Otherwise - as experience has shown - the quality promotion concept will not be introduced effectively. If individual objectives are not consistently determined, employees will not get a clear vision of their contribution towards overall organisational performance. Therefore, they will probably not feel responsible for achieving these aims and consequently will fail to take them seriously.

High staff turnover at management level can also create the impression that TQM lacks significance. As new managers are likely to shift their emphasis on quality strategy, it is often difficult to establish long-term continuity. This trend towards zigzagging can endanger a successful TQM process.

There are two more issues which have turned out to be crucial in practice when introducing a comprehensive quality concept. Both are related to the temporary dimension of this process:

❏ time for preparation

❏ time for implementation

As the idea of TQM has only spread slowly - though it has now become popular through the pressure of international competition - the concept is sometimes misunderstood. TQM is misinterpreted when its introduction mainly means establishing project teams that determine and work on weak points. Due to the lack of a systematic and coherent analysis of the present state (e.g. using self assessment based on the EFQM-Model), a strategy cannot be defined and definite aims cannot be set. The quality of the results is more or less coincidental. When the project work is completed, TQM or Business Excellence is also completed (which is, of course, impossible as Business Excellence is an ideal stage), which may frustrate the participants.

Introducing comprehensive organisational development that is clearly aligned with strategic objectives requires a thorough determination of the present state: an organisation has to know where it stands. It is worth spending time and resources in the preparatory phase so that implementation can be a success.

Compensation and recognition systems for management are mostly aligned with short-term successes. For introducing TQM, such a short-term vision often means defining tough schedules and deadlines that definitely cannot be kept to. Thus, it is often overlooked that communicating the aim and purpose of TQM requires several months if it is to be carried out by superiors and reach *all* employees. Even more time will be necessary if team-oriented work structures are implemented from scratch, because the employees then have to be trained in methodical and social skills. Of course, the period required for implementation can be cut if training and practical realisation are combined - this should, however, be carried out with a realistic perspective.

Furthermore, the success in introducing TQM depends on what else happens within the organisation. In many organisations, introducing new ideas and projects always depends on a small group of people. If they are engaged with other projects, implementing TQM will be delayed or carried out half-heartedly. In these cases, it might be better to wait half a year rather than to put too much strain on the company (and, in particular, their employees).

A feeling of being overloaded can also be caused by the way certification of the quality system according to DIN EN ISO 9000 is combined with the introduction of TQM. Although the scope of both concepts seems to suggest striving for certification first and then going for TQM, organisations have had conflicting experiences in this area. Some companies have introduced TQM first - and certification was achieved, so to speak, incidentally. Others got stuck with introducing TQM - and then succeeded through systematically dealing with processes for certification. Some experienced considerable acceptance problems when implementing TQM after certification: After all, they were certified to be a "quality company" - why then TQM? In any case, both aims should be combined for purely economical reasons. However, a company's vision must always go over and beyond certification. When dealing with processes, the focus must not only be on documentation, but also on their potential for improvement. Furthermore, this problem will be solved if the ISO 9000 series of standards is developed towards the quality understanding of TQM.

5.3   Summary assessment

The issues mentioned before can be summarised as follows:

- Introducing Total Quality Management is a long-term organisational development process.

- A shared corporate culture necessarily results in common priorities. These in turn are implemented through common aims for all employees.

- The necessary changes in behaviour cannot be achieved in the short-term. International experience shows that a period of between five and ten years is a realistic perspective.

- All participants need some feeling of success in the short-term. This can be achieved through improvement projects. However, care has to be taken that the quality approach is not reduced to a programme, as this damages the employees' motivation to participate.

- If the companies' strengths and areas for improvement are not known, it is difficult to set targets precisely. Therefore, it seems to be necessary and sensible to use self-assessment (e.g. based on the EFQM-Model) in order to determine the starting point, and to measure progress. This requires an internal audit, with the participation of experienced managers from different departments and functions in the company.

- However, the management's role is still the critical success factor. It has to act as a role model and be ready to provide resources. Furthermore, managers must credibly show their willingness and power to change structural conditions in order to realise Business Excellence. Several studies demonstrate that leadership is crucial. The following example comes from Develin and Partner, UK:

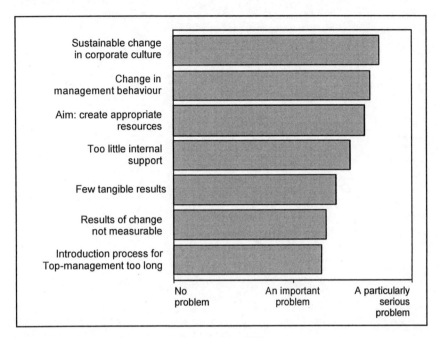

Fig. 56:   Problems when introducing TQM[130]

Success has been achieved when quality is no longer a special task, but an integral part of day-to-day business - in other words, when Total Quality Management has been realised in practice as an integrative management concept aiming at Business Excellence.

Part II:
The European Model for Business Excellence

1 Basics of the European Model for Business Excellence

At the end of the 80s, competition in the triad finally lead to a European initiative. The European Foundation for Quality Management (EFQM) was founded with the aim of bringing across to managers of European companies the idea of comprehensive Quality.

The Deming Prize in Japan and Malcolm Baldrige National Quality Award in the USA also had the same aim, to promote this process by a series of measures which had already been successfully applied. In addition to awards for doctoral and masters' theses and publications, there was also an award for extraordinary performances of managers. In 1992 this award was replaced by the "European Quality Award" (EQA) for companies.

This "main product" of the EFQM, which is also supported by the European Organisation for Quality (EOQ) and by the European Union (EU), is the subject of the following chapters.[131]

The basic model for the European Quality Award was developed on the one hand to provide an individual European direction and yet, on the other hand, to be comparable with existing assessment concepts.

By including more than 250 people from different institutions - among them also the founding members of the EFQM - a model was created which was intended to be flexible enough to be applicable within all branches, industries and sizes of companies as well as within the different cultural framework in Europe.

The model's basic structure differs from comparable approaches because of its two groups of criteria influencing businesses: "Enablers" and "Results". The fact that the emphasis lies with the results criteria comes from Tito Conti's work on "Company Quality Assessments". This orientation to the Results criteria can already be seen within the basic model.[132]

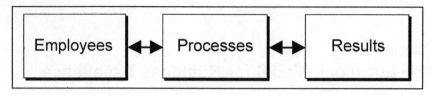

Fig. 57:   The basic EQA Model

or in words:

**"Better results by including all employees (people)
in the continuous improvement of their processes."**

These basic ideas can also be applied to many other concepts being discussed today (e.g. KAIZEN or Lean Management). However, the specific
characteristics of the European Model for Total Quality Management can
only be distinguished clearly when we examine the model's whole structure:

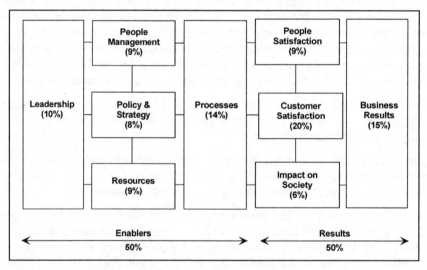

Fig. 58:   The European Model for Business Excellence

The Enablers "Leadership", "People Management", "Policy and Strategy",
"Resources" and "Processes" are distinguished from the Results criteria
"People Satisfaction", "Customer Satisfaction", "Impact on Society" and
"Business Results.

Whereas the Enablers include the essential factors of "Business Excellence", the Results criteria show that all efforts have to aim at improving
business results. This aim can only be achieved with satisfied customers

and employees (people). The institution's impact on society is also considered here.

The Enablers and Results criteria are given equal weight (each to 50 %). The weighting of the single criteria is the result of an intensive discussion in which the 14 founding members of the EFQM also participated.

In the following pages, we will give a detailed description of the contents of the criteria and their subcriteria, complemented by examples. The assessment process itself will be explained later.[133]

2 Elements of the European Model for Total Quality Management [134]

In contrast to the Malcolm Baldrige National Quality Award, the European Model does not use such detailed subdivision and description of the single elements. As mentioned before, the European Model chooses an "open" concept which can be applied by all kinds and sizes of organisations. Therefore the given sub-criteria or the listed details should only be understood as examples and suggestions which can be used if relevant and ignored where justifiable.

As the European Quality Award has only existed since 1992, the case studies shown here (each one marked with a grey "bar") do not only show EQA winners. They also consider Malcolm Baldrige National Quality Award winners as well as other companies with extraordinary performances in the field of TQM. [135]

The individual criteria will first be shown in an overview, and then described in more detail.

2.1 Leadership

Although Leadership is given "only" 10 % weight within the whole model, this criterion is a key factor for initiating and stabilising comprehensive quality concepts. Total Quality cannot be realised without the commitment of top management, and is therefore "condition sine qua non": without management's commitment, nothing will happen!

For that reason, the central issue here is "how the behaviour and actions of the executive team and all other leaders inspire, support and promote a culture of Total Quality Management."

Evidence is needed of "**how leaders**: [136]

1a: visibly demonstrate their commitment to a culture of Total Quality Management.

1b: support improvement and involvement by providing appropriate resources and assistance.

1c: are involved with customers, suppliers and other external organisations.

1d: recognise and appreciate people's efforts and achievements."

These sub-criteria can be described in more detail as follows:

1a: Visible demonstration of the leaders' commitment to a culture of Total Quality Management

A successful corporate culture which aims at supporting and promoting Total Quality can only be realised if the managers act as role models by developing and "living" the fixed values and norms. That means that they have to take on the leading role within the Total Quality process by ensuring that their commitment to all employees in the company and to their customers and suppliers is evident. This can, for example, be achieved by

❑ the top management (e.g. the company's owner, manager or CEO) being initiator and promoter,

❑ all relevant managers participating in regular meetings of a steering group which, for example, is responsible for formulating quality policy and coordinating quality activities within the entire company,

❑ managers carrying out regular review meetings within the single business units and analysing the actual measures already implemented,

❑ managers assuming the responsibility for the optimisation of business processes or taking on the realisation of single EQA elements,

❑ managers initiating improvement projects and investing time in participating in teams or taking on the team leadership.

The promotion of Total Quality demands the targeted qualification of all employees for specific groups. The managers' commitment can be shown clearly by

❑ their participation in training courses,

❑ undertaking training courses for employees and thus sharing their knowledge with employees (participating in training cascade),

❑ initiating or - if possible - carrying out special qualification measures (e.g. teaching the company-specific basic principles of Total Quality) for new employees,

❑ opening training courses on specific subjects and being available to answer questions in a final discussion.

In order to disseminate the quality concept, it is furthermore absolutely essential that the exchange of information between managers and employees functions correctly. Managers must be open and accessible for discussions, they have to listen to their staff and communicate with them.

This is the only way to ensure that comprehensive acceptance is achieved, that mutual comprehension is established and that employees with doubts are convinced. This can be achieved as follows:

- ❑ using regular staff meetings (e.g. works meetings) where the top management can inform employees on how far the Total Quality concept has been realised, where they can present results, where they can analyse quality targets and explain the planned action steps

- ❑ integrating the subject of Total Quality in the agenda of (regular) meetings on all levels

- ❑ communicating and disseminating the idea of Total Quality by different media (company newspapers, bulletin boards, video, direct letters to employees)

- ❑ providing opportunities for informal discussions between employees and managers

- ❑ assessing the efficiency of communication between managers and employees by using appropriate evaluation instruments

Ritz-Carlton[137]

- ❑ All managers participate in the TQM steering group.
- ❑ The top management itself ensures that products and services comply with customer requirements.
- ❑ Managers personally train new employees.
- ❑ The president personally presents the company's quality objectives within an intensive training course for new employees.
- ❑ Managers participate regularly in training for the support of TQM and consistently strive to make quality concepts more efficient.

Granite Rock[138]

- ❑ Granite Rock organises a celebration in each branch where all employees have the opportunity to communicate and discuss personally with the top managers.
- ❑ The manager's role is more a teacher or coach than a "traditional" manager.

BOC Special Gases[139]

❑ The company's TQM vision was formulated by BOC's CEO himself.

❑ When starting the TQM activities, all managers participated in a two-day awareness seminar.

❑ Top and middle management were involved when deciding on ways to implement the TQM approach.

Texas Instruments[140]

❑ The managers practise "Management by Walking Around" and personally disseminate the TQM idea.

❑ TI-managers participated personally in approx. 150 quality teams.

Beside personnel aspects like engagement and managers' personal commitment by giving an example to the employees, it is also very important how management succeeds in establishing Total Quality consistently and in the long term. This is a decisive factor in determining whether TQM will become or remain a (time-limited) quality programme or whether Total Quality success is to be made an integral part of daily work. Here, the main task of management is to create the appropriate structural framework to ensure that the change in the company's culture to TQM will remain long term. In particular, managers have to succeed in creating a special atmosphere within the company where all employees accept Total Quality as a fundamental principle of their own work which supports the company's development. To succeed, it is firstly necessary

❑ to develop a vision showing "the journey's destination" and clarify that TQM is a strategy to (better) achieve company goals.

❑ to transform the vision into missions (e.g. messages such as "improved customer orientation") making focused action possible and thus being the basis for the

❑ formulation of individual (quality) goals.

To stabilise and speed up TQM, it is essential to institutionalise appropriate reviews of this process. These can be carried out on different levels:

❑ Annual assessments e.g. on the basis of the European Quality Award, in order to determine main actions and targets on an individual level[141]

❑ Additional systematic data gathering (e.g. customer and employee surveys) which can also be used for Benchmarking

❑ Reviews within regular meetings of steering groups to consider issues such as the results of quality improvement teams

❑ A specific review of the TQM introduction process (incl. appropriate data collection)

❑ Regular discussions between managers and employees on all levels concerning quality issues

The risk of TQM only being understood as a programme can be reduced, and a continuous Total Quality culture built up if all essential activities are included in daily work. This means, for example, not differentiating between financial or quality parameters as a basis for target-group specific decisions; both parameters should be integrated in one suitable parameter system. Assessments should not only be seen as a basis for improvement projects, but rather used as controlling instrument and as basis for annual corporate plans.

In general, a Total Quality culture requires a change in the attitudes and behaviour of all employees. For this, appropriate reward and payment systems have to be introduced which consider the commitment to and achievement in Total Quality within the appraisal and promotion of staff at all levels. Usually, it is obligatory to change existing concepts for the assessment of performances.

The stabilisation of a quality culture by reinforcing customer and process orientation may lead to corresponding organisational consequences.[142]

Ritz-Carlton[143]

❑ Numerous training programmes exist for employees as well as for managers. These have been introduced to ensure the implementation of Total Quality.

❑ Each employee gets a short "set of instructions" including the essential measures for the promotion of customer satisfaction.

❑ The motto: "We Are Ladies and Gentlemen Serving Ladies and Gentlemen" demonstrates that customer satisfaction is the highest priority.

❑ Surveys conducted in the company show: 96% of the staff identify themselves with the quality goal "excellent customer service".

Granite Rock[144]

❏ Top Management has formulated quality goals and expectations, which focused on nine core elements. These elements reflect the strategy for the promotion of Total Quality.

❏ For these nine elements, targets are set annually and the managers check at regular meetings if those targets have been achieved.

❏ The results of the reviews are made accessible to all members of the organisation.

BOC Special Gases[145]

❏ The steering group, which includes managers of many different functional areas has worked on numerous activities concerning the implementation of Total Quality.

Some examples:

- Working out a training programme

- Listing necessary quality improvements

- Preparing and evaluating surveys within the market

- Supervising progress in the implementation of TQM

❏ Managers see themselves as role models for the realisation of TQM, and encourage their employees to actively participate in the implementation process.

Texas Instruments[146]

❏ Appreciation and rewards for individuals is subject to contributions to corporate values.

1b: Support of Total Quality through provision of appropriate resources and assistance

The implementation of comprehensive quality concepts demands the provision of personnel and financial resources and, in addition, active support from all managers at all levels. Active support here initially means personal participation, e.g.

❏ when defining priorities in improvement activities,

❏ in Self-Assessment after appropriate qualification,

❑ when moderating workshops,

❑ when implementing problem solutions (especially concerning problems which can only be solved from a certain position of power
or with responsibility for budgets) or

❑ when executing training activities.

This personal assistance for the support of Total Quality processes helps
to fulfil the function of being a role model.

Since TQM requires the active involvement of all employees in an organisation, an appropriate framework has to be created. This includes issues
such as

❑ actively supporting those taking appropriate improvement activities,

❑ releasing staff for quality discussions, work on projects, quality
circles or TQ training and

❑ providing suitable rooms with appropriate equipment for group
work.

Regardless of how resources are provided, they will initially have to be
seen as an investment (advance provision). The following questions are
therefore important:

❑ Is there a TQ budget, e.g. for the development and further development of a concept (with additional external support)?

❑ Are the investments for education and training independent of the
actual economic situation?

❑ Are there long-term resource allocation plans which are not exclusively defined by bureaucratic pay-back-periods?

❑ Can any positive trends be determined concerning investments
for TQ-specific subjects (e.g. customer and process orientation)?

❑ How do these investments develop in comparison to other competitors or Best-Practice-Examples?

❑ Is our company a benchmark for others?

BOC Special Gases[147]

❑ In addition to the TQM steering group there are two cross-
functional subgroups working on specific quality subjects in the
fields Marketing and Products.

❑ Managers invest 40 % of their working hours in TQM activities, e.g. for training, meetings and communication with staff.

Granite Rock[148]

❑ Managers participate actively in developing and realising internal and external qualification concepts.

❑ Moreover, a managers' tasks include the evaluation and improvement of the management system.

❑ There is a job rotation system for upper management. By these regular job changes between different business units and divisions, the development of new ideas is supported and the cooperation between different units and divisions is improved.

1c: Involvement with customers, suppliers and other external organisations

Comprehensive Quality Management cannot be undertaken exclusively within the company. The idea of prevention in a wider sense demands the involvement of customers and suppliers which depends on the personal commitment of managers. This can be achieved when

❑ managers invest much of their time in establishing and preserving good relations to customers and suppliers,

❑ managers try to get information on-site (systematic programme of visits),

❑ there is an appropriate assessment and feedback system (assessing suppliers/analyses of customer satisfaction) which is systematically used as a management instrument,

❑ the relation to suppliers and customers (e.g. traders) is based on partnership including training and consulting services and supporting communication throughout all management levels,

❑ special performances are honoured by the top management (e.g. Quality Excellence Award),

❑ complaints are an issue for the top-management,

❑ common improvement teams are established,

❑ customers and suppliers are partners within Quality Function Deployment and Simultaneous Engineering.

These common activities contribute considerably to improving communication between companies, increasing the effectivity of measures and supporting partnership - every aspect helping to achieve a common objective. Thus, the partners have the opportunity to learn and understand the wishes and needs of respective customers and suppliers and to find appropriate means to meet them. The reaction time needed to adapt to changes in customer needs and market situations can thus be shortened, which contributes considerably to better customer orientation.

Granite Rock[149]

❑ The company's organisation was restructured to support customer orientation which especially helped to establish closer relationships between top-management and customers.

❑ Customer surveys make it possible to meet customer wishes quickly, to maintain a high quality standard of products and services and thus to ensure customer satisfaction.

Milliken European Division[150]

❑ The Milliken Opportunity for Improvement (MOFI-)System for customer complaints lead to the average processing time being reduced from 40 to less than 2 days.

❑ Each employee of Milliken is obliged on principle to process complaints.

❑ Complaints are not seen as a chance to blame the person responsible, but as a chance for improvement.

❑ They have started activities for receiving suggestions for improvements from trading partners.

❑ Milliken draws up a supplier profile showing the on-time delivery of Miliken. The profiles are sent to the authorised dealers.

Another important factor for Total Quality is the relationship to the company's surrounding area and its impact on society. It is the management's task to take appropriate measures to make the essential ideas of the company's quality concept known outside and that these find expression in the company's relationship to its surrounding area. This can for example be achieved by company representatives (usually managers or experts) participating in events on the subject of TQM or actively cooperating with institutions working on aspects of Total Quality.

Below some examples:

- ❏ Cooperation with the EFQM or their national groups (e.g. D.E., the "German EFQM" group)

- ❏ Cooperation with specialist organisations (e.g. norm associations) or professional associations dealing with different Total Quality aspects

- ❏ Participation in or execution of industry-wide discussion groups on TQM

- ❏ Participation of top management in working groups supporting the competitiveness of industries or branches which e.g. can be initiated by ministries of commerce

- ❏ Execution of industry specific conferences on Total Quality which can be used for the exchange of information and experiences

One very effective way of disseminating the ideas of Total Quality concepts is the integration of basic approaches in external education and training concepts. This can be achieved by events initiated by the company itself or by external qualification measures. Some exemplary approaches are:

- ❏ Conception and execution of or participation in industry-wide seminars and training programmes on Total Quality issues

- ❏ Participation of the company's managers as speakers on quality subjects within lectures and exercises at MBA and/or regular university study courses

- ❏ Provision of information material (e.g. case studies) for education and training purposes

- ❏ Participation in the development of professional specific education programmes, e.g. at vocational and technical schools.

Another possibility for the promotion of Total Quality is specific public relations work. A company can support the dissemination of Total Quality concepts in the company's surrounding areas e.g. by

- ❏ Employees of the company publishing reports and articles on quality subjects,

- ❏ Company representatives being involved as speakers at congresses and seminars,

- ❏ Reporting on quality subjects within company internal magazines,

- ❏ Managers writing papers on quality subjects

The active support of the community concerning cultural, social and sporting fields also contributes to the promotion of Total Quality outside the company.[151]

Exemplary approaches are:

- ❏ Financial and material support of amateur theatre groups, youth centres and sports clubs

- ❏ Creation or support of meeting places or nursing wards for handicapped persons or people who are socially disadvantaged

Not only the managers but every single employee as a representative of the company and its quality philosophy is able to contribute to disseminating the TQ ideas and visions outside the company. Therefore the managers have to encourage their employees to undertake such activities and support their execution. In particular, staff should be prompted to participate in

- ❏ professional and specialised associations as well as in

- ❏ local organisations and institutions

and their commitment should be encouraged by management.

Milliken European Division[152]

- ❏ Milliken executes Open Days for CEO's (Chief Executive Officers) of the EFQM members.

- ❏ Within the EFQM's Guided Study Tour, Milliken organised a conference on the subject of Benchmarking.

Texas Instruments[153]

- ❏ TI actively supports the state of Texas in realising a TQM initiative.

- ❏ TI founded a TQM team which reports to external groups about experience gathered during the implementation of comprehensive quality concepts.

Robert Bosch[154]

- ❏ The company provides conference rooms for the German speaking group of the EFQM, the "German EFQM" (former "Frankfurter Forum").

❑ Within EFQM's Guided Study Tour, the Robert Bosch GmbH held a conference on "People Empowerment".

❑ The company participates in the "Programme Managing Total Quality" at the University of Kaiserslautern (Germany) by providing speakers and lecturers.

Rank Xerox[155]

❑ The company's management initiated publication of their application for the European Quality Award.

❑ The company's managers hold lectures at congresses and in other companies to Total Quality subjects.

❑ Managers of Rank Xerox participate in executing EFQM congresses.

1d: Recognition and appreciation of the efforts and achievements of people

Comprehensive concepts for change have to be supported and realised by people. Since the willingness for change is a slow process, it is essential to reinforce this process on all levels by recognition. Here, it is not only the people within the company who should be considered, but also suppliers and customers (if these are contributing to the implementation of the Total Quality culture). Everyone involved should get appropriate feedback showing how managers, customers or suppliers perceive their behaviour and performances. The main targets of feedback are:[156]

❑ to support and stabilise (quality) promoting behaviour by recognition

❑ to correct behaviour that is contrary to the aims of comprehensive quality promotion

❑ to clarify relations and requirements between internal and external customers and suppliers

❑ to activate a learning process making it possible to learn from each other

❑ to offer the possibility of self-critical reflection

❏ to inform and motivate in order to reduce uncertainty, and to provide conditions which ensure the success of quality-promoting activities.

In order to really achieve the aims of feedback, it is necessary to follow particular instructions:[157]

❏ Feedback has to be formulated in the right way, i.e. it has to include concrete details, reactions of the person giving the feedback and it has to show possible consequences.

❏ Feedback has to be suitable, i.e. it has to be oriented towards the person who gets the feedback and not the person who gives feedback.

❏ Feedback on behaviour must concern those areas which an individual is able to change.

❏ Feedback should be given as soon as possible.

❏ Feedback should not exert pressure on the individual. He/she decides personally whether he/she will change or not.

All other recommendations for employee feedback by giving recognition and criticism can of course be applied within Total Quality.[158]

With regard to recognition, the easiest way in which it can be given is to recognise the performance of an employee, or to have (top) managers present "on site" ("Management by Walking Around"). In this category, we can include examples such as thanking employees personally or by letter, as well as presenting cash or other rewards as special appreciation. In the case of certificates and presents, it is especially important to check carefully whether the recipient feels that this is appropriate recognition.

Recognition can, of course, be given for special success or effort, for achieving excellent quality, and can also be initiated by managers and customers. Below some examples:

❏ quick and effective solution of customer problems

❏ special success and effort of individuals or teams

❏ particular commitment to customers

❏ keeping to customer deadlines - even when conditions are difficult

❏ initiatives for identifying and solving quality-related problems.

However, one should take into consideration that standards of service and effort may vary according to different employees and it is therefore not encouraging if only "Olympian" performances are recognised.

Promoting the implementation of comprehensive quality concepts within the company can in addition be supported by the annual awarding of an internal quality prize. This can for example be initiated by customers or superiors from branches, business units, departments, by management or by the steering group. Every employee nominated who does not win the prize receives at least a certificate or some other kind of recognition for his/her special endeavours. Criteria and winners should be announced within the company as well as externally (e.g. in specialist magazines). These measures with their widespread impact reinforce the importance of such an award. For a limited period of time, a quality prize may also emphasise particular topics by using specific criteria within the assessment such as

❑ Contributions to improving customer orientation,

❑ Originality of worked out solutions for problems,

❑ Contributions to stabilising results in the long term,

❑ Optimisation of key processes,

❑ Excellent behaviour identified by customer or supplier feedback

❑ Special achievements with positive influence on business results.

Analogous to the awarding of an internal quality prize it may be an advantage to recognise the support of Total Quality with regard to cooperation between companies with a quality award for customers (especially for appointed retailers or wholesalers of the company) and suppliers. Such recognition should also consider customers' and suppliers' performances, as well as their endeavours regarding the dissemination of the Total Quality idea. Examples for criteria which could be used to select the winner are:

❑ customers and suppliers participating in training courses provided by the company

❑ adopting quality targets in their own corporate policy

❑ quality teams supported by customers and suppliers

❑ customers' and suppliers' activities aimed at increasing the satisfaction of the ultimate buyer.

Nomination of the respective partners can be made by management (especially persons who are responsible for purchase and sales). When selecting the jury members, it is not only managers who should be considered, but also external people, such as renowned experts or representatives from specialist associations. To promote awareness of the prizes, and to achieve widespread quality efforts from customers and suppliers, the quality prize has to have a special reputation. It may be promoted by public representatives awarding the prize and by reports about the winners in newspapers and specialist magazines.

The efficiency of these measures depends on a fundamental comprehensive reward concept which is reviewed regularly and benchmarked with "Best-Practice-Examples".

Milliken European Division [159]

- ❑ The management recognises successes which exceed an employee's "regular" duties with a thank-you letter or personal thanks.
- ❑ At Milliken, it is a special honour to be selected as "employee of the month" by staff election.
- ❑ Photographs of employees with exceptional performances are placed at central points in the company.

Ciba-Geigy [160]

- ❑ Payment of management is subject to achieving fixed targets.
- ❑ The corporate suggestion system was reorganised in line with the implementation of TQM.
- ❑ Improvements concerning "job duties" can be included in the suggestion system.
- ❑ Employees receive material or non-material appreciation for improvement suggestions.

2.2   Policy and strategy

The question of whether Total Quality Management is due to become a programme carried out within a certain time limit, as has happened with similar models in the past, is heavily dependent on the extent to which comprehensive quality is made an integral part of corporate policy. i.e., how it affects strategic orientation and its implementation in daily business. Here it is important to differentiate between those organisations that already have a vision and strategic corporate planning, and those - in particular smaller or medium-sized companies - in which the introduction of Total Quality Management leads to the formulation of appropriate statements and their implementation within the framework of a joint planning and target concept.

The following issues relating to policy and strategy are listed within the context of the European Model for Business Excellence:

2a: How policy and strategy are based on information which is relevant and comprehensive.

2b: How policy and strategy are developed.

2c: How policy and strategy are communicated and implemented.

2d: How policy and strategy are regularly updated and improved.

These issues can be detailed as follows:

2a: How policy and strategy are based on information which is relevant and comprehensive

Because "management by facts" is such an important component in the implementation of TQM, this must also be reflected in the formulation of policy and strategy.

In contrast to traditional management methods where only direct performance indicators delivered by the accounting and reporting department are considered, here also indirect indicators are regarded. Some examples for indirect indicators are:

❑ feedback from customers and suppliers,

❑ feedback from company employees,

❑ data relating to the performance of competitors and best-in-class companies (benchmarks) and

❑ data of social, political and legal significance.

IBM

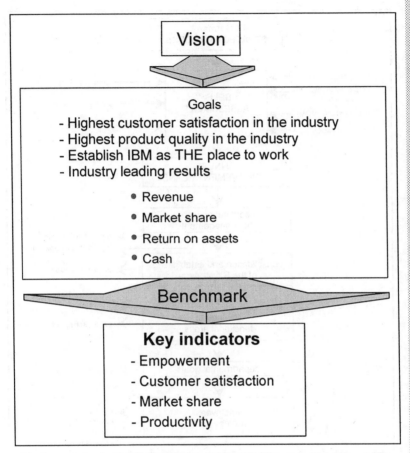

Fig. 59:   The derivation of relevant data for the creation of corporate plans for IBM[161]

In this context, the most important issue is the existence of a consistent process of data collection and its implementation within policy and strategy. A reorientation of strategic controlling is therefore required.

Rank Xerox

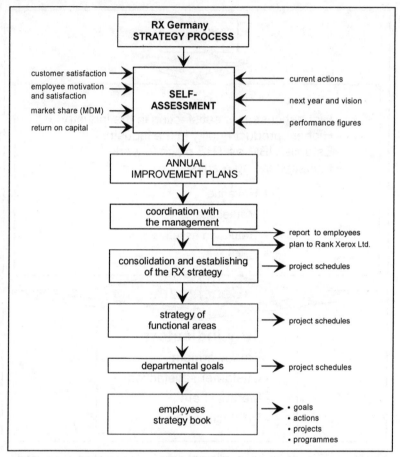

Fig. 60:   Policy deployment at Rank Xerox Germany Ltd[162]

2b: How policy and strategy are developed

If TQM is to act as a concept which targets business excellence, then there can be no difference between the corporate goal and the total quality approach. This assumes, however, that an extended and consolidated understanding already exists of how positive company results can be achieved in the long term, instead of in the short term to the cost of individual target groups (such as the employees or society).

Even in some of the standards, such as the design of DIN ISO 8402, connections such as these can be observed:

"For a corporate management method aimed at the involvement of all its members, which puts quality first and aims to achieve long term business success, as well as benefitting both the members of the organisation and society through customer satisfaction."

Long-term business success is therefore based upon long-term customer satisfaction combined with benefits - or at least contentment - on the part of the members of the organisation and the environment. This statement can also be found in the European Model for Business Excellence, whereby this additionally mentions which enablers are necessary to achieve it. A corporate vision and the missions that are derived from it explain the corporate goal and the values to be used as a basis for its realisation. They thus become a reflection of the way in which Business Excellence is understood - or show that the company or organisation has confused TQM with a quality improvement programme.

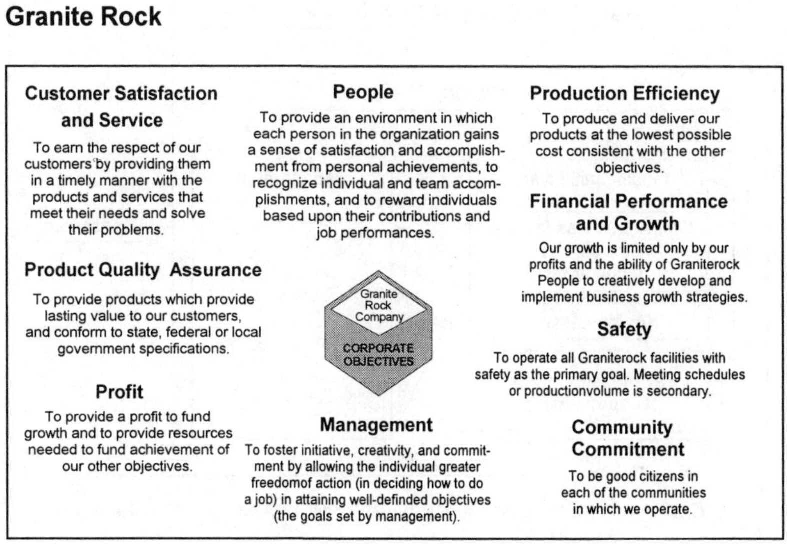

Granite Rock

Customer Satisfaction and Service	People	Production Efficiency
To earn the respect of our customers by providing them in a timely manner with the products and services that meet their needs and solve their problems.	To provide an environment in which each person in the organization gains a sense of satisfaction and accomplishment from personal achievements, to recognize individual and team accomplishments, and to reward individuals based upon their contributions and job performances.	To produce and deliver our products at the lowest possible cost consistent with the other objectives.

Product Quality Assurance

To provide products which provide lasting value to our customers, and conform to state, federal or local government specifications.

Financial Performance and Growth

Our growth is limited only by our profits and the ability of Graniterock People to creatively develop and implement business growth strategies.

Profit

To provide a profit to fund growth and to provide resources needed to fund achievement of our other objectives.

Safety

To operate all Graniterock facilities with safety as the primary goal. Meeting schedules or production volume is secondary.

Management

To foster initiative, creativity, and commitment by allowing the individual greater freedom of action (in deciding how to do a job) in attaining well-definded objectives (the goals set by management).

Community Commitment

To be good citizens in each of the communities in which we operate.

Fig. 61:   Corporate objectives as a basis of company policy and strategy[163]

❑ Agreement of quality and corporate planning

❑ Deployment of measurable area targets from the nine corporate goals:

- Responsibility of the area leader
- Quarterly progress check
- Annual evaluation of target achievement
- Annual reformulation taking into account customer surveys, benchmarks etc.

❑ Annual process evaluation

❑ Definition of requirements on the own division and on suppliers

IBM

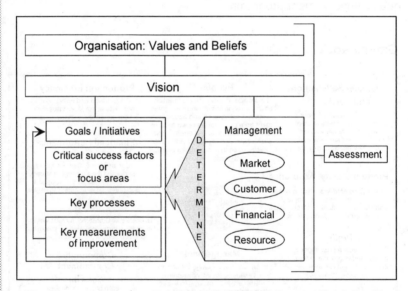

Fig. 62:   Policy and strategy at IBM based on a Total Quality Model[164]

Hewlett Packard

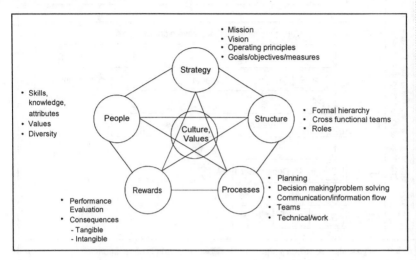

Fig. 63:   Policy and strategy as a part of a TQM-oriented organisa-
               tional model[165]

2c: How policy and strategy are communicated and implemented

Policy and strategy can only become reality if they are translated into a stringent planning process. Since planning is always based upon premises, and is therefore distanced from reality, it has to be constantly adapted. The interesting matter here is how this planning process can be systematically improved, and how changed priorities based on the data collection mentioned in 2b can lead to suitable adaptation processes.

Furthermore, it is also important to deal with the basic processes of transforming policy and strategy into defined corporate plans, and of deploying them. It is of particular significance that customer and process orientation are also applied through cross-functional deployment processes, and that they are not only oriented towards functional interests, as is so often the case with traditional management by objectives (compare fig. 64-65).[166]

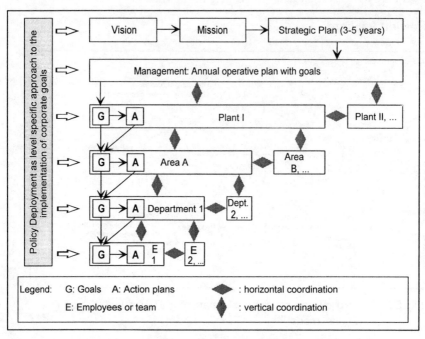

Fig. 64:   Policy deployment as an approach to the level-specific implementation of corporate goals (principles)

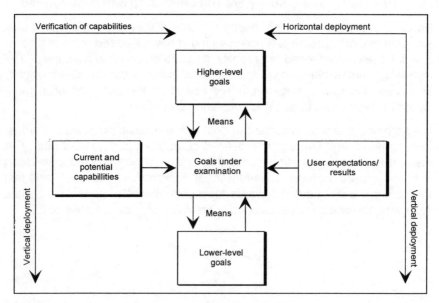

Fig. 65:   A close-up on the vertical/horizontal intersection and capabilities
check[167]

IBM

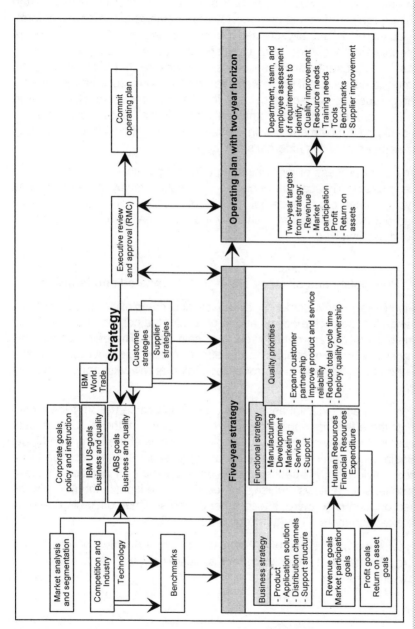

Fig. 66:   The Interrelationships of Company Policy and Strategy and
                the Business Planning at IBM[168]

The best vision and the tightest planning are of little use if they are not communicated. The way in which this is done is closely related to the planning process: If this is oriented towards participation, then an "information cascade" is actually created during the process. Of course, every imaginable media source (e.g. circulars, company newspapers, posters, videos, slide-presentations) can be used to ensure that ideas have been communicated. Different communication methods are suitable for different target groups e.g. kick-off meetings for the top management, or on-site visits for (top)management, combined with suitable information seminars. This could be supplemented with cross-level informal communication (e.g. in the canteen or within external seminars).

As any other process of disseminating information , this one, too, needs a success check. This can be achieved by regular employee surveys, or at intervals, carried out by external assessors. Occasional on-site interviews carried out by top managers generally lead to a feeling of surprise on the part of those involved.

2d: How policy and strategy are regularly updated and improved

The increase in environmental dynamics and complexity in recent years demands that corporate policy, and in particular the corporate strategy and its implementation, are not allowed to remain static. Therefore, companies need new methods of evaluating the effectivity and relevance of their policies and strategies, and new processes aimed at reworking and improving them.

Both internal and external assessment methods can be used for the evaluation of the effectivity and efficiency of a strategy - methods such as self-assessment, surveys or benchmarking on the basis of the European Model for Business Excellence. The results of this assessment process lead to a strategy review and, if necessary, to an adaptation. In addition to these comprehensive reviews, which, for economic reasons, should only be carried out annually, there is also a need for less time-consuming reviews to be executed more often (quarterly or biannually).

The review-process is part of a PDCA-Cycle[169] or a Hoshin planning[170] procedure. Furthermore, it is important to also deal with a review of the review-process.

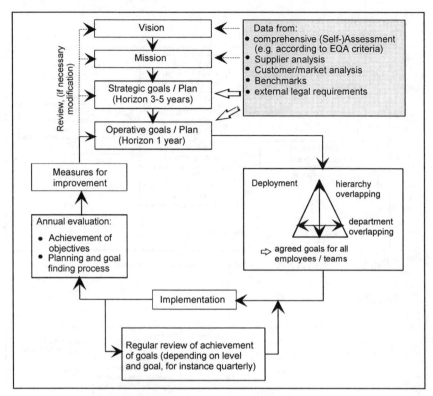

Fig. 67:   Policy and strategy as a continuous process

IBM

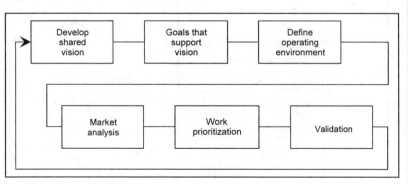

Fig. 68:   Strategic planning as a continuous process at IBM[171]

Royal Mail

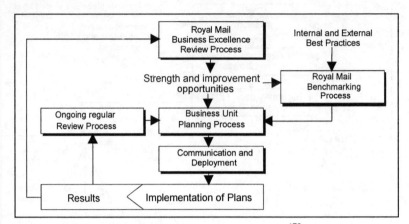

Fig. 69:   Royal Mail Business Excellence process[172]

Toyota

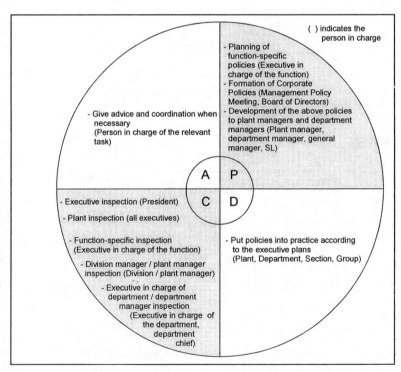

Fig. 70:   Continuous improvement of company policy and strategy
             through the PDCA-cycle at Toyota[173]

2.3   People management

The basic model of the European Quality Award presented initially has already demonstrated that the goal should be the involvement of all employees. This in turn explains the "Total" in TQM. However, the general target of continuous improvement also affects the processes of employee management. The success of these measures also filters down into all result criteria. In contrast to many of the older or more recent management concepts, which also claim employee orientation or people-centred management for themselves, both of the world-wide quality assessment concepts, (MBNQA and EQA), additionally include an evaluation of these methods by the employees themselves in the form of regular employee surveys.

Employee orientation within the European Model for Total Quality aims in particular to include all employees across the company in the continuous improvement process.

Broken down into individual units, this can mean:

3a: How people resources are planned and improved.

3b: How people capabilities are sustained and developed.

3c: How people agree targets and continuously review performance.

3d: How people are involved, empowered and recognised.

3e: How people and the organisation have an effective dialogue.

3f: How people are cared for.

These criteria can be specified as follows:

3a: How people resources are planned and improved

If it is assumed (in production plants as well as in others) that quality is generated by people, then a basic element of every management concept must be the continuous development of human resources. Accordingly, professional, methodical and social skills aimed at better problem solving have to be developed using improved concepts and methods.

This includes for example the regular and systematic examination of all processes within personnel management (e.g. personnel planning, recruitment, personnel placement, personnel development, performance appraisal and payment concepts) as well as their adaptation to changes in general conditions. If new requirements for superiors arise or if they change (e.g. in the creation of a guilt-free atmosphere, the promotion of cooperation through teamwork or an open doors policy) then this must be reflected in the personnel recruitment procedure and in performance appraisal. Only by changing structural conditions such as these it is also possible to change management attitudes.

Further important issues are the systematic analysis of the results of staff surveys and the safeguarding of these results through renewed interviews dealing with the same issues. Additional feedback opportunities arise in regular talks between superior and employee and annual councelling.

Finally, none of these points can come to fruition unless personnel policy is closely linked to a company policy which, in turn, contains total quality aspects itself. As with company policy, here too, it is a question of how strictly personnel policy is implemented in personnel planning, and in applicable measures.

The question of what personnel or organisational position this controlling function is assigned (whether "only" in the personnel department or whether a high-ranking "Human Resource Committee" is created) gives a good indication of the significance attached to this issue in the company - similar to the implementation of benchmarking.

BMW

The round table discussion concept at BMW [174]

❑ goal:

- organisation of continuous improvement concerning personnel

❑ characteristics:

- individual departmental discussions with a superior
- role of personnel management

  - initiation and organisation of processes

  - management of information (e.g. analysis and documentation of the personnel situation of the respective organisation units and problem-oriented selection of information)

  - personnel consultation (while creating individual and collective measures)

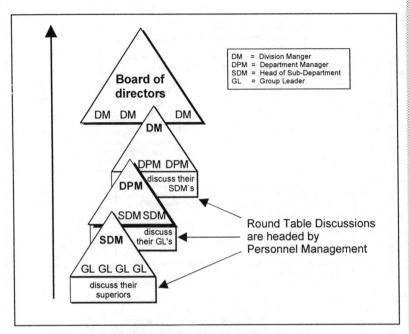

Fig. 71:   Organisation of the BMW round table discussion con-
              cept[175]

❑ procedure

- focal point of subject

  - current personnel structure

  - target personnel structure (e.g. with regard to quali-
    fications required in future)

  - assessment of performance and potential

  - measures based on target performance analysis:

    ⇨ short-term measures agreed upon immediately

    ⇨ global personnel political decisions within result
      discussions

- individual department "bottom up" discussions of personnel
  problems moderated by the relevant personnel official

- "top down" result discussions

- using the degree of fulfilment of the agreements as the
  input for discussions in the following year

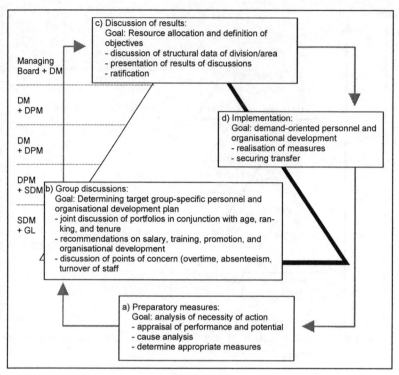

Fig. 72:   The procedure of round table discussions at BMW[176]

3b: How people capabilities are sustained and developed

As shown above, it must be possible to measure how stringent the implementation of a total quality-oriented personnel policy is by examining the change in the individual task areas of human resource management.

This begins with the implementation of personnel policy in short, medium and long-term personnel planning. It is particularly important for long-term considerations to develop a target in accordance with qualitative personnel planning. This should be preferably oriented towards the critical success factors of the company or the organisation. From these success factors, it is then possible to derive the necessary key qualifications.

Bertelsmann

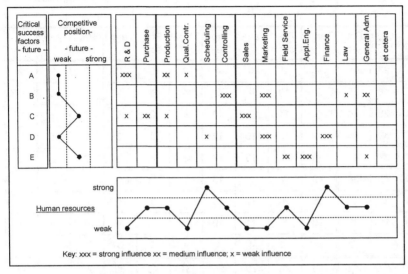

Fig. 73:   Analysis of the significance of human resources for competitiveness at Bertelsmann[177]

In order to recognise a need for action, the competencies in the current situation need to be analysed (qualification demand analysis). From this analysis, it is possible to derive consequences for personnel recruitment and development (see Fig. 74).

Alongside the continuous adjustment of changing qualification demands profiles, the quality of procedures is equally important. In this way, so-called assessment-centre-concepts are considerably more valid than traditional personnel recruitment methods. Another advantage is its team-orientation, since, on one hand, it is a group selection method, and on the other hand, places special emphasis on checking the ability to work in a team.

Personnel development means in-company training focused on the company-related targets, closing the gap between the actual state-of-the-art and the target state through qualitative personnel planning, and supporting and realising career planning with personnel-related targets. In this context, one should differentiate between planning for the new generation of executives and a more general personnel development plan which is based, for example, upon annual assessment interviews.

Number of employees			Professional Competence									
			High (e.g. University graduates)						Low (e.g. semi-skilled)			
			5		4		3		2		1	
Age	Target	Present	Target	Present	Target	Present	Target	Present	Target	Present	Target	Present
< 25	23	18	11	2	5	4	3	8	2	2	2	2
25-29	18	21	9	10	4	3	4	5	1	3	0	0
30-34	25	26	6	11	7	10	4	0	5	2	3	3
35-39	30	35	12	12	10	12	2	3	2	6	4	2
40-44	37	41	13	10	15	17	3	4	5	7	1	3
45-49	40	38	18	6	7	15	6	11	6	1	3	5
50-54	35	40	15	26	10	11	3	3	4	0	3	0
55-59	25	32	10	5	11	19	2	6	2	0	0	2
≥ 60	17	24	5	11	4	4	4	8	3	1	1	0
Total	250	275	99	93	73	95	31	48	30	22	17	17

Fig. 74: Example for qualitative personnel planning (corresponding for methodical and social competence)

In addition to the existence of target group-specific and problem-oriented personnel development, there is also the issue of its effectivity and supervision. This is not only necessary for immediate economic reasons, but also for indirect reasons: overqualification or general qualification that is not applied often leads to dissatisfaction and therefore hinders motivation rather than increasing it.

The seriousness of personnel development measures can be recognised on one hand by the budget and its alteration (in particular during economically difficult times) and on the other hand by the personal dedication not only of the operating department but also the line executive.

If teamwork and employee participation are basic elements of a total quality approach, as emphasised, for example, by Ishikawa[178], then personnel development concepts must attach great importance to its contents. This applies to every target group in the company (employees and executives), and demands corresponding structural framework where such behaviour is worthwhile, as well as qualification in the sense of imparting methodical and social skills. The number of teams or the time spent in teamwork are an initial, yet superficial, indication of how far this type of cooperation has succeeded. This purely quantitative measure must by complemented by a qualitative, result-oriented evaluation.

BOC Special Gases

Skill analysis at BOC Special Gases as an element of a qualitative personnel concept[179]

❑ Premise:

⇨ Efficient employees possess "superior" behaviour and special skills (especially social skills)

❑ Goals:

- Create a model for "superior" behaviour
- Survey of abilities and behaviour during the "better" execution of an activity
- Work out the "basic skills" of the employees

❑ Procedure:

1. Assessment of all employees in the department according to formal criteria (two target groups with different performances)

2. Organisation of behavioural event-interviews with these two target groups (description of the way in which the activities are carried out)

3. Objective evaluation of the collected information with work skills analysis

4. Determining crucial skills by comparing better employees with average employees

5. Detailed review of the competence models determined for individual areas of activity, using this to prepare a general job description

❑ Application of results:

- personnel planning and development by comparing the current and the target-skills of employees
- Performance assessment, determining remuneration

Hewlett Packard

Integration of new employees

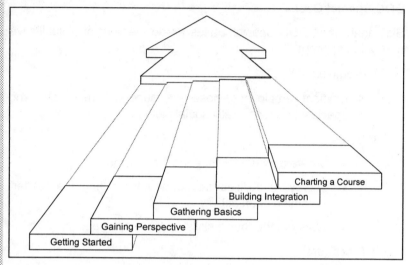

Fig. 75:   Integration of new employees at Hewlett Packard[180]

1.   Start (before entry - first day)
     Receive necessary information in order to ensure a pleasant transfer into the HP community and the new work surroundings

2.   Gain impressions (first month)
     Gain impressions of expectations of superiors, department purpose and goals, and the relationship to the whole organisation

3.   Acquire basic knowledge of company purpose and goals, rough overview of philosophy and essential processes at HP

4.   Achieve integration (fourth to sixth months)
     In-depth understanding of processes and philosophy at HP, as well as integration into these of one's own role. Also understanding of the achievement assessment processes and opportunities for involvement in individual development plans

5.   Determine further development (seventh tc twelfth months)
     Gain knowledge of, experience with and access to resources necessary for continuous development and qualification

Methods:
     Workshops, experiences, check lists, achievement feedback, information material, (structured and informal) talks with superior and colleagues

Granite Rock

IPDP at Granite Rock (Individual Professional Development Plan)[181]

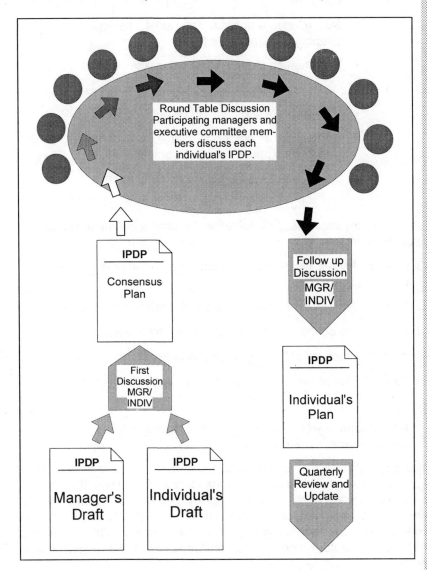

Fig. 76:   Human Resource Development at Granite Rock

❏ Principles:

- Every position is available to every employee on principle.

- Every employee can participate in seminars and further training courses relating to every area within the company.

- No (over) emphasis on past performances, but orientation towards the future.

- The creation of an IPDP is voluntary.

❑ Goals:

- Integration of company and employee ideas

- Agreement of corporate plans (e.g. company results, quality) and personnel development

- Basis for determining training requirements

In conclusion, the main issues involved in Personnel planning, recruitment and development are:

❑ how employees' knowledge is assessed and compared with company requirements

❑ how recruitment, promotion, transfers and release are planned

❑ how training concepts are worked out and implemented

❑ how the effectivity of training programs is assessed

❑ how employees can be trained further through team work.

3c: How people agree targets and continuously review performance

As has already been mentioned within the context of the criteria of policy and strategy, the deployment of corporate targets to the level of teams and individual employees is an essential step towards the achievement of total quality. On the one hand, one must ensure that corporate targets are deployed functionally and stringently, but that, on the other, customer-oriented, and therefore more general and cross-functional targets are not neglected.

Taking these issues into consideration leads to the weaknesses of older concepts such as Management by Objectives, which are dominated by functional orientation, meaning that other aspects are only dealt with implicitly. Solutions for arising target conflicts are therefore also not dealt with individually.

Hewlett Packard

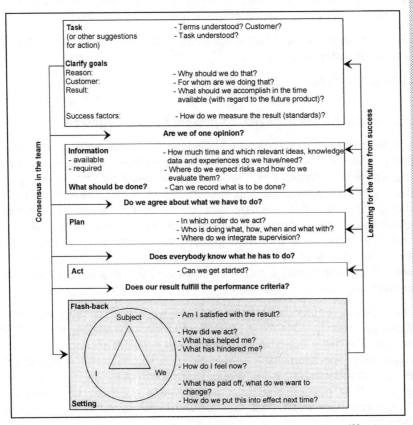

Fig. 77:   Operating procedure "goal-oriented work in teams"[182]

The agreement of individual and group targets with corporate targets is dependent, on the one hand, on the goal development *process* which ensures formal congruence and, on the other hand, on whether there really is *agreement* on the target, which then allows the partners to contribute their own ideas. Goal agreement concepts on the individual level cannot be efficient unless there is a functioning system of regular feedback, and if consequences are to be expected in the case of goal deviation. Such consequences could be the adjustment of qualification requirements for employees, thus creating a direct connection to the personnel development components discussed earlier.

Furthermore, a reviewing process which incorporates the work of the quality improvement team is essential for functional and cross-functional target agreement.

In conclusion, therefore, the main issues are

❑ how targets for individual employees and teams are agreed upon and brought in line with corporate targets,

❑ how targets for individual employees or teams are checked and implemented, and

❑ how employees are assessed and supported.

3d: How people are involved, empowered and recognised

Participation in continuous improvement programs does not happen automatically, and therefore requires a suitable framework. This is even more the case now than decades ago, when it was usual in industry to delegate problem-solving to specialists and specific departments. There is also the additional problem that management in particular tends to interpret suggestions for improvement as criticism or evidence of their own in-activity. Therefore, it is this management and executive culture which needs to be changed, in order to show employees that continuous improvement is (once again) a part of their job, and that this leads to positive rather than negative consequences.

For this reason, appropriate public relations work is necessary at every available opportunity. This must be evident in implementation, e.g. in that employees are given the time to participate in problem-solving groups, or that types of cooperation which enable more participation at the workplace (such as self-managing work groups) are promoted. In this context, questions about occupational health and safety are also becoming increasingly important. In the past, they too were considered to be the task of a specialist.

The participation of individuals in the continuous improvement process should also be strengthened by further development of the company suggestion system. Here, it is especially important to reduce the lengthy and unclear appraisal methods that often require much more effort than the actual bonus deserves. In such instances, systems should be introduced which can be used there and then, and which can clarify the relation between (additional) performance and the bonus. The bonus - for successful team work, too - does not have to be of a material nature. Public recognition and the integration of success-reports into regular meetings also contribute to the reward. Successful work requires the appropriate training, which can, of course, differ between target groups. Thus, we can imagine special training courses for employees who regularly deal with (external) customers.

Ciba Geigy

CIGENIUS - decentralised suggestion scheme[183]

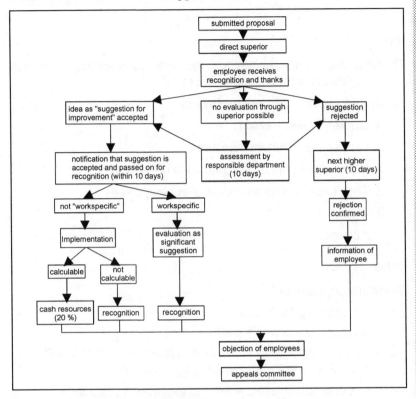

Fig. 78:   Decentralised suggestion system at Ciba-Geigy

❑ Characteristics of the company suggestion scheme:

- Suggestions are formally submitted ideas for the improvement of existing practices and processes which aid the company and its employees.
- Suggestions can be submitted by individuals or groups.
- Suggestions can relate to one's own work or to other areas (aim: tapping existing expert knowledge).
- Bonuses can be of a material or non-material nature. Suggestions relating to one's own tasks, and therefore termed as occupational duty, are only rewarded with a non-material bonus.
- The suggestion scheme is decentralised. Every suggestion goes to the direct superior, who assesses the suggestion.

- within ten working days. Thanking the employee is a matter of course (thanking culture). If a suggestion is rejected, this must be checked by a superior within ten working days.

IBM

The best way to improve quality is the participation of the employees in the continuous improvement process:[184]

❑ **Participation of the employees**	**76%**
❑ Quality-related training	33%
❑ Quality improvement measures	26%
❑ Improvement of the relationship to the suppliers	16%
❑ Task exceeding qualification of the employees	18%
❑ Statistical methods	12%
❑ Automation	7%

BMW

Guidelines to "Lernstatt":[185]

1. Overcoming Taylorism
2. Inclusion of the whole person
3. Independent activity of the participants (help towards self-help)
4. Freedom for the group (relative self control)
5. Direct inclusion of the junior management as facilitator
6. Indirect inclusion of the other superiors
7. Balance between subject orientation, group activity and the individual
8. Strive for a mature relationship with each other
9. Full consideration of the relationship in interpersonal behaviour (disturbances have priority)
10. Working in ways that are closely related to target groups (no training)
11. Work as close to the site as possible
12. Full use of visual communication devices
13. Fair and methodical settlement and solution of conflicts
14. Transfer principle: "It is not important what you aim for, but what you do"

The implementation of the solution to the problem is often simplified if high ranking executives take on the role of a promoter.

The extent of employee participation in this sort of cooperation is to a large extent dependent on how far their skills and abilities are acknowledged in problem-solving or self-managing work groups. As with other corporate processes, employee participation should undergo a regular review, e.g. using employee surveys, and if necessary be adapted to altered conditions. A comparison with best-practice-examples could also be useful.

In order to promote employee participation, a differentiated draft should be available, relating to different needs (and experiences). This concerns not only the extent of participation (from awareness of a problem to the implementation of the solution), but also the way in which it is organised (e.g. individual or group work). The increasing participation of employees in the planning and decision-making processes, and the corresponding authorisation to individual responsible actions is known as people empowerment.

Ritz Carlton[186]

People Empowerment

- ❑ The great significance of the employees is demonstrated in the company vision: "We are ladies and gentlemen serving ladies and gentlemen"
- ❑ Teams on all company levels are employed to set up goals and deployment plans
- ❑ All levels are orientated towards the vision and the targets
- ❑ All employees are encouraged to think beyond what is required of them
- ❑ Communication is promoted between functions
- ❑ Simultaneous, integrated problem-solving
- ❑ Task plans should be clear and easy to understand in their implementation
- ❑ Orientation of new employees by trainers and superiors
  - Setting an example in procedure and behaviour ("gold standards and methods")
  - Permanent success check (learning check)
  - Certification of new employees as soon as they meet all requirements

⇨ standards are developed by teams of employees from the relevant department

❑ Competence of the employee

⇨ Every employee has the authority to spend up to $2000 to satisfy the customer in the case of complaints

Robert Bosch[187]

Team-oriented production (TOP)

❑ Goals:

- Increase in flexibility and economic efficiency
- Increase in employee motivation and identification with the job

❑ Guidelines:

- Joint, integral tasks for the production team
- Decision-making at the lowest possible level
- Continuous improvement as a continuous task
- Clear goals
- Integral and task-relevant information and communication
- Qualified and flexibly employees

❑ Teams as a basic element of TOP

- 8-15 employees
- Highest possible continuity concerning the line-up
- A selected team leader:
  - Also works productively in the team
  - Leads team discussions (normally 1h/week) and continuous improvement circles
  - Carries out measures for the continuous improvement of processes
  - Is the contact person for team relevant affairs

❑   Realisation:

- Teams have a joint task, which is differentiated according to the contents (the professional task as a priority, with indirect activities and internal self-organisation). They have the necessary resources and empowerment as well as responsibility for the result

- Team-related goals which have been set or agreed upon have to be comprehensible, influenceable, achievable and assessable by the team

  - Time-, quality-, cost- and quantity targets

  - Goals related to CIP activities

- Information for the teams (e.g. goals, actual situation) are continuously updated and visualised

- Effort involved in overcoming interfaces is minimised by affiliation of production-related, indirect functions

- Independent realisation of the continuous improvement process

- Rewards dependent on the work in the team on the basis of job evaluation; in addition a team-related element

3e: How people and the organisation have an effective dialogue

In this issue, we must firstly deal with the presentation of traditional communication methods within the context of meetings, team briefings and regular feedback. Alongside the assessment of how timely and comprehensive top-down communication actually is, it is also interesting to observe whether effective bottom-up information and communication exists.

In relation to the method of feedback, it is also necessary to clarify to what extent this is received "neutrally", or whether selective perception takes place (e.g. if the feedback comes from a superior).

In addition to a benefit analysis of the "management by walking around" (e.g. as an attempt to collect information about the degree of acceptance of the total quality idea), it is also important not to forget the introduction of visual management concepts (e.g. within self-managing group activities). Visualising the most important goals and the current stage or degree of realisation normally raises interest in the possibilities of influencing them.

IBM

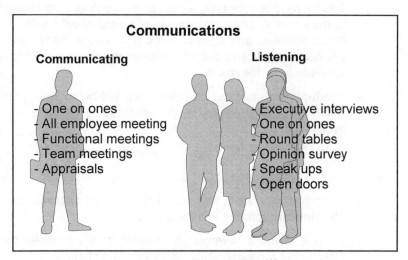

Fig. 79:   Beginnings of verbal communication[188]

The systematic use of information and communication techniques is also an issue here, even if only to present daily topics (e.g. expected visitors, canteen menu) on TV-monitors. In connection with this, we must also mention all computer-aided feedback systems that help groups to optimise their decisions.

Finally, one could also include communication requirement analysis in this section.

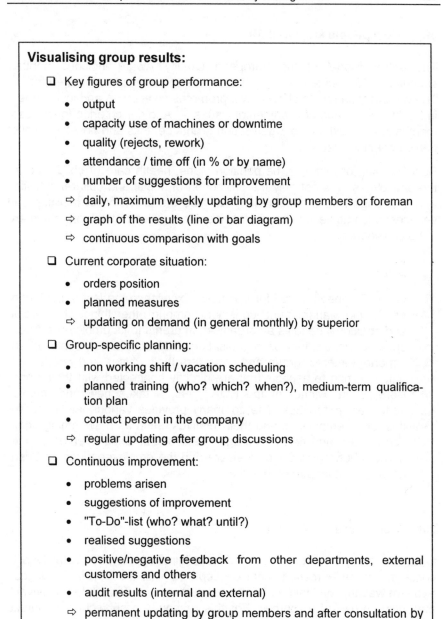

Visualising group results:

❑ Key figures of group performance:

- output
- capacity use of machines or downtime
- quality (rejects, rework)
- attendance / time off (in % or by name)
- number of suggestions for improvement
- ⇨ daily, maximum weekly updating by group members or foreman
- ⇨ graph of the results (line or bar diagram)
- ⇨ continuous comparison with goals

❑ Current corporate situation:

- orders position
- planned measures
- ⇨ updating on demand (in general monthly) by superior

❑ Group-specific planning:

- non working shift / vacation scheduling
- planned training (who? which? when?), medium-term qualification plan
- contact person in the company
- ⇨ regular updating after group discussions

❑ Continuous improvement:

- problems arisen
- suggestions of improvement
- "To-Do"-list (who? what? until?)
- realised suggestions
- positive/negative feedback from other departments, external customers and others
- audit results (internal and external)
- ⇨ permanent updating by group members and after consultation by external

Fig. 80:   Visualising group results on information displays

3f: How people are cared for

The actual Model of the European Quality Award includes another subcriterion (3f), added in 1997. It analyses "how people are cared for".[189] The organisation has to show how it promotes awareness and involvement in health, safety and environmental issues.[190] Another criterion for assessment is to what extent the organisation grants benefits and how the level of these benefits is set.

Benefits can, for example, be pension plans, health care or child care for the employees. It is not only the promotion of social and cultural activities which belongs to this subcriterion, but also the provision of facilities and services, such as flexible hours or transport facilities to the work place are to be considered.

Brisa

In the European Model for Business Excellence the last subcriterion of "People Management" considers, among other things, the social and additional benefits an organisation grants to its employees. They show to what extent an organisation understands its people as an important interest group and considers their whises and needs, not only referring to aspects that are directly connected with their work. Here, Brisa, winner of the EQA 1996,[191] takes new and unconventional approaches. The company provides various leisure facilities for its employees and their relatives, such as a swimming pool, sports halls and fields. Through these offers, Brisa overcomes the barriers between work and leisure and the employees identify Brisa as an important part of their life.

2.4   Resources

One particularly important factor in the original "Japanese" Total Quality concept, and other management concepts (e.g. in the Toyota Production System) was the avoidance of any wastefulness - or, formulated positively, the optimum use of resources. For this reason, the subject of resources has been increasingly focused on in recent years. It was not only the use of material resources, buildings and equipment that were considered, but also the use of technologies, particularly concerning the aspect of capital tie-up. It is therefore a necessary and logical consequence when partial concepts such as these are part of comprehensive Quality Management.

The management of resources within the European Model for Business Excellence attaches special importance to the aspects of "Support of Policy and Strategy", and "Continuous Improvement". In detail the following factors are considered:

4a: Management of financial resources

4b: Management of information resources

4c: Management of supplier relationships and materials

4d: Management of buildings, equipment and other assets

4e: Management of technology and intellectual property

A more detailed description can be found in the following:

4a: Management of financial resources

A company's ability to survive depends, in the short term, on securing its liquidity and, in the middle and long term, on stabilising its profit situation, enabling it to permanently fulfil its obligations to shareholders, employees and society.

Thus, a company has to strive for long-term optimisation - e.g. by trying to achieve a continuous increase in the "Shareholder Value". This requires the integration of financial planning in corporate planning, and the creation of a systematic approach to formulating targets. If the company's objectives reflect the idea of Total Quality Management e.g. through improved customer orientation, then this will also have to find expression in the allocation of financial resources. An indicator for this can be the share of financial resources spent on securing the company's future (e.g. investment, research, training) and continuous improvement (e.g. reduction in the average capital tie-up or in processing time).

In this context, a word of criticism - in Germany, at least the desired pursuit of long-term targets has usually been counteracted by the short-term considerations of management.

In addition to determining the contents of financial plans, they should also be regularly reviewed and improved. In general, a systematic inspection concept should include financial parameters such as cash flow and floating assets based on traditional accounting and reporting. Data concerning customer and process orientation are usually not considered. It is therefore important to check to what extent e.g. approaches of an activity based costing should be taken into account (see Fig. 81). Thus, the main issue is to see how currently existing approaches can continuously be developed and new approaches be tested (e.g. the systematic simulation of options on financial assets). Systematic reviews should be undertaken with appropriate attention to detail. Should there be a "closer" relation to quality, then a quality costs concept should be used which is not limited to the cost of errors. A sensitivity has to be developed for mainly low (initial) expenses for preventive measures concerning quality assurance.[192] The main goal here is not to develop a highly detailed system of cost recording, but to make it possible to compare the relation of particular "types of quality costs" (internal and external costs for mistakes, testing, assessment and prevention).

In summary, the handling of financial resources includes how

❑ financial strategies support policy and strategy,

❑ financial strategies and practices are reviewed and improved,

❑ financial parameters such as cash flow, profitability, costs and margins, assets, working capital and shareholder value are managed for improvement,

❑ investment decisions are evaluated and

❑ "quality cost" concepts are used.

Porsche

Main processes and Cost-Drivers in purchasing (extract)[193]

MAIN PROCESSES	**COST DRIVER**
placing orders	
• Series material through long-term contracts	Number of long-term contracts
• Series material through individual orders	Number of individual orders
• Non-production material through individual orders	Number of individual orders
Material disposition	
• For JIT-parts	Number of JIT-part numbers
For ABC-parts	Number of ABC-part numbers

Acceptance of goods

- Material for high-shelved   Number of supplied part
  storage (HSS) / Small   numbers. HSS/ SPS

  parts storage (SPS))

- Special storage   Number of supplied part
                                                numbers. Special storage

Storage of goods HSS   Number of containers High-
                                                shelved storage

Storage and handling of car
body and metal parts   Number of containers for metal parts

Ascertaining the unit cost of sub processes in the cost centre "purchasing"						
(1) Processes	(2) Parameter	(3) Planned output	(4) Planned cost	(5a) Process cost unit rate (1)	(5b) Distributed process cost per unit (2)	(5c) Total process cost rate
		(units)	(DM)	(DM)	(DM)	(DM)
Obtaining (a) offers	Number of offers	1 200	300 000	250.00	21.27	271.27
Submitting (a) orders	Number of orders	3 500	70 000	20.00	1.70	21.70
Handling of (a) complaints	Number of complaints	100	100 000	1 000.00	85.10	1 085.10
Department (b) control			40 000			
(a): depending on planned output (b): independent from planned output						

Fig. 81:   Process cost unit rate in the purchase department of
                    Porsche[194] [oa: output assigned; on: output neutral]

St. Gobain

External errors	Internal errors
- Returns	- Rate of capacity utilisation
- Warranty	- Break downs
- Substitute deliveries	- Deficiencies
- Compensation deliveries	- Defect material
- Cost of customer service	- Waste/Rejects
(e.g. travelling expenses)	- Repairs
- Delays	- Special checks
- Incomplete deliveries	- Storage, various losses
- Loss of customers	- Planning error
	- Error in handling deliveries
	- Absenteeism
	- Work accidents
	- Strikes
Inspection	**Error prevention**
- Laboratory, raw materials,	- Well considered plans /
finished products	constructions
- Equipment control	- Training, quality plan
- Observation instruments	- Evaluation of suppliers
- Quality service	- Internal auditor, maintenance
- Certificates	- Safety plan
- External fees	

Fig. 82:   Indication list itemising quality costs[195]

4b: Management of information resources

Optimising the management of information resources has recently been particularly discussed within the context of comprehensive computer concepts. For both CIM (Computer-Integrated Manufacturing) and CIB (Computer-Integrated Business), the aim was to reduce the time needed by making it possible to use the same data for different applications (e.g. in construction and in accounting). This was planned to be used in connection with the vision of a "deserted plant". However, one important fault within the practical realisation of this aim was to suppose that the successful use of computers could be achieved without creating new structures or restructuring the organisation (see Fig. 83). In addition to some mistakes made in the application (e.g. PPS-systems), a complexity was furthermore generated which hardly could be handled.

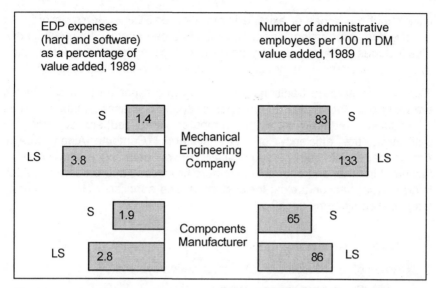

EDP expenses
(hard and software)
as a percentage of
value added, 1989

Number of administrative
employees per 100 m DM
value added, 1989

S   1.4

Mechanical
Engineering
Company

LS   3.8

83   S

133   LS

S   1.9

Components
Manufacturer

LS   2.8

65   S

86   LS

Fig. 83:   Productivity advantages through automation of efficient and
comprehensible processes - successful (S) versus less
successful (LS) companies[196]

IBM

Other worldwide IBM
manufacturing and
development locations

Marketing & Service

Rochester manufacturing
development and support

Customers

Suppliers

Business partners

Fig. 84:   Informational networks[197]

The implementation of Total Quality in a company generally leads to
organisational consequences (e.g. increased object or customer orientation
rather than orientation towards corporate functions) making it necessary to

think about the sense of existing information or EDP systems. In order to achieve this, information is needed which has been neglected up until now. This includes data for judging processes in their entirety or an information system for assessing the organisation's customer orientation (see Fig. 84).

This is in contrast to traditional accounting and reporting methods, which are more orientated towards functions or costs. Self-assessment concepts in production require appropriate computer-aided feedback systems. Up until now, the efficiency of CAQ systems (Computer-Aided Quality Assurance) should be regarded critically. How is data concerning the satisfaction of internal and external customers processed and prepared? Which informational networks exist for customers and suppliers? How are knowledge-based systems used?

Texas Instruments

Areas of application within the information system:[198]

❑ Solving customer problems:

- Employees with contact to customers can fall back on actual data and carry out analyses in order to make necessary decisions (Electronic Customer Support)

❑ Process improvement:

- Constant analysis and statistical evaluation of process parameters
- Reduction in processing time (door-to-door time)

❑ Increase in the level of productivity and safety

❑ Integration of the information management system in the strategic planning process

❑ Determination of action strategies

IBM

Information System "Electronic Customer Support" for the promotion of customer orientation:[199]

❑ target:

- analysis of customer satisfaction
- direct reaction to customer satisfaction

❑ dual function:

- problem management:
  if problems arise supporting customers by direct provision of information

- gathering customer wishes:
  by systematically analysing this data, trends can be recognised earlier.

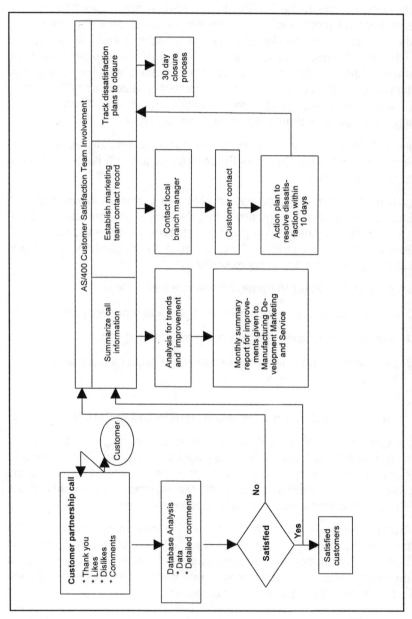

Fig. 85:   Customer-oriented information management at IBM[200]

These few examples demonstrate that a Total Quality company also needs appropriate information strategies and systems which reflect and support company goals.

In this context, *quality orientation* in a wider sense cannot mean that systems become more and more complex: instead, customer orientation stands for increased user-friendliness. As positive trends in relation to hardware have been observed in recent years, this now applies particularly to software. Another aspect of this subject is accessibility, characterised by the number of available terminals or by the real-time data transfer in companies with functional units at different places. Improvement projects concerning response time should likewise not be forgotten.

Finally, software packages providing assistance to employees within improvement projects (e.g. Business Process Management) have to be mentioned in this context.

Supposing an information and data processing concept already exists to continuously support the company's targets, one must then ask whether this too is being continuously improved, e.g. based on the results of Self-Assessment or Benchmarking. This can also be applied to information validity, integrity, security and accessibility.

In summary, it is possible to name the main issues as how

❑ appropriate and relevant information is made more accessible,

❑ information strategies support policy and strategy and

❑ information validity, integrity, security and scope are assured and improved.

4c: Management of supplier relationships and materials

This subject, too, has been discussed in depth in recent years. Partial concepts coming from Japan, such as Just-in-Time and Kanban lead to stock-reductions. These strategies were then finally integrated during the discussion on Lean Production or Lean Management, as a result of the MIT-study on the world-wide state of the automotive industry.

The Muda Principle (avoiding waste of any kind) mentioned above leads for example to the concept of "lean production" with drastic reductions in preparation times, material inventories and stockage area. Quick feedback and the pressure to systematically eliminate errors, along with zero-defect-production, create the ideal prerequisites for this.

	Japanese plants in Japan	Japanese plants in North America	American plants in North America	All plants in Europe
LAYOUT				
Area (sm / car / year)	0.5	0.8	0.7	0.7
Size of repairing area (% of assembly area)	4.1	4.9	12.9	14.4
Supplier/Assembler Relations				
Inventory level (days, for 8 parts)	0.2	1.6	2.9	2
Number of suppliers per assembly plant	170	238	509	442
Proportion of parts single sourced (%)	12.1	98.0	69.3	32.9

	Toyota Takaoka	GM Framingham
LAYOUT		
Assembly area per car	0.45	0.75
Stock of parts (average)	2 hours	2 weeks

Fig. 86:   Comparing assembly area and relationship with suppliers[201]

The strategy "Simplifying before automation", i.e. to gain advantages in productivity through stable processes and better product design instead of automation - should also be included here. The "lean purchasing" is another consequence of these thoughts, which had already been discussed by Taichi Ohno (Toyota) in the 50s. The depth of production is reduced (e.g. only own-production of key components), and then the greatly reduced number of suppliers (system suppliers) are worked with intensively. The aim here is to achieve a concept based on long-term contracts and - if possible - financial shares. This requires, among other things, a comprehensive approach to supplier assessment.

This cooperation extends to common product development (e.g. with Simultaneous Engineering), as well as the common determination of target costs, taking into account a learning curve for cost reduction. In the automotive industry, this intensifying of cooperation which also includes the introduction of a quality management system has existed for many years. Outside Japan, Ford took on a kind of exploratory role (see the following example). For example, the type of job-sharing between producer and supplier becomes evident within the concept of the self-confirming supplier.

Continuous Improvement within cooperation with suppliers is, however, often only achievable by cross-functional and industry-wide teams. In this context the management of such a process and the continuous deter- mining of results (also through Benchmarking) are important factors. In addition one should also discuss how

❑ management of supplier relationships reflects policy and strategy,

❑ the supply chain is managed for improvement,

❑ material inventories are optimised,

❑ global non-renewable resources are conserved, recycled, and waste minimised.

Ford

Supplier Assessment System:[202]

Criteria and assessment elements	Points
Adequacy of the suppliers' quality assurance system	30
• 20 questions for checking the system	
The managers' quality awareness and their attitude to quality	20
• Continuous improvement (understanding/ attitude, training, supervision by management)	
• Reaction if quality complaints arise	
Continuous quality performance	50
• Quality of products and services	
	TOTAL: 100

Classification of suppliers:[203]

Classification and area of scores	Code
PREFERRED	E
• 85-100 (it is possible to be honoured as Q1-supplier)	
SUITABLE	S
• 70-84	
NOT SUITABLE	U
• less than 70	

Rank Xerox

The number of suppliers has been reduced in the past ten years from 5 000 to 400[204]

Granite Rock

Partnership with suppliers for mutual benefit:[205]

❑ On-going Supplier Quality Performance Tracking System for assessment

❑ Golden Chain Award for suppliers

Ritz-Carlton

On-time delivery for all types of material when furnishing and equipping new hotels increased from 60 % in 1989 to 100 % in 1991[206]

Texas Instruments

Integrated information system with 800 suppliers[207]

❑ Regular assessment of performance and quality, documentation in performance reports

❑ Implementation of customer-supplier-teams

❑ On-time delivery raised by 46 % during the past 4 years

Strategic alliances and reduction in number of suppliers

4d: Management of buildings, equipment and other assets

In the EFQM model for 1997, the management of buildings, equipment and other assets is discussed under a special criterion.[208] Optimising fixed assets in concurrence with company policy and strategy is seen as a starting point.[209] In addition, the efficient utilisation of operating resources as well as concepts are dealt with such as maintenance to increase life span or total operating performance.

In this context, the Total Productive Maintenance (TPM) concept is still useful. TPM aims to maximise equipment effectiveness. This is achieved by establishing a thorough system of preventive maintenance for the equipment's entire life span. Furthermore, TPM involves every single employee, from top management to workers on the shop floor. It encourages self-managing work group activities by promoting preventive maintenance through motivation management.[210]

In addition, the organisation has to disclose how it assesses the impact on society and on its employees, as well as how it handles safety issues.

IDEMITSU KOSAN[211]

Parts of the modern TPM concept were discussed in Japan as early as the mid-1950s. As a reaction to the general setting, which seemed particularly critical from a technical perspective, the management of Idemitsu Kosan refinery decided to introduce TPM in 1988. Crucial specific problem areas include:

❑ "hazardous" production in huge plants

❑ the absolute necessity of maintenance because of extremely sensitive production processes

❑ large production areas and a small number of employees

❑ stringent security regulations

Besides improving on-the-job safety and increasing employee performance, the effective utilisation of production equipment had to be ensured. Therefore, small groups were established which were supported and coordinated by a TPM-promotion committee. Each small group took care of a number of measures with specific objectives:

❑ measures to enforce the efficient utilisation of production equipment

- maintain planned operating rate

- increase fuel production

❑ self-initiated maintenance measures

- increase number of suggestions for improvements

- improve employees' ability to diagnose problems

❑ scheduling maintenance

- increase production equipment reliability

- develop scheduling system

- integration of scheduling and maintenance requirements

❑ preventive maintenance

- improve construction and planning process

- prepare preventive concept

- set up production equipment to fulfil maintenance
  requirements

❑ measures to increase on-the-job safety

- assess danger potential

- increase employee awareness and sensitise attitudes

❑ increase employee performance with respect to technical
requirements

- develop training programme for production workers

See figure 87 for initial results of small group activities.

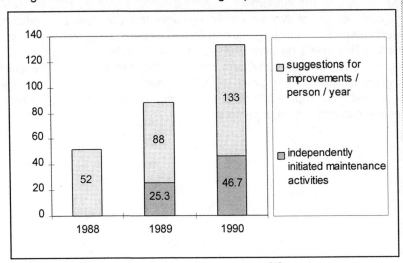

Fig. 87:   Initial Results of the TPM-Introduction[212]

4e: Management of technology and intellectual property

Whereas in 4b, the issues of information and communication technologies were dealt with, here the subject is process and product innovation in a general sense.

Securing markets in the long term will generally not be possible without the innovation of products and services, and this often requires process innovation. Some of the companies which began a "comprehensive TQM-programme" were less successful because they optimised their processes for the sake of process-optimisation, and thereby purely and simply forgot about product innovations.

Therefore, the primary aim in this context must be to achieve, maintain and increase skills and leadership in key technologies - e.g. in cooperation with external partners and research institutes. Leadership in technology, however, also requires the appropriate qualifications. This aim has to be integrated into the strategic planning of human resources and its realisation.

It is certainly not the goal to create "Happy Engineering", i.e. to use all possibilities without evaluating the consequences for the customer (contribution to solving the customers' problems) or for business results. Here, the difficulty is to resolve as far as possible the potential contradiction between restriction through systematically managed processes, and creativity. (This could be achieved e.g. by strictly differentiating basic research with the "utmost liberty" and more regulated research and development which is applicable in practice.) When creating innovations, the most important aspect is their systematic use or marketing and the protection of intellectual property e.g. with patents.

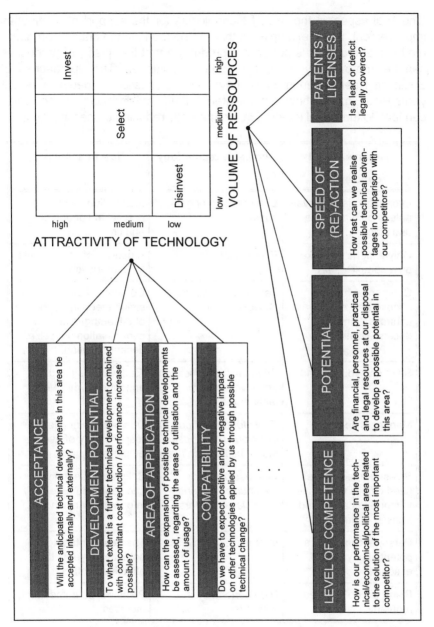

Fig. 88:   Technology-Portfolio according to Pfeiffer[213]

In order to support process and product innovations, it is necessary to implement and describe a process in the same way as new or alternative technologies are identified and assessed in relation to the effects they could have on the company (see Fig. 88).

One final aspect is the use of technologies for the support of continuous improvement. Some examples of this can be found in the chapter on "information resources". It is not only in production that the quality of processes can be improved by using appropriate techniques. The approaches of Business Reengineering which have been discussed in depth in recent years (see Fig. 89) show that the intelligent use of information technologies can lead to functional integration, dramatically reducing processing time.

Organisational deficiencies	Available technology	New possibilities
Information is only available at a certain time and place.	Common use of data bases	Information can be used parallel at various places and times.
Only experts can take on a complex job.	Expert systems	A generalist can execute the experts job.
Companies have to choose between centralisation and decentralisation.	Telecommunication networks	Companies can simultaneously make use of advantages of centralisation as well as decentralisation.
Seek and you will find.	Automatic identification and investigation techniques	That which is sought announces where it is.
Managers decide.	Tools for the support of decisions (data bases, model building software)	Decision making is the responsibility of every employee.
Sales representatives need offices to receive, to store, to call on and to transfer information.	Wireless data communication and portable computers	Sales representatives can send and receive information anywhere.
Personal contact to a potential buyer is essential.	Interactive video disks	The best contact to a potential buyer is the - effective contact.
Plans will be adapted regularly.	High performance computers	Plans will be immediately modified.

Fig. 89: Overcoming organisational barrier through new technologies[214]

In conclusion, the keeping of the EFQM-criterion Resources

- ❑ "exploits existing technology and protects competitive advantages

- ❏ identifies and evaluates alternative and emerging technologies in the light of policy and strategy, and their impact on the business and on society

- ❏ harnesses technology in support of improvement in processes, information systems and other systems

- ❏ exploits and protects intellectual property."[215]

2.5   Processes

It is not only the subject of resources that has become more significant. Processes too have started to attract greater attention. On the one hand, it is possible to observe an increasing interest in the certification of Quality Management systems which automatically requires the comprehensive documentation of processes. On the other, concepts such as Lean Production, Lean Management and "Business Reengineering" are strongly orientated towards processes. In contrast to the current version of the DIN EN ISO, weight is placed here on the aspect of value-adding and the elimination of all non-value-adding activities. Total Quality concepts also integrate systematic process analyses, but use an approach which is more concentrated and yet more comprehensive.

In one sense, this approach is more restricted because - e.g. in contrast to the DIN EN ISO - not all processes are discussed, but rather those processes which are considered to be fundamental to securing the critical success factors (key processes). Whereas the DIN EN ISO 9000 is predominantly internally oriented, the emphasis here when selecting key processes is on external orientation and, therefore, customer orientation.

However, this approach is also more comprehensive because it is not restricted to one single analysis of a process's contribution to the net product and to the documentation of processes. Instead, the approach includes the continuous management, review and improvement of processes. Moreover, it includes the creation of feedback systems which take into account customer, supplier and employee information within the continuous improvement process.

While the dangers of bureaucracy are often discussed within the context of certification, this approach explicitly demands innovation and creativity.

This topic can be broken down into the following aspects:

5a: How processes key to the success of the business are identified

5b: How processes are systematically managed

5c: How processes are reviewed and targets set for improvement

5d: How processes are changed and the benefits evaluated

5e: How the organisation implements process changes and evaluates the benefits

5a: How processes key to the success of the business are identified

The main task here is to recognise the critical success factors and identify the key processes influencing these factors. As only the top management can work out solutions, it is they who will have to give the impetus. The solutions could vary greatly according to specific industries or companies (e.g. the protection of the environment may have a different relevance in the chemical industry than in other industries).

In contrast to other concepts for optimising processes, the customer's requirements are the focus of attention here, and may therefore lead to a reorganisation of processes. The subprocesses derived from key processes may possibly have to be adapted to the local framework. In addition to the matter of identifying these processes (if a systematic and consistent approach already exists), it is also necessary to determine which processes actually belong to the key processes.

IBM

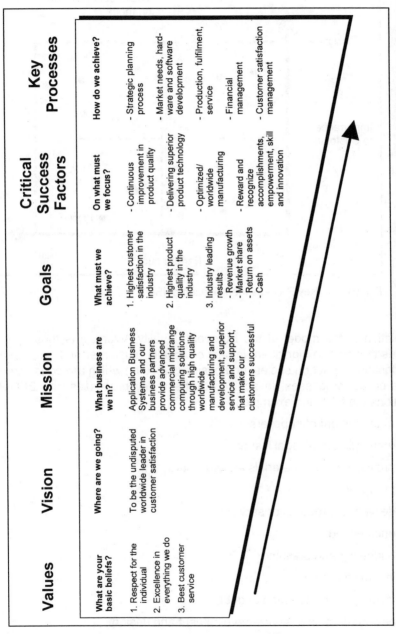

Fig. 90:   Identification of key processes at IBM[216]

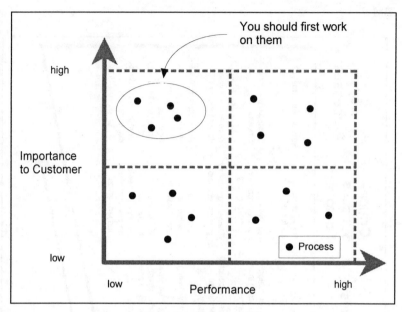

Fig. 91:   Key Process Identification at IBM[217]

In relation to the model of the European Quality Award, it is those processes that have a significant impact on results (customer and employee
satisfaction, impact on society and business results) which are considered
to be critical processes. In addition to these key processes, the EFQM
mentions the following examples:

- ❑ management of suppliers
- ❑ management of legal issues
- ❑ provision of raw materials and suppliers
- ❑ production
- ❑ delivery of products or services
- ❑ engineering
- ❑ budgeting and planning
- ❑ incoming orders
- ❑ invoicing and collection of debt
- ❑ new product and service development and design
- ❑ marketing and sales
- ❑ management of safety and health and of environmental issues

Badenwerk

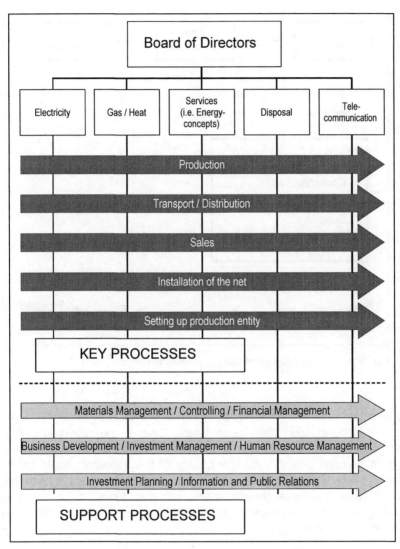

Fig. 92:   Key and support processes at Badenwerk[218]

Ubisa

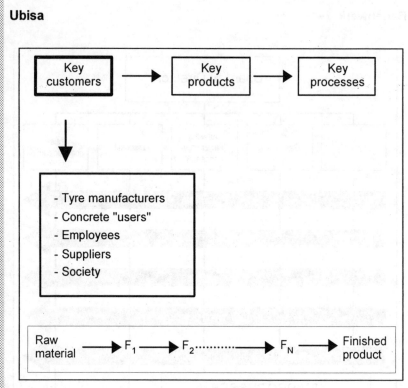

Fig. 93:   Identification of key processes at Ubisa[219]

Since process-oriented observation generally involves several departments, interface issues often arise which have to be resolved. When
choosing a solution, it is important to differentiate between long-term or
short-term process orientation. The quality of the solution should be reviewed regularly. As all activities within a Total Quality concept ultimately
aim to improve business results, these will also have to be called to
account. Examples of measures may be customer satisfaction, cycle times,
zero defects and efficiency.

Texas Instruments

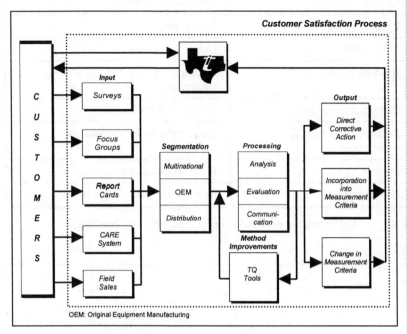

Fig. 94: Customer satisfaction process[220]

In summary, the most important aspects are how

❑ key processes are defined,

❑ the method of identification of key processes is conducted,

❑ the impact of key processes on the business is evaluated.

Analysing processes on the basis of the current DIN EN ISO 9000 will generally not comply with these requirements.

5b: How processes are systematically managed

In order to achieve long-term stability of cross-departmental processes in particular, (such as the execution of an order), an appropriate framework has to be established. Here preventive concepts such as Quality Function Deployment or Process-FMEA could be mentioned.

Process steps	Indicators
Contract release	Contract corrections
Process order	Faulty input
Place order	Delivery not on time
Receive goods	Incomplete/faulty accompanying documents
Store/distribute goods	Wrong delivery
Installations/material movements	Incomplete/faulty installation documents
Invoice	Invoice corrections
Process payments	Incomplete/faulty payment documents

Fig. 95:   Indicators for selected subprocesses in order handling[221]

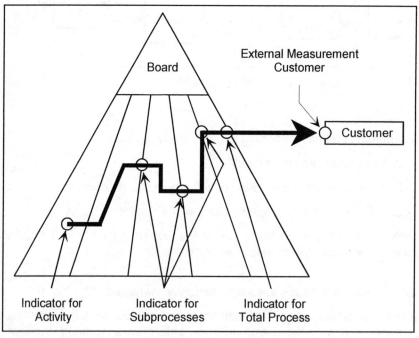

Fig. 96:   Differentiation of measurement indices for process management[222]

[A1]	Order processing	
[A11]	Check customer order, order confirmation	Cycle time: Receipt of order to confirmation of order
[A111]	Receive order, copy and distribute, initiate check	Number of offers followed by an order
[A112]	Administrative/technical review, record	Cycle time
[A113]	Apply for export permit	Number of unqueried export permits
[A114]	Order confirmation	Number of achievable deadlines
[A12]	Placing internal order	
[A121]	Transfer customer order into internal order	Number of correct internal orders
[A122]	Sign internal order	Cycle time
[A123]	Copy internal order, distribute and declare	Number of correct internal orders

Fig. 97:   Measurement indices for subprocess "Execution of customer order" in order processing

The steps taken in these processes require the existence of performance data and parameters. Concepts for continuous improvement (such as Deming's PDCA cycle) are also based on this data. Here, improvement targets for certain performance parameters are defined, based on the results of regular internal audits. Benchmarking methods can be used to support these processes, and particularly for determining parameters for key processes.

In this context, certification can be the lead-in, in as much as pressure to "re-certify" can lead to such a system. Within a company-specific assessment concept based on the MBNQA or EQA, not only the framework, but also the effects of the changes on results can be determined.

The adequate management of cross-departmental processes requires an appropriate organisational framework. Cross-functional teams and the concept of process-ownership are solutions which can often be found in practice.

IBM

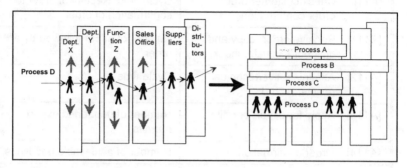

Fig. 98:   Cross-Functional Teams at IBM[223]

The systematic management of processes could include how

❏ process ownership and process management are established.

❏ standards of operation are established and monitored.

❏ performance measurements are used in process management.

❏ systems standards, health and safety systems are applied in process management,

❏ interface issues inside the organisation and with external partners are resolved.

5c: How processes are reviewed and targets set for improvement

Total Quality Management as "Management by Facts" defines quality as being measurable. Correspondingly, the relevant processes are described using parameters which are fundamental for regular reviews and improvements. In contrast to traditional management concepts, this data does not only refer to economical aspects but is also concerned with those aspects which have indirect influence, such as customer and employee satisfaction. Within the notion of a comprehensive approach, data from suppliers and competitors is also included.

The continuous improvement of processes also requires a system which may be included in Cross Auditing, Benchmarking and Policy Deployment. Here, the setting of priorities and the way in which they influence those processes that are essential for the company should be made clear. Essential here means an orientation to the future and thus to customers.

Continuous improvement means that future targets can (also) be derived from past data. They thus show continuity, but also promote improved prevention.

The relevance of improvements often depends on the challenging nature of the targets: challenging targets obviously motivate people more - especially if there is an appropriate framework for achieving those targets.

Hewlett Packard

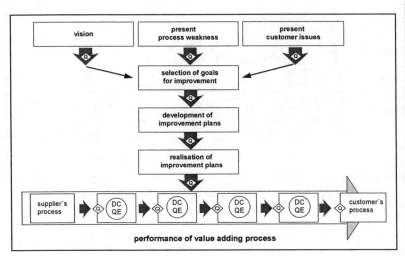

Fig. 99:   Derivation of process improvement goals[224]

For continuous, on-site reviewing and managing processes, it is, on the one hand, advantageous if the process owner (on a subprocess level) has been empowered to intervene. On the other hand, however, the management of processes requires the user-friendly visualisation of parameters and measures.

Therefore, this checklist includes all approaches describing how

❑ methods of improvement, both incremental and breakthrough, are identified and prioritised.

❑ information from employees, customers, suppliers, other stakeholders, competitors and society, and data from benchmarking is used in setting targets for improvements.

❑ current performance measurements and targets for improvement are related to past achievement

❑ challenging targets to support policy and strategy are identified and agreed upon.

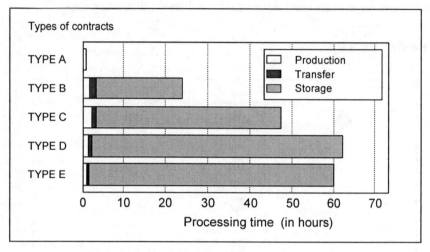

Fig. 100:   Analysis of the distribution of processing time depending on various types of contracts[225]

IBM

Continuous Improvement in "Cross-Functional Teams":

❑ Tasks:

- Improving processes
- Choosing tools for securing processes

❑ Procedure:

- Describing problems
- Analysing trends (frequency of errors, evaluation of SPC charts)
- Correlation of trends with already changed processes:
  - procedure
  - material

- • Systematic determination of causes
    - – cause and effect diagram
    - – practical experiments
- ❑ Targets:
    - • Cost reduction
    - • Reduction in processing times
    - • Reduction in defect-rate through prevention
- ❑ Results:
    - • Reduction in processing time (80 %) and in stock (55 %)
    - • Reduction in storage area (30 %)

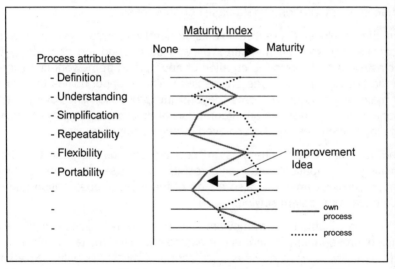

Fig. 101:   Process improvement with cross-functional teams[226]

5d: How processes are improved using innovation and creativity

As already mentioned in the introduction, the systematic analysis and documentation of processes is often associated with the prejudice of bureaucracy. It is therefore especially important to mention innovation and creativity in this context.

Here, we focus on three issues:

❑ How are (process-related) innovations (e.g. new construction principles or altered management techniques) introduced into the organisation?

❑ How are the creative talents of employees promoted in incremental and breakthrough improvements?

❑ How are organisational structures changed to encourage innovation and creativity?

The first of the above-mentioned questions surely represents the greatest challenge and will have to be described under the heading "transfer of technology". This therefore points to transfer institutions such as universities and other research institutes. However, the exchange of experiences with Best Practice Companies or the use of national and international networks (also within TQM) should not be forgotten. In addition, one can include the implementation of suitable processes such as the systematic evaluation of (international) data bases or congresses.

Using the employees' creative talents generally requires investments in educational and training measures as well as offering the opportunity to participate - in addition to the creation of appropriate framework conditions (see the section on employee satisfaction). These opportunities to participate may be provided by teams "beyond the production line" or by "self-managing work groups" as an integral part of daily work. Employee motivation may sometimes also be achieved through competitions.

If and to what extent one has succeeded can be determined when examining participation rates and results. The use of many applied methods and instruments is also a sign of the level of qualification and of the potential for problem solving.

The change in structural framework can best be recognised in the existence of cross-functional teams (for example within Simultaneous Engineering), as these support process orientation the most. Not only the variety of teams but also the restructuring of the corporate suggestion scheme represent structural adjustments. Nevertheless, all these approaches are more like a "cosmetic" touching-up of the old system. Radical restructuring e.g. in the sense of a constant process-oriented division of labour with a strong reduction or restructuring of existing "departments" or new decentralisation concepts is rarely found in practice.

Iveco Magirus

Start-up talks - a company-specific model of process innovation teams:[227]

❏ employee participation when starting a new product line

❏ fortnightly approx. 30 minutes in 20 areas

❏ either, if possible, gather problems and weaknesses as well as solutions for problems, or otherwise transferring to specialised departments

❏ presented by junior managers or foremen

❏ voluntary participation

❏ pilot phase:

⇨ April 1991 - Sept. 1992 with 266 subjects in 101 start-up talks

⇨ until Sept. 1992: 172 solutions for problems implemented

⇨ participation rate: 246 out of 1462 employees (16.8 %)

❏ phase of continuation:

⇨ Sept. 1992 - July 1994 with 352 subjects in a further 197 start-up talks

❏ targets for start-up talks

• early guarantee of product quality:

- reduced reject rates

- lower correction costs

• increase in productivity:

- optimising production methods and work processes

- fewer downtimes

• positive attitude of employees towards changes

BMW

Module teams at BMW:[228]

❏ new organisation of product and process development:

• spatial combination of all those who are involved in development

• arrangement of those involved according to mental flow of material

❏ promotion of interdisciplinary communication

❏ intensification and improvement of organisational connections

❏ introduction of flexible organisational forms according to the principles of project management

❏ simultaneous and global project processing by teams

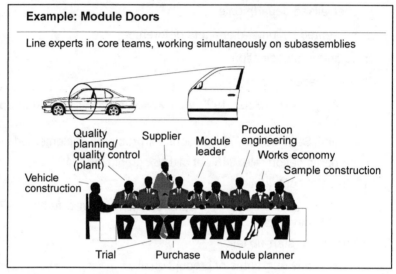

Example: Module Doors

Line experts in core teams, working simultaneously on subassemblies

Fig. 102:   Process-oriented product development[229]

❏ Targets of module work:

  • improvement of quality

  • reduction in product and process development times

  • reduction in one-off tasks

  • improving cooperation within the whole process chain

  • comprehensive and object-specific observation

❏ Determination of standard modules of a vehicle

❏ Process orientation in product development - from functional to process-oriented teams

❑ Experiences until now:

- reduction of time, energy and costs for development
- improvement of product / process quality
- effective simultaneous work
- improvement in the solving of complex and comprehensive problems
- early recognition of problems
- direct and quick solving of problems
- high motivation of team members

5e: How processes are changed and the benefits evaluated

If the continuous improvement of processes is our focus, then there must also be a "process" for introducing and assessing improved and new processes. This process should fulfil at least three tasks:

❑ to check if new or changed processes are suitable for the envisaged target by executing a pilot study complying with a framework that is transferable and that guarantees a systematic procedure. In this context, the inclusion of the people affected is an aspect of employee orientation.

❑ timely and comprehensive information on and adequate qualification for process changes. This requires a timely analysis of the need for training so that qualification can be provided when it is needed.

❑ to check the results of a changed process (especially in relation to the envisaged targets) with an adequate audit system including the essential aspects of a TQM philosophy. The use of an appropriate concept for project management is recommended, especially regarding considerable changes in key processes. In order to ensure that the envisaged benefit is achieved, an assessment model may be supportive.

IBM

New design of development process for the system AS 400:[230]

❑ Installing Early Manufacturing Involvement Teams (EMI) by involving suppliers and customers

❑ Targets of new design of the product development process AS 400:

- early determination of product requirements

- avoiding errors in product and process design

- lower number of changes concerning hard and software

- delineation of process steps

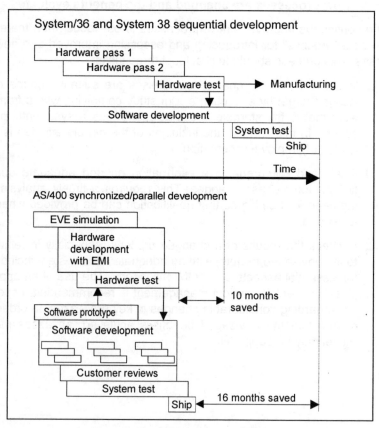

Fig. 103:   Comparing System/3X with AS/400[231]

ABB

T 50 Programme at ABB:[232]

❑ Increasing customer satisfaction through:

- reduction in processing time

- decentralisation of corporate structure

- further development of the employees' skills

❑ Targets of programme:

- to reduce processing time by at least 50 %

- to improve on-time delivery (target: 95-100 %)

- to reduce stock by 30 %

- to increase productivity of corporate processes by at least 20 %

❑ Beginning in 1990

❑ Implementation of a process-oriented form of organisation:

- work is organised in process teams in order to fulfil the following tasks:

    – product development

    – organisation of projects (looking after customer orders)

- self-managing work groups on the executive level

⇨ use of "Target Oriented Teams"

- implementing the programme in 130 companies (26 300 employees) of the company group ABB

Target oriented teams at ABB:

❑ characteristics:

- teamwork with trained employees (e.g. Process-Mapping)

- analysis of processes

- orientation to net product (reducing waiting times and ex-penditures for corrections within the process)

- improving the effectivity and quality of corporate processes between suppliers and customers

❑ Results achieved through process changes up to 1993:

- reduction of processing time from receipt of order until delivery according to type of product by 45 up to 70 % (average: 47 %)

- reduction of time for product development by 25 up to 80 % according to type of product

- Improvement of on-time delivery (average: 94 %)

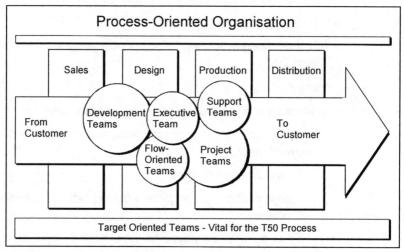

Fig. 104:   Target-oriented teams at ABB[233]

2.6   Customer satisfaction

The satisfaction of all external customers is considered by the European Model for Business Excellence to be the most important result criterion. However, while this should be regarded as a natural prerequisite within a free market economy, it was obviously all too often forgotten during economic boom periods related to "Quasi-Monopolies" (as can sometimes be found in trade). And it is for this reason that all TQM Assessment Concepts (e.g. also the MBNQA) place special emphasis on this aspect. The customer is also being rediscovered in a variety of other concepts (e.g. Lean Management or Business Reengineering) as well as in various publications. The most important advantage of the TQM approach in the European Model for Business Excellence is the orientation to results, which means that positive developments caused through changes in customer satisfaction can really be proved. While the Results criterion "Employee Satisfaction" finds its complement within the Enablers, namely "Employee Orientation", the same cannot be said for the Results criterion "Customer Satisfaction". Because of the obvious importance of customer orientation, this criterion is an implicit element in all Enabler criteria.

Due to the special importance of this subject, there are some important aspects which should be mentioned and integrated here (as they have similarly been included in former versions of the American MBNQA). These are:[234]

❏ knowledge of customers and markets

❏ management of customer relations

❏ commitment to the customer (customer orientation in its original sense)

❏ determination of customer satisfaction

❏ development of customer satisfaction

❏ benchmarking results with competitors

Current and future customer requirements need to be an essential part of corporate policy and strategy if the company intends to contribute to the optimisation of the customer's interests. It is therefore important to know

❏ how (also potential) customer groups / market segments will be defined,

❏ which data will be collected, how often, and by which methods (e.g. customer workshops), and how their objectivity and validity will be ensured,

❏ how specific product or service features and their relevance for different target groups will be collected or determined,

❏ how other customer-related data (e.g. complaints, losing or winning contracts, performance parameters concerning products and services) are used.

The aspect of future customer requirements requires additional answers:

❏ What period of time has been considered?

❑ How important is changing the framework (e.g. technology, competition, society, ecology, economic and social developments) for the influence on customers' future behaviour?

❑ How important are potential customers - including our competitors'?

❑ What does the projection of the most essential product and service features look like?

❑ To what extent have changing and new market segments and their effects on actual products and services been considered?

Perhaps some of this data is collected by customer satisfaction analyses. However, these analyses are more likely to be product or attribute-oriented, relating to the past or present. New solutions for customer problems which do not yet exist are only rarely included in satisfaction analyses.

Granite Rock

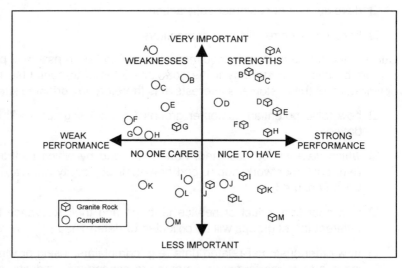

Fig. 105:   Granite Rock portfolio concept: importance of product and service quality [235]

As already mentioned in the context of processes, the continuous evaluation and improvement of processes for determining the customer's requirements and expectations are also important here. This includes the following aspects:

❑ improvement of survey's design,

❑ ensuring that information on customers is appropriate,

❑ simultaneously using different methods for obtaining information,

❑ considering the greater or lesser importance of target group specific product / service features.

One key process of customer-oriented companies is the management of customer relationships, also referred to as the process for optimising customer benefits[236]. Optimising this process requires - as with all other processes - a whole range of activities:

❑ measures to enable the customer to find support and to give feedback easily

❑ investment in the selection and training of employees with direct customer contact

❑ defining key requirements that have to be met in order to maintain and increase the customer's connection, and the translation of these into parameters

❑ defining service standards derived from these key parameters, and the use of these in the improvement of customer orientation

❑ ensuring follow-up measures

❑ effective and prompt processing of formal and informal complaints

❑ continuous improvement of processes.

Case-Study MBNQA

❑ Definition of service standards for telephone calls[237]

❑ Taking the call before the third ring,

❑ Immediate identification of the customer calling by the employee,

❑ Immediate notation of the phone number in order to be able to call back if call is unexpectedly interrupted,

❑ Avoiding internal connections to other employees, or at least checking if customer agrees to be connected,

❑ In case of complex information or comprehensive investigations promising to call back within two hours,

- ❑ "Follow up" call must be executed by the employee who took the first call,
- ❑ No customer should have to wait more than 45 seconds.

IBM

Follow up service at IBM:[238]

- ❑ Contact customer by telephone 90 days after sale of product,

- ❑ Gather recognition, criticism and general comments,

- ❑ Feed information into data base,

- ❑ Analyse data base,

- ❑ Distribute regularly to development, programming, marketing, production and service departments,

- ❑ Marketing department should contact dissatisfied customers,

- ❑ Understand and solve the problem,

- ❑ Contact customer again by telephone after a further 30 days.

IBM

Customer Complaint Management at IBM:[239]

- ❑ Receipt of complaints by
  - works manager,
  - product director
  - other top management
- ❑ Dealing complaints:
  - customer satisfaction management team
  - naming one responsible person for each complaint
  - solution within 2 weeks
  - documentation and evaluation of each complaint
- ❑ Using complaints for improvement of products and services

Milliken European Division

Feedback system of Milliken European Division for informing customers:[240]

<u>current year:</u> (customer xy)

number of orders	63
square meters (sales volume)	16 311
number of on-time deliveries	63
share of on-time deliveries	**100 %**

<u>compared to past year:</u> (whole company, cumulative)

	current year	past year
total number of orders	759	564
square meters (in total)	159 237	177 295
number of on-time deliveries	756	563
total share of on-time deliveries	**99.6%**	**99.0%**

Customer orientation in its narrowest sense includes the obligations of a company to increase the customers' confidence in products and services. As mentioned earlier, this also requires the personal commitment of top management.

The acid test for whether obligations have been met is seen when defects or problems arise, when dealing with guarantees and service, when the customer has been poorly informed, and when conflicts in interests arise (e.g. on-time-delivery versus product quality) etc.

To fulfil requirements agreed on (e.g. meeting delivery dates), it is also very important to regularly communicate with the customer and to inform him of all relevant aspects (e.g. progress made in the problem-solving process).

The investigation of customer satisfaction has to include all relevant fact-ors. The following factors are mentioned within the application documents of the European Quality Award:

❑ overall image:

   – accessibility

   – communication

   – flexibility

   – pro-active behaviour

   – responsiveness.

❑ products and services:

   – conformance quality

   – delivery

   – design

   – environmental profile

   – innovation

   – price

   – reliability.

If the achievement of continuos improvement and the measuring of this achievement are key elements of TQM, then customer satisfaction must be investigated and determined on a regular basis. Objectivity and validity of data also depend on how it is obtained. Data gathering executed by in-stitutes working in the market is more likely to lead to "desired" results than data gathering carried out by external professional companies using anonymous customer interviews. According to the company size and customer structure (target groups), different methods may be applied which can be simultaneously used to verify the quality of the data.

IBM

Methods for determining customer satisfaction:[241]

❑ Telephone survey by independent institute:

   • assessing the relevant importance of current and planned products / services

   • objectivity (client should not be mentioned)

   • possibility of giving comments on "questions not posed"

- advantages:
  - economical method
  - questions can easily be modified
  - high percentage of response
  - quick availability of information
  - possibility of concentrating on specific problems
- disadvantages:
  - no complex questions / multiple choice
  - no use of figures and charts

❑ written survey by independent institute:

- assessing the relevant importance of current and planned products / services
- objectivity (client should not be mentioned)
- possibility of giving comments on "questions not posed"
- advantages:
  - costs can be controlled
  - possibility of using figures and charts
  - complex questions / multiple choice possible
- disadvantages:
  - sometimes low response rate
  - no testing questions possible or pretest necessary
  - no deeper knowledge of persons who answer
  - data cannot be gathered short-term

❑ customer workshops:

- concentration on key customers
- demands neutral facilitation
- advantages:
- detailed analysis of customer problems
  - search for solution is already part of workshop
  - exact knowledge of participating persons

- disadvantages:
    - cost and time intensive procedure
    - only wise for key customers
- ❑ customer survey by questionnaires / response cards attached to the product:
    - advantages:
        - very low costs
        - general statements on product quality and delivery problems
    - disadvantages:
        - very low response rate
        - mostly used by dissatisfied customers
        - no detailed knowledge of persons who answer
        - complex questions practically impossible
        - impossible to time availability of data
        - often misunderstood as certificate of guarantee
- ❑ interviews by service personnel:
    - regular interviews or interview directly after service was "delivered"
    - "face-to-face-interview"
    - advantages:
        - complex questions / multiple choice
        - very flexible method
        - use of charts and figures
        - highest response rate
        - possibility of targeted selection of persons interviewed
    - disadvantages:
        - method demanding the most time and perhaps also the highest costs
        - interviewers' influence cannot be excluded

Olivetti

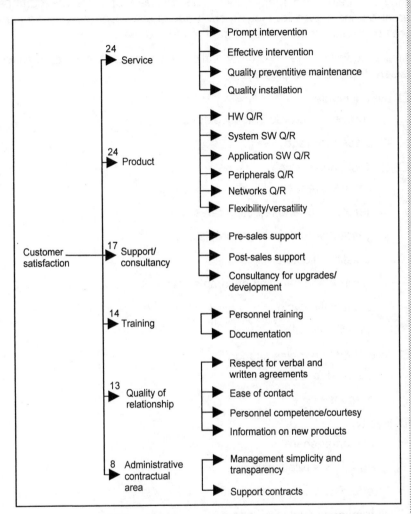

Fig. 106:   Example of customer satisfaction tree for medium-large users of information technology systems, with weighted first-level branches (source Olivetti, Q/R = Quality/Reliability)[242]

One of the key questions which has to be answered before starting is: Who is the customer? This question takes into consideration that a product's quality, for example a car's paint, is judged by very different target groups. This starts with the buyer of an automobile company and ends with the consumer. Between them are the application consultant, the person processing the paint, and many more. This shows that there are perhaps different competencies for judging such questions, which have to be considered by bearing in mind the different target groups.

Additional indicators for customer satisfaction may, of course, also be considered. Some examples are:

- ❏ overall image:
  - − number of awards and accolades
  - − press coverage
- ❏ product and services:
  - − competitiveness
  - − defect, error and rejection rates
  - − guarantee and warranty provisions
  - − logistic indicators
  - − number and handling of complaints
  - − product life cycle
  - − time to market.
- ❏ sales and after sales support:
  - − demand for training
  - − response rate.
- ❏ loyalty:
  - − customer share
  - − duration of relationship
  - − effective recommendations
  - − frequency / value of orders
  - − life time value
  - − new or lost business
  - − repeat business.

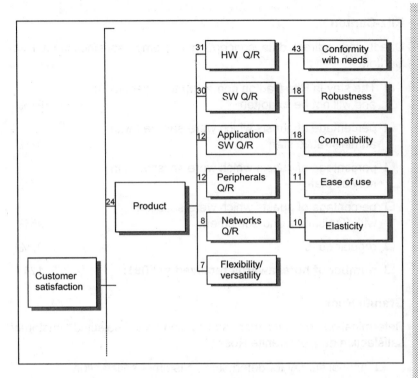

Fig. 107:   Example of extension of branches, weighted to the third level
             (medium-large users of information technology systems,
             source Olivetti, Q/R = Quality/Reliability)[243]

Moreover, supplier assessment programmes of main customers provide a
further source of comprehensive data.

Apart from the execution of a regular customer survey, it is also important
to determine how many customers of different categories (e.g. A, B or C
customers) should be included in data gathering.

The consequences of the survey are equally important: Is there a systematic concept for analysing data? What has been implemented, and how?
Which targets were determined? Were they achieved or surpassed? How
have complaints and guarantee costs developed? Which continuous improvements are being made in connection with data gathering?

Finally, it is necessary to compare one's own data with that of competitors
to check if the company comes off well or badly in comparative studies by
externals.

Ritz-Carlton

Direct and indirect data concerning customer satisfaction at Ritz-Carlton:[244]

❑ The stay in Ritz-Carlton comes up to expectations
  and will not be forgotten: 97%

❑ percentage of guests which were satisfied with
  administrative staff: 97%

❑ percentage of guests which were satisfied with
  service staff: 97%

❑ percentage of guests which were satisfied
  with furnishings and equipment: 95%

❑ regular guests: 97%

❑ **number of hotel awards received in 1991:   121**

Granite Rock

Determination of customer satisfaction and selected customer satisfaction data at Granite Rock:[245]

❑ annual survey for determining customer satisfaction

❑ considering own customers and those of competitors

❑ benchmarking with companies of other industries (e.g. food industry, production industry)

❑ customer satisfaction data:

  • reduction in customer complaints by 31 % in 3 years

  • expenditures for processing complaints: 0.2 % of turnover (average in industry: 2 %)

IBM

Solution of problems arisen: effects on customer satisfaction / multiplier effect (n=2 400)[246]

❑ No problem arose. The customer is satisfied with product and service:

  • "I would buy the product again."   84 %

  • "I would recommend the product to others."   91 %

  multiplier: 3

❏ A problem arose and was resolved:

- "I would buy the product again."   92 %
- "I would recommend the product to others." 94 %

multiplier: 3

❏ A problem arose, but was not resolved:

- "I would buy the product again."   46 %
- "I would recommend the product to others." 48 %

multiplier: 7

Management system for determining customer satisfaction at IBM:[247]

❏ knowing and comprehending customer requirements and wishes

❏ creating a ratio system for determining customer satisfaction

❏ creating a close customer-feedback-system

❏ providing statements of customer satisfaction

❏ defining and eliminating causes for dissatisfaction

2.7   Employee satisfaction

If we agree with the general theory that satisfied employees produce satisfied customers, then the logical consequence is a regular survey of employee satisfaction. The appropriate contents of such a questionnaire have been discussed in the chapter on employee orientation: personnel planning, recruitment and development, goal agreement, progress and development control, participation and competence, top-down and bottom-up communication, and finally, continuous improvement of all aspects of personnel management. Within the context of employee satisfaction criteria, the question to focus on is the opinion of the employees concerning the performance of the company with regard to the satisfaction of all persons involved. Firstly, here, the direct assessment of the company using employee surveys must be distinguished from the indirect indications of employee satisfaction or dissatisfaction, such as absence rates.[248]

❏   If possible the entire staff should be included in the survey
      (or at least a representative sample)

❏   Regular surveys (e.g. annually) in order to track developments

❏   Assure and keep anonymity

❏   Include works council and superiors from
      the development of the assessment instrument

❏   Targeted selection, training and supervision of the interviewers

❏   Avoid too many questions

❏   Easily comprehensible questions

❏   Each question ought to consist of multiple-choice (guided
      questions) and an area for voluntary, further comments (open
      questions)

❏   Final question: "Are there any points of concern which
      we have either dealt with too superficially or not at all?

Fig. 108:   Recommendations for the structuring of employee surveys

Assessments carried out by employees can be conducted using employee surveys, discussion groups, annual appraisal interviews and other methods. For such an assessment, the following possibilities are available:

❏ free interviews (Exploration, in-depth interviews)

❏ standardised interviews (set questions that are posed orally with
   the help of a questionnaire or checklist)

❏ group discussions

❏ questionnaires that are left with the person to be interviewed:

- request to return completed questionnaires

- ad hoc answering in group situations

❏ multiple choice etc.

Employee surveys should contain the following important groups of questions regardless of how the survey is realised:

❏ Questions on general satisfaction (relating to the company) and specific work satisfaction (relating to ones' own department)

❏ Difficulties and positive aspects at work (as an open question)

❏ Satisfaction with specific conditions at work place (framework and work organisation)

❏ Desires for change in specific conditions at work place

❏ Payment and behaviour of superiors

❏ Potential for motivation of the current activity (questions concerning work contents, information and awareness of interrelatedness)

❏ Willingness to develop (independent from the current activity)

❏ Individual or group workplace / cooperation with colleagues

❏ Statistical data on the individual

Hewlett Packard

Management method "Employee surveys"[249]

❏ Structuring of the survey:

- 68 questions covering 13 areas:

  management, supervision, communication, relations, work conditions, performance, development, recognition, tasks, corporate management, salary, rewards, quality

- 20 specific / individual statements on effectivity

- room for personal comments

- time taken for survey: 45-60 minutes

❑ Application of employee surveys for continuous improvement:

    ↳ survey ⇨ analysis ⇨ presentation of results ⇨ implementation of improvement projects ⇨ application of employee surveys and other statements to evaluate projects ⇨ renewed surveys

❑ Employee surveys are a management instrument aimed at

- improving communication
- identifying and analysing problem areas
- determining employee-oriented priorities
- evaluating the effectivity of measures and practices
- functioning as an early warning system
- making sound decisions

In their self-assessment brochure, the EFQM suggests the following contents for an employee survey:

❑ motivation

- career development
- communication
- empowerment
- equal opportunities
- involvement
- leadership
- opportunity to learn and achieve
- recognition
- target setting and appraisal
- the organisation's values, mission, vision, policy and strategy
- training and education.

❑ satisfaction:

- company administration
- employment conditions
- facilities and services

- health and safety conditions
- job security
- pay and benefits
- peer relationships
- the management of change
- the organisation's environmental policy and impact
- the organisation's role in the community and society
- working environment.

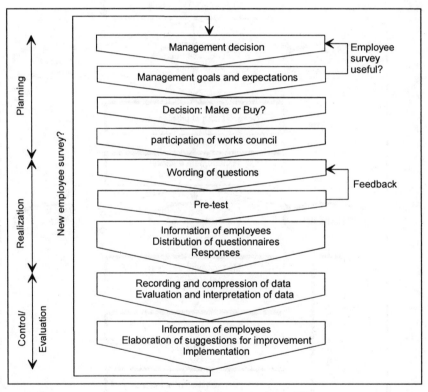

Fig. 109:   Principle course of an employee survey[250]

The subject of employee surveys shows particularly clearly that total quality management must be combined with continuous improvement. Without the dedicated will to use the results of a survey as a basis for the introduction of an improvement process, it becomes a dangerous instrument: The disappointment of raised expectations leads to frustration and demotivation.

This means that in such cases it would be better to have no survey at all. This applies equally to customer surveys.

Hewlett Packard

Feedback-Groups[251]

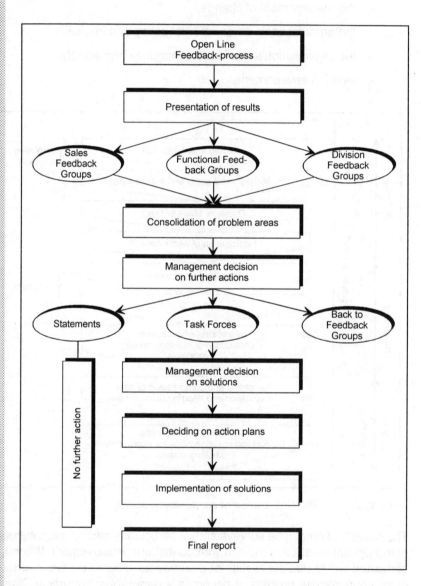

Fig. 110 :   Use of Feedback-Groups at Hewlett Packard

❑ Aim:

- Reappraisal of employee surveys

❑ Participants:

- 5 - 10 employees and 1 chairperson from the personnel department

❑ Tasks:

- To identify problem areas
- To describe the problem areas in detail
- To analyse possible causes
- To work out suggestions for solutions

In addition, the objectivity and validity of the obtained data must be ensured. This generally requires data collection by an external institution which is able to fulfil these demands, in particular when using a written survey. Furthermore, the following areas can also prove problematic when dealing with employee surveys:

❑ Wording of the questions (have to be worded neutrally) and of the questionnaire,

❑ Distortion that can occur during interviews (due to the interviewer's influence),

❑ Interpretation of the consciously (rationalised) opinions expressed, and the unconscious motive that may have determined it (pretext or stereotyped opinions etc.),

❑ Forecast of the relation between the expressed opinion and future behaviour,

❑ Danger of systematic mistakes.

It seems especially important that there is a chance for area and level specific assessments. Here it might be necessary to deal with the contradiction between absolute anonymity and the potential to recognise and solve target group specific problems. Anonymity of the individual must definitely be protected.

Since employee surveys fall under the co-determination law in Germany, the works council has to be included. Ideally, the works council itself also contributes, e.g. by assessing the customer orientation of their own work. The works council's active support promotes further acceptance, should this be necessary.

IBM

Excerpt from the quality survey[252]   1984   1986

1. To what extent are you aware of the current
    efforts being made concerning quality?
    1. Very   ⇨ 69%   75%
    2. Quite   ⬈
    3. A little
    4. Hardly
    5. Not at all

2. I have the impression that quality is important for my
    management.
    1. Totally agree   ⇨ 83%   100%
    2. Basically agree   ⬈
    3. Neither/nor
    4. Tend to disagree
    5. Completely disagree

3. To what extent have you understood the quality
   requirements in your department?
    1. Completely   ⇨ 74%   91%
    2. Mostly   ⬈
    3. Partly
    4. Hardly
    5. Not at all
    6. I cannot answer this question.

4. All in all, how would you evaluate the performance quality in
    your department (service and/or products)?
    1. Very good   ⇨ 78%   83%
    2. Good   ⬈
    3. Average
    4. Poor
    5. Very poor
6. I cannot evaluate it.

When evaluating the results, the first question to arise is: how representative are they? Additionally, one must examine how far continuous impro-

vement already exists. Here, what is particularly interesting is in how far these improvements can be traced back to total quality activities, and how far the aims laid down there have been achieved. At the same time, information can also be obtained about how far total quality ideas pervade the company, and the degree of one's own active participation.

Project group "Employee survey"

❑ Working group with representatives of various companies (among others BASF AG, Bertelsmann, 3M Deutschland GmbH, Hamburg-Mannheimer Versicherungs-AG, Hewlett Packard GmbH, IBM Deutschland GmbH) and scientists

❑ Goal:

  • Possibility of benchmarking

  • Cost saving through validated survey instrument

  • Use of employee survey as a management instrument

❑ Development of a standard questionnaire extendable according to company specific requirements:

No.	Core area	Number of questions
1	Work place	2 (+ 1 Statistics)
2	Work situation	8
3	Information	3
4	Education, training and development	4
5	Leadership	16
6	Cooperation/Coordination	4
7	Income and social benefits	5
8	Company image	3
9	Commitment to the company	2
10	Statistics	9
11	Open questions	1
	Total	57

Fig. 111:   Project group "Employee survey" [253]

It is also possible to use benchmarking here when meaningful, e.g. through cooperation with professional associations such as the Deutsche Gesellschaft für Personalführung (German Association of Personnel Management). The ideal has been achieved when you yourself are used as a benchmark.

General Indicator	Formula
Applicants training placement (attractivity)	$$\frac{\text{Number of applicants}}{\text{Number of places of training}}$$
Indicator for company suggestion system:	
Rate of suggestions for improvement	$$\frac{\text{Submitted suggestions for improvement} \times 100}{\text{Average number of employees}}$$
Structure of submitting employees	$$\frac{\text{Submitting employees with the characteristics } i \times 100}{\text{Total number of submitting employees}}$$
Cycle time per suggestion	$$\frac{\Sigma \text{ Cycle time}}{\text{Number of suggestions}}$$
Rate of acceptance	$$\frac{\text{Number of accepted suggestions} \times 100}{\text{Number of submitted suggestions}}$$
Rate of realisation	$$\frac{\text{Realised suggestions} \times 100}{\text{Accepted suggestions}}$$
Average bonus	$$\frac{\text{Gross bonus}}{\text{Awarded Suggestions}}$$
Rate of cost saving	$$\frac{\Sigma \text{ Cost savings resulting from suggestions}}{\text{Number of awarded suggestions}}$$

Fig. 112:   Ratio of employee-oriented activities (I)[254]

Alongside the direct evaluation of the company by the employees, it is also possible to use indirect indicators to help determine employee satisfaction. Here, a comparison with the branch average or the "best-in-class" can be useful:

❑ motivation and involvement:

- involvement in improvement teams
- involvement in suggestion schemes
- levels of training and development
- measurable benefits of teamwork
- recognition of individuals and teams
- response rates to people surveys.

❑ satisfaction:

- absenteeism and sickness

- accident levels
- grievances
- recruitment trends
- staff turnover
- strikes
- use of benefits
- use of facilities provided by the organisation (e.g. recreational, crêche).

Indicator for PD / Education:	Formula
Cost of training per employee	Total cost for training courses / Total number of participation
Cost per training hour	Total cost of training hours / Total number of training hours
Time for education and training per employee	Σ (Training hours x number of participants) / Total number of participants
Training effectiveness	Number of trained employees / Total number of staff
Satisfaction of participants	Number of satisfied participants / Number of submitted training evaluations
Improvement of performance after training	$\varnothing$ Average improvement of job performance (difference between pre-test and post-test for each course)
Indicator for employee satisfaction:	
Staff turnover	Employees who left on a voluntary basis x 100 / Average number of staff
Average time of company affiliation	Σ Time of company affiliation / Total number of employees
Frequency of stress-based illnesses	Lost days through stress-based illnesses x 100 / Planned working time in days
Number of relocation requests after short period of work	Number of relocation requests
Results of employee survey	Qualitative as well as quantitative

Fig. 113:   Ratio of employee-oriented activities (II)[255]

2.8   Impact on society

In contrast to the Japanese and US-American Quality Assessment Models, the European Model includes a criteria which pays particular attention to the environmental effects of managerial action.

This complies with an increasing awareness for such questions in Europe. In accordance with the ever-increasing desire for certification of quality assurance systems, an environmental certification system has been developed in Europe which now has to be converted into national law on the basis of an EC decree of 1995. This EC-eco-audit aims to achieve the voluntary participation of commercial companies in a mutually beneficial system for environmental management and environmental audits.[256]

Individual targets are[257]:

❑ Determination and implementation of site-specific environmental policy, programmes and management systems by the companies,

❑ Systematic, objective and regular assessment of the performance of these instruments,

❑ Informing the public of company environmental efforts.

The benefits of eco-audits on business management can be seen in:

❑ the potential for economising on raw materials, water and energy,

❑ a reduction in waste

❑ a reduction in insurance premiums against environmental risk,

❑ a decrease in the personal liability risk for business management and the responsible employees,

❑ minimising the risk of legal conflicts as well as court costs and fines,

❑ Improvement of the company's image with

• official authorities,

• customers,

• consumers,

• and employees.

Kunert

Introduction of an eco-balance sheet:[258]

In 1991, Kunert, a producer of trousers and other garments, was the first German company to introduce an eco-balance sheet. According to their own experiences, this internal eco-balance sheet has created a "solid basis for an environmental management system where cost-cutting for ecology is now exceeding one million marks". The eco-balance sheet records the input and output flows of the company via the flow of energy and materials. In the eco-report published by Kunert, the listed accounts are broken down into individual ones and interpreted before the "consequences and goals" are finally described

INPUT		1991	1992
1	Circulating goods (kg)	15 771 320	12 006 223
1.1	Raw materials	5 311 896	4 243 238
1.2	Semi-finished and finished goods	2 655 422	2 114 895
1.3	Auxiliary materials	5 954 169	4 115 455
1.4	Ancillary	1 849 833	1 532 635
2	Plant and Equipment (piece)	not recorded	16 246
2.1	Buildings		n.e.
2.2	Production machines		6 573
2.3	Office equipment		7 010
2.4	Office and comm. machines		2 490
2.5	Vehicle fleet		173
2.6	Others		n.e.
3	Energy (kWh)	185 039 982	157 709 097
3.1	Gas	15 749 655	20 536 032
3.2	Electricity	54 809 172	46 465 919
3.3	Fuel oil	97 754 180	71 677 150
3.4	District heating	1 615 625	2 391 466
3.5	Fuel	15 111 350	16 638 530
4	Water (m^3)	672 110	530 541
4.1	Tap water	451 936	338 583
4.2	Untreated water	220 174	191 958
5	Air	n.e.	n.e.
6	Land (m^2)	752 257	771 991
6.1	Sealed	70 066	76 069
6.2	Green	529 745	534 794
6.3	Built over	152 446	161 128
6.4	Utilizable area	206 618	222 771

Fig. 114:   Eco-balance sheet Kunert`s 1991/92 (Input)[259]

OUTPUT			1991	1992
O	1	Products (kg)	9 280 253	7 997 075
	1.1	Hosiery	5 786 896	5 153 663
	1.2	Outer wear	175 962	164 446
	1.3	Transport packaging	309 437	117 273
	1.4	Product packaging	3 007 958	2 561 693
O	2	Waste (kg)	3 124 629	3 069 063
	2.1	Hazardous waste	26 475	27 738
	2.2	Recyclables	1 963 477	2 260 672
	2.3	Residual waste	1 134 677	780 653
O	3	Waste heat (kWh)	185 039 982	157 709 097
	3.1	Utilizable energy	not stated (n.s.)	
	3.2	Unused Energy		n.s.
	3.3	Noise		n.s.
O	4	Waste water (m^3)	487 770	388 189
	4.1	Quantity	487 770	388 189
	4.2	Pollution		n.s.
O	5	Used air (kg)		n.s.
	5.1	Quantity		n.s.
	5.2	Air emission	29 387 121	23 465 129
O	6	Floor loading		n.s.

Fig. 115: Eco-balance sheet Kunert`s 1991/92 (Output)[260]

In addition, it is also economically wise to integrate further issues - such as impact on society - into a total quality concept which also requires similar introduction and integration. This also corresponds to an extensive under-standing of quality.[261]

It is for this reason that the following issues can be found in the exemplary explanation of the EFQM for the European Quality Award:

❑ Reporting on activities to assist in the preservation and sustain-ability of resources:

- choice of transport
- ecological impact
- reduction and elimination of waste and packaging
- substitution of raw materials or other inputs and
- usage of energy, virgin and recycled materials.

Bischof & Klein

Environmental protection as a management task:[262]

As producers of paper and plastic packaging materials, Bischof and Klein have a particular obligation towards the environmental compatibility of its products and production. The background for the environmental efforts of the company is, in particular, the current discussion on waste management, which primarily involves producers of packaging material.

Bischof & Klein reacted to this development at a relatively early stage and have undertaken the following extensive measures for ecologically oriented management:

- ❑ Environmental protection as company goal (since 1985),
- ❑ Introduction of material lists from suppliers in order to obtain information on supplied fabricated materials (since 1987),
- ❑ Obligation of executive staff to practice environmental protection by adding a clause to the contract.

In addition, internal seminars are provided on environmental issues, in particular techniques, purchasing and sales.

Texas Instruments

Improvement of environmental protection (e.g. energy saving):[263]

The "Defence Systems & Electronics"-Group of Texas Instruments has undertaken measures for environmental protection at various US locations of the company. The result has been a series of improvements, such as:

- ❑ Austin: Avoidance of dangerous residual waste disposal by recycling.
- ❑ Lewisville: The US Navy quotes a programme and a data base (TIESYS) from Texas Instruments as the "best method" for surveillance of dangerous chemicals.
- ❑ Forest Lane: In 1991, Forest Lane was named "the energy project of the year" by the Association of Energy Engineers (AEE).

Expressway: achieved a 64% percent reduction in ozone-destroying chemicals in 1991.

❑ Mc Kinney, Lemmon Avenue, Lewisville: the elimination of dangerous CFC's and trichloroethanes from metal processing.

❑ In addition to these measures, Texas Instruments has an extensive recycling programme for metal scrap, paper, manmade materials, corrugated card and wood.

Kunert

Reduction of waste (reducing packaging):[264]

When examining the packaging of products (the subgroup of process materials in the eco-balance sheet) it became clear that, because price labels were pasted onto the polypropylene bags, the soft packaging round stockings could not be recycled.

Now that the price is printed directly onto the packaging foils, 500 000 price labels can be saved. Because of this new technology, 30 000 kg of paper and glue could be saved in 1993.

In the "consequences and goals" section of the eco-report, it was agreed to cut the average percentage of packaging used, and to test recyclable box packaging.[265] Kunert's real ecological effort, however, lies not in the drawing-up of an eco-balance sheet, but primarily in the goals which can be derived from it, which are written down and can be checked at any time.

In March 1992, Kunert enterprises were awarded the "Environmental Award of the National Association for German Industry" for its ecological efforts. In the same year, Rainer Michel, chairman of the board at Kunert, was awarded the Alternative Marketing Prize, the ASU Environment Award and the Bavarian Environment Medal.

❑ Activities to reduce and prevent nuisance and harm from its operations and/or within the life cycle of its products:

- health risks and accidents,

- noise and odour,

- hazards (safety),

- pollution and toxic emission.

Rasselstein

Efficient prevention of accidents:[266]

Accidents caused by wrong behaviour can only partially be avoided by methods such as plant security control, accident analyses, rules and regulations. Rasselstein, a producer of tinplate, has therefore integrated occupational health and safety cross-functionally into the corporate structure, including all employees in the process. The responsible department is directly subordinate to the board.

The task of the department for occupational health and safety/ergonomics includes all important operational and organisational processes and ranges from the planning of new buildings to maintenance and repair work.

A few of the numerous tasks of this department are:

❑ Technology-related measures (e.g. measuring hazardous substances and noise, examination of tools and equipment, inspection rounds)

❑ Organisational measures (risk analysis, accident analysis, safety talks, etc.)

❑ Co-operation with the works council

❑ Co-operation with the supervisory authorities

❑ Fire protection (not only object-related, but also as personal protection)

❑ Fire fighting (two-year period of training to gain the qualification "full-time factory fireman"),

❑ Suggestion system.

The top management supports this extensive safety program which not only helps to prevent possible nuisance and damage in the neighbourhood, but also, and in particular, reduces the risk of industrial accidents.

In this context, top management has stressed to the staff several times: "In our company, people come first. The health of our employees takes precedence over quality and quantity of production".

❑ Involvement in the communities where it operates:

• involvement in education and training

• support for medical and welfare provision

- support for sport and leisure

- voluntary work and philanthropy.

IBM

Working with sheltered workshops for people with disabilities:[267]

IBM promotes the improvement of living conditions for people with disabilities in various projects. IBM concentrates primarily on the development of new products which can provide the disabled with new perspectives for working and living conditions. In addition, IBM management instructed the purchasing department in 1979 "to give more orders to the sheltered workshops in order to make the social duties of the company more evident". In the first year alone, turnover reached 0.8m Deutsche mark. By 1993, it has increased to 10.5m DM. This, in turn, secured 1 100 jobs. This turnover is divided between 54 workshops nationally.

However, this cooperation is not limited to passing on orders. IBM purchasers also passed on their knowledge to the workshops, so that new, high quality products and services could be produced.

One example of this is that an intensive training course at one workshop enabled some disabled people to carry out micro-scopically precise tests of printed circuit boards for computer systems. Simultaneously, they were able to carry out complicated touch-up work on electronic bridges.

Contributing to the improvement of quality of life also includes the creation and organisation of work conditions considering the aspects of human work. These include

- ❑ ease of execution

- ❑ lack of risk to health

- ❑ bearableness

- ❑ promotion of personal growth.

and they are also important within the Result criteria "People Satisfaction". Their effects on society (e.g. inability to work, early retirement) become especially evident here.

Alongside these points, other, indirect aspects can be used to assess the company, such as:

- ❑ Accolades and awards received.

❑ The number of violations against national and international norms.

❑ The number of complaints.

❑ The number of safety-related accidents.

❑ Reports by external inspectors.

In addition to a clear policy on safety and environment, a regular, subjective (survey in the company environment) and objective (e.g. physical data) assessment, and to the targeted improvement derived from these assessments, it is also necessary to assess how dedicated the company is to the community in which it is operating. Here, activities can be included such as:

❑ Charities/ sponsoring

❑ Training

❑ Medical aid and care and

❑ Sport and leisure.

This can be made by releasing employees or providing financial or non-financial resources.

IBM

Release of employees for activities in community organisations:[268]

In order to increase their active commitment to society, IBM Germany has created various specialised programmes. In so-called "secondments", employees are "loaned out" to a community organisation for months, or even years at the company's expense. By providing their knowledge and experience they help to initiate new projects that would normally have little chance of success. The secondees are placed in different areas: environmental protection and education, training, social projects which particularly benefit the disabled, culture, and sport.

In this way, an "Information network for the depollution of the Elbe" was set up with the secondments -- a concept that planned the organisation and implementation of concrete clean-up measures for the heavily polluted Elbe based on reliable data. The necessary steps could finally be taken in October 1990, after the changes in Eastern Europe. Alongside the release of employees, IBM also took on the financing of the hardware (24 IBM systems and 6 IBM notebooks), standard software and the programming of the application software.

On the whole, it is important that , on the one hand, there is a unified policy and strategy in the area of "impact on society" which, e.g., also includes suppliers. On the other hand, it is also essential to be able to show continuous improvements based on "closed feedback systems". Finally, it should also be possible to relate the remaining results to each other.

2.9   Business Results

All measures executed within TQM aim to ensure and improve long-term business results. In contrast to short-term profit maximisation strategies, TQM places emphasis on increasing the long-term company value, which includes various aspects (e.g. increase in human capital or shareholder value). The necessary preconditions already described in connection with the Enablers usually have to be created from scratch. This begins with the process-oriented restructuring of the organisation and also includes changes in reward systems (also for management) and reorganisation of reporting and accounting. The results can therefore only be partly shown in (direct) financial parameters. For this reason, they include all results criteria and refer to measures and ratios reflecting corporate policy and strategy which go far beyond traditional commercial data. As with the integration of the Total Quality philosophy (e.g. aspects such as customers, employees and society) in corporate policy, this integration is also vital for the reporting and assessment of results. Traditional audit concepts and approaches for company assessment therefore have to be developed accordingly. A basis for this can be provided by the self-assessment concepts of the Malcolm Baldrige National Quality Award and the European Quality Award.

TQM as a "Management by Facts" means being able to demonstrate what effects the application of potentials has on the development of results, and learning to understand them. Naturally, there is only a limited number of mono-causal relations. However, the effects of specific design concepts can be assessed by applying sensitivity analysis. Similarly, the influence of individual economic measures is rather limited in certain areas. Nevertheless, it is possible to show that the effects of macroeconomic developments can also be limited e.g. by the creation of systematically advanced feedback systems (also in the sense of early-warning systems). However, this presupposes that the management reward system is not exclusively based on short-term financial figures.

The issues mentioned above apply equally to the evaluation of the results data:

❑ How did results develop, absolutely and relatively, in comparison to the past (in particular positive trends)?

❑ How do the results appear in relation to formulated targets?

❑ How can results be judged when compared with competitors?

❑ How great is the distance to internationally leading companies?

❑ How complete is this data?

In principle, all factors can be included in the results discussed here (which have not already been taken into account in the other results criteria) to serve to assess the designing of enablers.

On the whole, it is possible to formulate general guidelines for measuring and dealing with all results. These can be found below in the form of a checklist:

❑ Subject of presentation:

- to consider and show relevance and effects of data
- to show own performance
- to show progress
- to show trends
- to present targets and the achievement of them
- to prove realisation of targets
- to consider performance of competitors and best-in-class-companies

❑ Manner of presentation:

- complete, simple and clear
- period of time: the longer, the better
- meaningful figures with respective comments, all elements should be explained (e.g. different divisions, relative measures "world-class", freak values, when using selective presentation: selection criteria)

Case-Study MBNQA

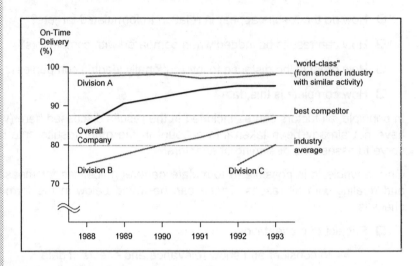

Fig. 116:   Example for a meaningful "Result"-Figure for Product-/
            Service-Quality[269]

This figure demonstrates how results can be meaningfully presented in graphs while considering important elements. This graph presents trends for a success factor over a longer period of time compared to benchmarks. For financial and non-financial variables, the documentation of the European Quality Award mentions the following as examples.

Financial measures for corporate success could include:

❑ profit and loss account items including:

– gross margins

– net profit

– sales.

❑ balance sheet items including:

– long term borrowing

– shareholders' funds

– total assets

– working capital (including inventory turnover).

❑ cash flow items including:

   – capital expenditure

   – financing cash flows

   – operating cash flow

❑ other relevant indicators including:

   – return on equity

   – return on net assets

   – credit ratings

   – long-term shareholder value (total shareholder returns)

   – value added.

Rank Xerox

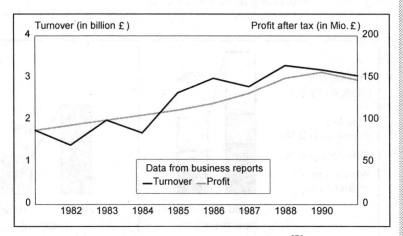

Fig. 117:   Presentation of profit and turnover trends[270]

IBM

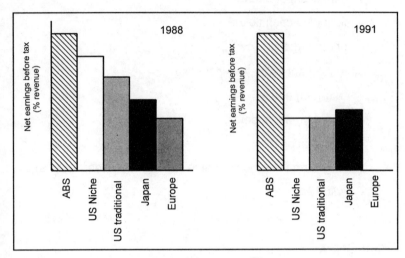

Fig. 118:   Profitability by competitor group[271]

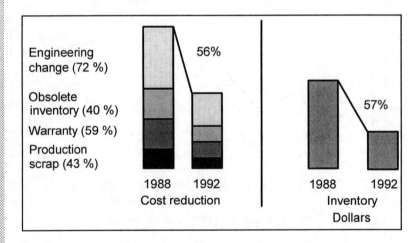

Fig. 119:   Economic use through Quality Improvements: Costs and Inventory[272]

These details may be given in absolute figures, as ratio per capital unit, or as ratio per employee.

The following examples show that a combined presentation of financial and non-financial indicators may also be advisable.

IBM

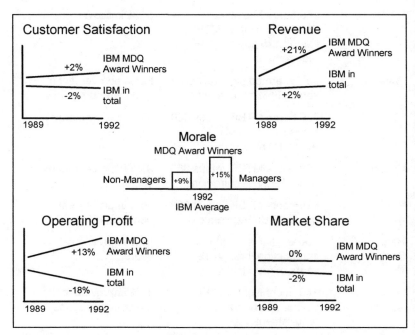

Fig. 120:   Combined presentation of financial and non-financial performance measures at IBM[273]

Texas Instruments

Reliability and costs: key data for main products [274]

Programme	Reliability	Costs
HARM	550 hours Meantime Between Failures (MTBF) versus 125 hours MTBF requirement	81 % improvement
Paveway	99,6% armed flight reliability versus 96% requirement	82% improvement in working hours per sy
TTS	780 hours MTBF versus 400 hours minimum MTBF requirement	85% improvement ov years
Chapparal	600 hours MTBF versus 350 hours MTBF requirement	95% improvement ov years
P-3 FLIR	629 hours MTBF versus 300 hours MTBF requirement	26% improvement between 1985 and 1
Harpoon / Seeker	100% reliability during introduction through 12 years of production	91% improvement ov years
F-111	140 hours flight MTBF versus 206 hours Test requirement	19% improvement ac 4 production series
LANTRIN	1 100 hours Test MTBF versus 206 hours Test requirement	67% improvement between 1988 and 1
P-3 ISAR	113 hours flight MTBF versus 75 hours MTBF requirement	Production costs: 30 improvement betwee 1988 and 1990
TOW 2	744 hours MTBF versus 450 hours MTBF requirement	Defect costs: 72% improvement in 2 yea
Javelin	predicted reliability of instruction issue unit = four times requirement	89% improvement

The non-financial variables of the organisation's success include aspects related to the internal economy and efficiency decisive for the long-term success of a company. Many of these variables are related to the critical processes already mentioned in the chapter "Processes".

Areas to address could include:

- ❑ overall performance:
  - – market share.
- ❑ key processes:
  - – cycle time
  - – defect rate
  - – maturity
  - – productivity
  - – time to market.
- ❑ information:
  - – accessibility
  - – integrity
  - – relevance
  - – timeliness.
- ❑ suppliers and materials:
  - – defect rate
  - – general performance
  - – inventory turnover
  - – price
  - – response time
  - – utility consumption.
- ❑ assets:
  - – depreciation
  - – maintenance costs
  - – utilisation.
- ❑ technology:
  - – innovation rate
  - – patents
  - – royalties.

Rank Xerox

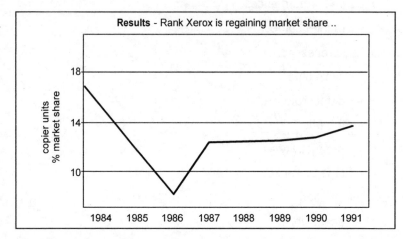

Fig. 121:   Market share development: Example for the presentation of trends[275]

IBM

Improving cycle times:

❑ reduction of 50 % in product development

❑ reduction of 60 % of processing time

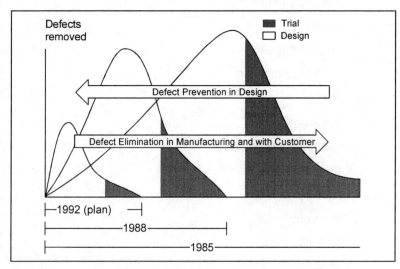

Fig. 122:   Benefit of Defect Prevention at IBM[276]

IBM

Supplier A			
Supplier benefits		**IBM benefits**	
Personnel reduced	46 %	Leadtime reduced	62 %
Space reduced	43 %	Inventory reduced	$ 534
Inventory reduced	75 %		
Cycle time reduced	80 %		
Supplier B			
Supplier benefits		**IBM benefits**	
Personnel reduced	10 %	Leadtime reduced	42 %
Space reduced	25 %	Inventory reduced	$ 705
Inventory reduced	$ 125	Transportation cost reduced	$ 200
Cycle time reduced	50 %		

Fig. 123:   Performance of suppliers: Profit-Improvement at IBM and their suppliers from two examples (in thousand US$)[277]

Milliken European Division

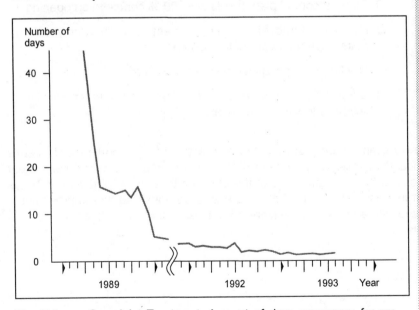

Fig. 124:   Complaint Treatment: Amount of days necessary for processing a Milliken Opportunity for Improvement (MOFI)[278]

In addition to the above-mentioned examples given by the European Quality Award, many other results may of course be of importance for a company. For Rank Xerox[279] it is as important to reduce the number of suppliers from 5 000 to 400 in the sense of a Single Sourcing as it is to reduce the inventory of raw materials by 80 % or the number of defective components by 99 % within the same period of time.

Ritz-Carlton

The following data concerning Ritz Carlton Hotels[280] is a good example of non-financial indicators in a typical service industry. These indicators are also not explicitly mentioned in the European Quality Award:

❑ For six years, they have been the benchmark for hotel products and services in the USA

❑ For two years, they have achieved the highest classification from hotel testers

❑ On-time delivery of all types of material when furnishing and equipping hotels has been increased from 60 % in 1989 to 100 % in 1991

❑ Start-up control plan: hotels are 100 % complete on opening

❑ Personnel turnover: an improvement of 46 %, today 16 % better than the best-in-class-competitor

❑ Leader concerning income per hotel room

❑ Cooperation with suppliers: reduction in delivery time for five key products from five to one day

The following figure shows the development of non-financial results (product) reliability and on-time delivery compared with cost development for one of the main products of the Malcolm Baldrige Award winner Texas Instruments.[281] The aim of the figure is to demonstrate that improvements in reliability and on-time delivery do not necessarily lead to an increase in costs.

Texas Instruments

If we examine the development of defect rates in the drawing-up of contracts or the duration of security checks for new employees at Texas Instruments Defense Systems and Electronics Group (DSEG)[282], it becomes clear that non-financial results can genuinely be related to supportive processes such as the administrative process mentioned above.

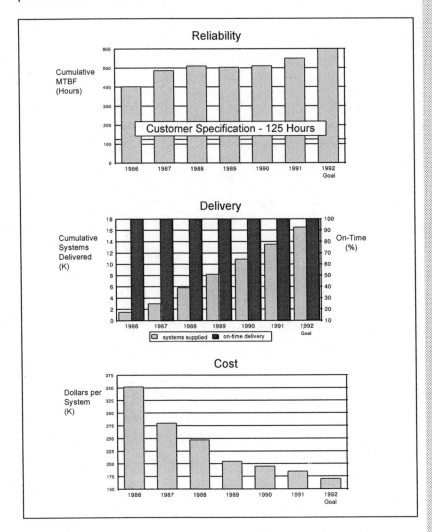

Fig. 125:   HARM-Flying object program shown with reliability, delivery and cost [283]

3 Implicit assumptions - or what remains to be considered

Although it has been repeatedly mentioned in previous chapters, it is perhaps wise, due to the wide-ranging spectrum of the subject, to once more explicitly state:

Concerning the Enablers, the European Model for Business Excellence considers two main aspects to be implicit or integral parts of the criteria of leadership, employees, policy and planning, resources and processes. These are:

❑ Customer orientation

❑ Product innovation

During the last recession, it was precisely these two aspects which played an essential role, in as much as they were entirely absent or barely noticeable within the consultancy concepts popular at the time (innovation crisis). Whether we talk of lean management or business reengineering, practical implementation was dominated by inward orientation which could be briefly presented under the heading: cost reduction by process optimisation.

Although it is necessary and makes sense to reduce internal planning and overheads, these are not the right concepts to secure the future of businesses. But here it should also not be supposed that these issues are of no importance at all. For this reason, the European Model also includes the criteria of resources and processes. First of all, however, process optimisation has to become a continuous process, radically changed, (and should thus avoid being the one-off project that the above-mentioned concepts became). Secondly, the reorganisation of the processes should be customer-oriented (e.g. cutting reaction time).

Optimal processes alone will not, however, secure long-term survival, even with customer orientation. This can only be achieved through new and better solutions (products and/or services) to customer problems. In this sense, product innovation also naturally means customer orientation - and it is then that TQM had been achieved. The European Model for Business Excellence offers a host of ideas for achieving this goal.

Part III:
Selected Managerial Methods in Context of Total Quality

1   Self-Assessment

1.1   Importance within TQM

Assessing a company is once more becoming increasingly important, not only because of the growing relevance and acceptance of international quality awards.[284] Thus, the Malcolm Baldrige National Quality Award, the European Quality Award and the DEMING PRIZE demand that all quality endeavours are regularly checked and improved by management. The ISO 9000 series - an assessment-system for quality management systems - also includes at least one management review within the QM-Element "Responsibility of Management". One of its central themes is the assessment of the progress and adequacy of the quality policy and the goals set by top management.[285]

Those systems do not explicitly demand a Self-Assessment, and only the European Foundation for Quality Management provides "concrete guide-lines" for the execution of a Self-Assessment. But especially winners of international quality awards use the instrument of a systematic and regular Self-Assessment - not least because they have to verify their quality and business results for at least three years.[286]

However, before discussing goals, frame conditions, execution and prac-tical relevance of this tool, it is necessary to position and to delimit the term "Self-Assessment" - paying particular attention to its tasks within business management.

The starting point for a company's new orientation may often be a vision - a comprehensive and foresighted imagination of purposes and ways to achieve them.

The vision is the basis for corporate policy which is oriented to the ideas of Total Quality Management. It may for example concentrate on customer orientation and satisfaction as a general goal and code of conduct for the company. The corporate policy thus creates a target system to put into concrete terms the long, middle and short-term goals for all company areas and functions within the frame of a strategic and operative management. These goals may be individual objectives for managers, teams and sometimes even individual employees, and they are reviewed regularly. In company practice this systematic and regular operationalisation of company "politics" is known as "Policy Deployment". Figure 126 shows such a process of goal setting carried out by Rank Xerox, the first winner of the European Quality Award.

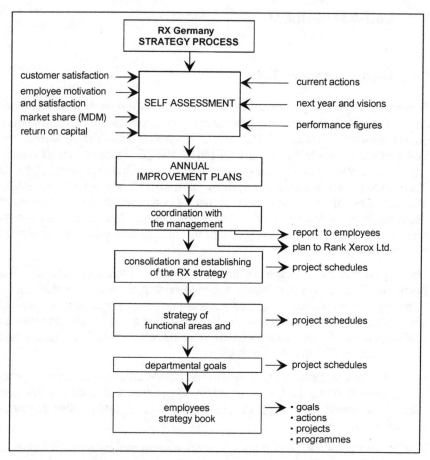

Fig. 126:   Policy Deployment at Rank Xerox Deutschland GmbH[287]

Business management theories also attach great importance to goal setting systems in order to make sure that corporate policy, general company goals and objectives of individual decision-makers concur.[288] In this context, one model which is often mentioned and which can in practice be found in different forms is Management by Objectives. Since it has been critisised due to its strong orientation to functional aspects, some multi-dimensional concepts for setting and realising goals as "Hoshin Planning" or "Goal Deployment" have established themselves.

On the basis of the classification of goal setting and assessment tasks within the company, Self-Assessment (e.g. within comprehensive quality concepts) can be characterised as follows:

❑ as a tool based on a multi-dimensional target system (e.g. criteria models of DEMING PRIZE, European Quality Award, Malcolm Baldrige National Quality Award),

❑ as an assessment method which can be carried out by the organisation itself or as an "internal" third party assessment,

❑ as a basis for strategic and operative management,

❑ as a prerequisite for benchmarking.

Self-Assessment is therefore the starting point for a regular strategic or operative planning process within the company and should ensure a continuous (quality) improvement.[289]

1.2 Goals and frame conditions of Self-Assessment within TQM - some fundamental remarks

As previously mentioned the importance of Self-Assessment approaches has increased because of the rising relevance of international quality awards. Such an assessment approach can therefore be used for preparing an award application. Moreover, the following aspects can outline important goals of Self-Assessment:

❑ identifying the current state of quality endeavours within the company before implementing TQM,

❑ creating a basis for future concentration on a company-specific approach,

❑ comparing the results to former assessments as a basis for initiating the next improvement cycle (control of efforts),[290]

- ❏ initiating a learning process, especially for management, by a detailed examination of the TQM-model[291] and

- ❏ identifying specific areas for improvement within the company, individual units or company functions (as a result of the Self-Assessment).

A consequence of these aspects is the involvement of all managers: a main prerequisite for the acceptance and the success of the Assessment tool. In this context it must be pointed out that - in practice - the term Self-Assessment is interpreted in different ways:

First of all the term "Self-Assessment" is used if the company itself starts the initiative (e.g. not the customer) and if the assessment is not carried out by third parties, but by people of their own company.[292]

Thus, Self-Assessment can be executed in such a way that for example independent business units assess themselves and derive their own improvement projects.[293] One also uses the term Self-Assessment if, for example, an individual unit of a bigger company is assessed by managers of another business unit of this company - i.e. an internal "third party" assessment.[294]

Irrespective of those two different ways of understanding Self-Assessment, its implementation and regular execution demand appropriate frame conditions, for example

- ❏ an existing corporate policy with visions, missions or company goals including the basic ideas of Total Quality Management,

- ❏ detailed information for the management on pros and cons of Self-Assessment and the necessary frame conditions (e.g. resource requirements, time needed for implementation, regular reviews),

- ❏ involving top management in the conception of the analysis and assessment instruments (e.g. during a workshop, if necessary supported by external consultants),

- ❏ involving the company's relevant functional areas in the conception and handling of the analysis and assessment instruments (e.g. the Quality Assurance Dept. to ensure that instruments comply with the existing certification measures or the human resources department to use any existing performance appraisal systems),

- ❏ provision of resources for the implementation of the tool (time and personnel: assessors for the assessment process and - if necessary - additional finances for external consultants and training),

❑ qualification of all managers involved in the assessment process (e.g. training of the Management concerning the understanding of the assessment criteria and the handling of the assessment instrument, training of assessors and promotors supporting the assessment process),

❑ informing people of targets, execution and consequences of the Self-Assessment,

❑ regular additional "third party assessments" in the sense of external assessments in order to gain additional ideas for the continuous improvement process,[295]

❑ continuous adjustment of the assessment instrument to changes identified by regularly reviewing corporate policy and the way in which the Self-Assessment is executed.[296]

The design of the assessment instrument is heavily dependent on review cycles and the area in which it is used. Normally, comprehensive and very detailed assessments are executed by support of an assessment team and these serve as a basis for strategic and operative planning. Questionnaires and additional interviews can be helpful here. At the same time or instead of this it is also possible to apply smaller check lists which can be used by management without any additional support and within shorter review cycles. Thus it is possible to roughly define the position of the respective functional area within the current business process.[297]

Already existing data should in particular be intensively used for the assessment process and as additional information for the goal setting process.[298] Some examples are:

❑ data resulting from customer surveys, customer complaint statistics, marketing strategies,

❑ data resulting from employee surveys, work safety statistics, illness rates, absenteeism and fluctuation, human resources development plans,

❑ data in connection with processes concerning processing time or process liability, projects and gained improvements,

❑ data in connection with products concerning error rate, life duration and failure rates as well as

❑ financial data, e.g. trends concerning profits, sales volume, ROI, quality costs.

1.3   EFQM Self-Assessment Concept

1.3.1   Basics

When drawing up a possible method for the implementation of a Self-Assessment the following questions have to be taken into consideration:

❑ Where are the strengths to be preserved or optimised with existing processes, or where can we find approaches for additional improvements?

❑ Which areas for improvement were identified, which of them are part of the company's bottom line and are therefore very relevant for key improvement measures?

❑ How do we observe the progression concerning the improvements agreed?

As shown in Figure 127, the starting point for a Self-Assessment according to the EFQM concept is the will of top management to support such an assessment process and to actively participate. Here, it is obligatory to offer special information workshops and training courses for corporate management.

Once the decision has been made to carry out a Self-Assessment, appropriate business units for a "Pilot-Assessment" should be selected. Because of trend-setting effects on the whole company, one should choose units with the will to participate actively. The "unit" chosen should have considerable influence on all elements of the European Quality Award (EQA).

Assessment teams have to be set up in the respective business unit, including people from all relevant management levels and corporate functions. In that phase, teams have to work out or select suitable existing instruments (e.g. questionnaires, check lists) and determine an appropriate assessment method (scoring scheme).

The units concerned then have to be informed of the forthcoming Self-Assessment, suitable managers have to be chosen as assessors or promotors, and have to be trained accordingly. Then the task of the

managers in the selected pilot units is to explain the assessment model
with the help of case studies. The managers of the respective areas carry
out assessments, collect data and determine the strengths and areas for
improvement by using the elaborated or selected interview guide lines and
check lists. If several areas are participating in such an assessment cycle,
the results will be collected and discussed on a higher level.

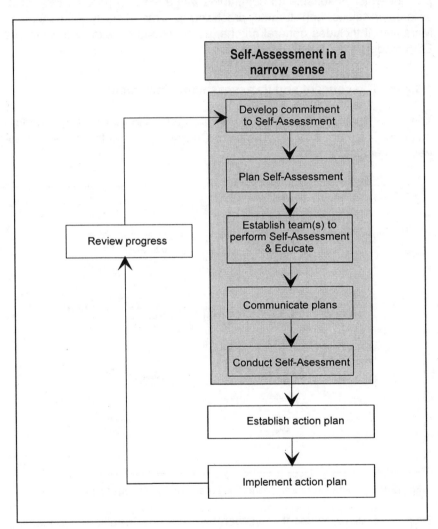

Fig. 127:   The Self-Assessment process[299]

After the Self-Assessment process itself, the projecting of improvement
measures has to start. The results will be action plans with clearly defined

priorities, projects and milestones. It is essential that appropriate resources are provided.

For future runs, the assessment process will provide the basis for a permanent progress control carried out by top management .

The action steps shown here are characteristic for a Self-Assessment process which is suitable for companies with a fixed corporate policy, clear visions, missions and targets practicing a Total Quality Management. Moreover, it includes general criteria, as described for example within the EQA-model.

1.3.2   The concept and its assessment dimensions

The Total Quality Model of the European Foundation for Quality Management (EFQM) - used for the European Quality Award - is the basis for Self-Assessment in Europe.

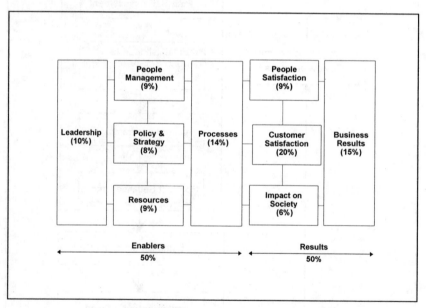

Fig. 128:   The European Model for Total Quality Management

Such a Self-Assessment considerably exceeds traditional Controlling concepts. Whereas financial data are normally the only background to controlling instruments, this model has three other "result" dimensions apart from the financial data within the criterion "Business Results". Besides non-financial improvements in the business results, such as reducing cycle times, the results criteria also includes "Customer and People Satisfaction" as well as "Impacts on Society" of running a business.

Apart from these results criteria, it is just as important - or perhaps even more so - to assess the future potential of the company: the behavior of management, investment in people, corporate policy and strategy and a reasonable use of resources, as well as the optimum design of key business processes. Altogether, traditional Controlling methods are strictly oriented to the past, whereas these Self-Assessment concepts try to concentrate on factors vital for surviving in future competition.

The "enabler criteria" and the "results criteria" differ in their structure:

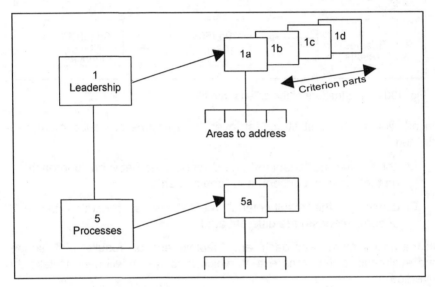

Fig. 129:   Structure of the criteria: enablers

Concerning enablers, every criterion is subdivided into a number of sub-criteria (four to six), all having the same weighting. To every single sub-criterion, some examples are provided to make the content more tangible.

The result criteria are only subdivided in a) and b). The following percentages are allocated to the sub criteria:

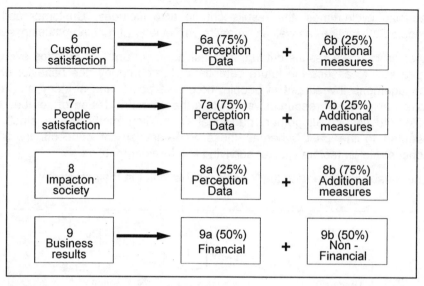

Fig. 130:   Structure of the criteria: results

In addition to this first structural level, both groups are once more sub-divided:

❑ concerning the "enablers" one distinguishes between "approach" (in the sense of concept) and "deployment",

❑ concerning the "result criteria" "results" and "scope" (in the sense of completeness) are differentiated.

In the assessment, "approach" and "deployment" or "results" and "scope" are evaluated to the same extent, which means one will have to take the average.

However, it may sometimes be necessary to make distinctions between approach ("desk jockeys") and deployment, in order to consider that developing a concept is relatively easy, in contrast to the more difficult consequent realisation of the concept.

This problem is currently being considered within one of EFQM's Task Forces.

The idea of continuous improvement can be found in all of the assessment dimensions:

for the "Enablers" one has to prove:

- ❑ the adequacy of methods, instruments and techniques used,
- ❑ the extent to which the concept is systematic and preventive,
- ❑ the use of review cycles,
- ❑ the realisation of improvements resulting from the review cycles and
- ❑ the extent to which the concept is integrated in daily work.

Assessing deployment means checking how adequately and effectively the approach was used:

- ❑ vertically through all relevant levels,
- ❑ horizontally to all areas and activities,
- ❑ in all relevant processes,
- ❑ concerning all relevant products and services.

Assessing the results includes the following factors:

- ❑ existing positive trends,
- ❑ comparing them with own targets,
- ❑ comparing them with the performance of competitors and "best in class" organisations,
- ❑ details proving that the results are produced by the approach,
- ❑ the ability of the organisation to maintain its leading position.

The scope of the results can be determined by:

- ❑ the extent to which all relevant areas of the company are covered,
- ❑ the extent to which the parameters chosen to measure results are shown,
- ❑ the extent to which the relevance of the shown results can be understood.

1.4   Methods and instruments for Self-Assessment

In the Self-Assessment documents of the European Foundation for Quality Management, one can find different methods and instruments which can be used for Self-Assessment:

❑ a workshop approach to Self-Assessment,

❑ a pro forma approach to Self-Assessment,

❑ a questionnaire approach to Self-Assessment,

❑ a matrix chart approach to Self-Assessment,

❑ a peer involvement approach to Self-Assessment and

❑ an award simulation approach to Self-Assessment.

1.4.1   A workshop approach to Self-Assessment

The advantage of this approach is that it requires the active involvement of the management team of the business unit performing the Self-Assessment.

The management team is responsible for gathering data and presenting to peers the evidence gathered at a workshop. This provides the starting point for the management team to reach consensus. Experience has shown that two people, fully trained as assessors, are required to facilitate the process and that, ideally, one of the assessors should be from the part of the organisation being assessed and the other from another part of the organisation ("neutral").

There are 5 components to the process: training, data gathering, scoring workshop, agreeing improvement actions and reviewing progress against action plans. These should be carried out regularly to achieve continuous improvement.

Training

Training for the management team begins with some homework - about 3 hours of preparatory reading of an EFQM case study extract prior to attendance at a training day. In the morning session of the training day, all team members are given an overview of the European Quality Award criteria and scoring system and then work through the case study pre-work. In the afternoon they experience a brief simulation of the scoring workshop which enables them to agree the issues to be addressed that will ensure an effective workshop event to be held approximately 4 - 6 weeks later.

Data gathering

Experience of organisations using the workshop approach has shown that data gathering can be one of the early learning opportunities for the management team. Sufficient time should be allowed for the management team to perform this task.

Consensus workshop

A typical agenda resembles the following:

1 Introduction by business unit leader

2 Process introduced by facilitators

3 Working through the nine criteria of the EQA-model

4 Review of the process

5 Confirmation of next steps

Typically, business units complete the workshop in one or one and a half days - depending on the experiences of facilitator and participants. Results criteria take less time than Enablers.

In general, a systematic analysis of the criteria includes the following aspects:

☐ Criterion part described by member of management team.

☐ Information gathered beforehand is presented to other members of the team in the form of strengths and areas for improvement.

☐ A check is made with the rest of the team to see if anything that is of relevance to the criterion part has been missed out.

☐ Discussion and agreement on strengths and areas for improvement.

☐ Team members score individually.

☐ Individual scores shared.

☐ Consensus gained.

Agreeing improvement actions

At the end of the workshop, it is probably inappropriate to move immediately into the action planning phase; the workshops are demanding events. However, apart of thus process a further date should be set by the management team at which action plans will be agreed. Usually, individual members of the team will take ownership of specific areas related to outputs from the Self-Assessment workshop and develop a set of proposals to be presented at the subsequent action planning workshop.

Reviewing progress

It is vital to ensure that reviewing progress against action plans is part of the normal business review process of the organisation and not a separate activity.

1.4.2   A pro forma approach to Self-Assessment

One way of reducing the amount of work in undertaking and documenting a Self-Assessment is to create a set of pro formas, for example, one page for each of the criterion parts, making 33 in total.

Criterion I. Leadership

How the behaviour and actions of the executive team and all other leaders inspire, support and promote a culture of Total Quality Management.

❏ **Criterion part I a:**

How leaders visibly demonstrate their commitment to a culture of Total Quality Management..

Areas to address*): How leaders ...

- act as role models leading by example,
- make themselves accessible, listen and respond to their people,
- are active and personally involved in improvement activities,
- review and improve the effectiveness of their own leadership.

Strengths:

- *Leadership role taken by President;*
- *managers first to attend TQM training then lead training;*
- *effectiveness assessed by employee survey.*

Areas for improvement:

- *No integrated process to manage activities;*
- *activities not subject to regular review.*

Evidence:

- *President's statements on TQM;*
- *visit by President to various locations, customers and suppliers;*
- *the number of leaders involved in TQM training;*
- *perceptions of staff on their leaders behaviours from surveys of 1988, 1990, 1992, 1994.*

Approach:	Deployment:	Overall Score:
40 %	*60 %*	*50 %*

*) The areas below are selected by the organisation engaged in Self-Assessment, they would have particular relevance to its activities.

Fig. 131:   Example for the design of a pro forma[300]

The description of the criterion part would be printed at the top of the page with areas to address beneath it. The rest of the page would be sub-divided into sections for strengths, areas for improvement and evidence.

An example of an already completed form is shown in Figure 131. The Self-Assessment document could be prepared by individuals or teams from within the organisation and scored by trained assessors. Often, provision will be made for the results of Self-Assessment to be checked by teams external to the organisation.

A well-constructed set of pro formas is particularly suited to addressing the Enablers criteria. For larger organisations comprising several business units, the pro formas from the various units can be collated and the common strengths and areas for improvement identified.

From this, current strategy can be reviewed and organisation-wide improvement plans developed.

As with other approaches, the process should be repeated at appropriate intervals for continuous improvement.

1.4.3   A questionnaire approach to Self-Assessment

The use of questionnaires is another valid approach to Self-Assessment.

Some organisations use simple yes/no questionnaires as a method for widespread data gathering in support of more elaborate Self-Assessment processes such as the workshop approach mentioned above.

Other companies use more sophisticated questionnaires as the prime method for analysing strengths and areas for improvement and establishing the basis for the business improvement plan. In these questionnaires, multiple choice answers rather than yes/no responses are required.

1.4.4   A matrix chart approach to Self-Assessment

This involves the creation of a company-specific achievement matrix within the framework of The European Model for Total Quality Management. It typically consists of a series of statements of achievement against a number of points on a scale 0 - 10 or similar.

Although every organisation is different and may face different issues, these matrix diagrams can help in understanding the criteria in a more practical way and offer teams a means to assess their progress quickly and simply.

The matrix chart approach can be used at any level within the organisation, either by the management team or by a representative cross-section of the people from the business unit undergoing the Self-Assessment.

	CUSTOMER SATISFACTION
10	There is a positive trend in customer satisfaction. Targets are being met. There are some Benchmarking targets across the industry.
9	75 % of customer satisfaction targets are being met.
8	50 % of customer satisfaction targets are being met.
7	All employees understand targets relating to customer satisfaction.
6	The drivers for customer satisfaction have been identified and are used to modify targets.
5	Compare customer satisfaction levels within the Company. Results have a positive trend and some are meeting targets.
4	The relevance of targets to customer satisfaction can be demonstrated.
3	Targets are set for improvement.
2	Data is used to plot trends of customer complaints.
1	Customer complaints are logged and reacted to on an ad hoc basis.

Fig. 132:   Matrix chart on "Customer Satisfaction"

Matrix charts can also be used within a workshop approach. Here, it is necessary to carry out a preparation briefing where the respective instrument and the requirements of the assessment process are explained. At the briefing, each team member receives a copy of the Business Improvement Matrix in which they mark their own rating of the unit being assessed. Approximately one week later, the team meets for a full day consensus workshop assisted by a trained facilitator. Although the facilitator is a fully trained assessor, his/her role is not to decide the rating, but to use questioning techniques and facilitation skills to help the team agree on their rating of the unit. The final step is the action planning meeting in which the assessment team use their consensus rating and discussion notes as a basis for producing and implementing an action plan for improvement. It will be beneficial to repeat the workshop every six to twelve months to serve as an input for continuous review of progress.

Considering all aspects, this method seems to be too superficial to be suitable for an application. At the most, it can only be used for the first step into Self-Assessment.

1.4.5   A peer involvement approach to Self-Assessment

This approach has many similarities to the award simulation approach but allows the business unit undertaking the Self-Assessment complete freedom in putting together its "submission", which may at one extreme be a set of existing documents, reports, graphs, etc. and at the other something very close to a genuine award application document.

It combines extensive involvement from within the unit with a contribution from trained assessors drawn from managers external to the unit. Their role is to help the unit see itself objectively, rather than to arbitrarily judge advise or consult.

The combination of business unit involvement and a structured site visit can lead to a very high degree of accuracy in scores and feedback, a high level of commitment from the business units and a high level of cross-functional learning for the assessors. The action-plan may be as follows:

Step 1:	INITIATION	• Review request
		• Scheduling
		• Team selection
Step 2:	UNIT EXECUTIVE TEAM WORKSHOP	• Process overview
		• Initial self-score
		• Unit planning
Step 3:	UNIT DATA COLLECTION	• Existing unit's data
		• Random questionnaires
Step 4:	REVIEW PLANNING MEETING	• Assessors meeting for:
		− Review of data,
		− Identification of issues,
		− Assignments of responsibilities.
Step 5:	SITE VISIT DATA COLLECTION	• Executive team interviews
		• Management team interviews
		• Front-line discussion groups
Step 6:	SCORING AND CONSENSUS	• Individual analysis and scoring
		• Consensus process
		• Feedback-report
Step 7:	FEEDBACK OF RESULTS	• Discussion and clarification of results with executive team
Step 8:	ACTION-PLANNING	• Business unit planning:
		− short term action plans,
		• Incorporation into Business Planning Process.

This process should be periodically carried out, allowing sufficient time for significant improvements to be made. For maximum benefit, as with the other processes described, commitment is needed from the top of the organisation and this is achieved through the assessors being senior line managers from different areas of the company.

1.4.6   An award simulation approach to Self-Assessment

The action plan suggested by the EFQM for an award simulation approach to Self-Assessment can be seen in the following Figure:

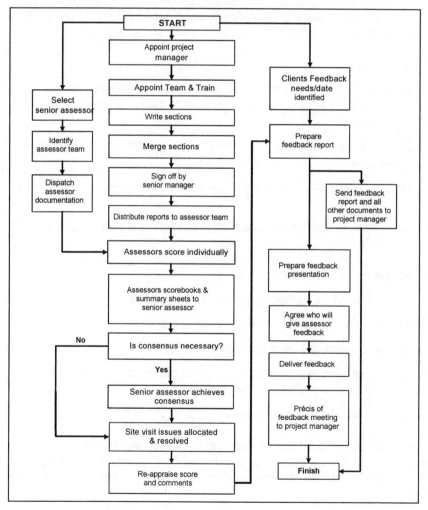

Fig. 133:   An Award Simulation Approach

1.5   General comments on Self-Assessment

Self-Assessment usually includes an individual scoring of the assessors, a consensus scoring within a team, a detailed on-site analysis and the final feedback report. Some comments on these points can be found in the following:

Comments on individual assessment and consensus scoring

The used data have to deliver useful information.

- ❑ Scoring charts should not always be taken as a guideline; however, the assessment of deployment, for example, depends on systematic approaches, regular reviews and integration.

Incomplete data:

- ❑ It is insufficient to say that a criterion or criterion part is not relevant to an organisation, convincing reasons have to be presented.
- ❑ If it is not relevant, the criterion will not be considered when scoring.
- ❑ It is valid to calculate the average on the number of remaining criteria.
- ❑ If reasons cannot be accepted, the criterion will be scored with 0 points.

Scoring is no exact science:

- ❑ An initial 3:1 variation in scoring is not unusual.
- ❑ People's perceptions of excellence are different.
- ❑ The scoring can be prejudiced or dogmatic.
- ❑ Taking the average does not support understanding. Reasons for different scoring have to be understood.
- ❑ Start with 50 % and then vary to higher or lower percentage.

Since the EQA-model was conceived for comprehensive use, an "exact" scoring can only be achieved in a team. Quality and acceptance of the results are dependent on the qualification and acceptance of the assessors.

Purpose, preparation and execution of a site-visit

The purpose of a site-visit is:

- ❏ to confirm the validity of the application,

- ❏ to clarify any unclear aspects of the application and rescore, if necessary, to take account of what is seen,

- ❏ to gain a sense of the atmosphere in the organisation and test whether the applicant could be a role model.

Preparatory measures:

- ❏ Planning of the site-visit begins during the consensus meeting.

- ❏ Fixing of site-visit date and distributing list of criteria with special relevance.

- ❏ Execution of a preparatory meeting including the following points:

  - – Who will be involved?

  - – What information is needed?

  - – Which questions will be posed and how will they be asked?

  - – Who carries out the interviews?

  - – What information should be given beforehand?

- ❏ Passing on general information to the applicant before the visit, especially if specific individuals will be interviewed.

Writing a Feedback-Report

- ❏ description of assessment process,

- ❏ brief overview of application (1 page),

- ❏ for each criterion part:

  - – strengths,

  - – areas for improvements,

  - – score band in terms of total points for application (e.g. 0 - 100, 101 - 200),

  - – score band (%) for each criterion (e.g. 0 - 10 %, 10 % - 20 %).

- ❏ address key issues focusing on strengths and areas for improvement,

- ❏ use the applicant's words,
- ❏ formulate according to the assessment,
- ❏ write in short sentences,
- ❏ if possible confine comments to areas directly related to the application, the criteria and score cards,
- ❏ the report must be understood by the applicant.

1.6   Example: The Royal Mail Business Excellence Review Process

Royal Mail's assessment process (see Figure 133) is integrated in the continuous improvement process (which began in 1988) based upon consistent customer orientation. Self-Assessment is the starting point for a regular business excellence process[301], being controlled by the top management and the management of the different business units.[302] Two important aspects were considered when working out the process:[303]

- ❏ the analysis of best practice examples of winners and finalists of the Malcolm Baldrige National Quality Award,
- ❏ the decentralisation of Royal Mail into 18 business units and a superordinated management almost exclusively fulfilling strategic tasks (Strategic Headquarters).

The assessment's objective is - in accordance with the EFQM model - to identify strengths and areas for improvement of the respective unit; it therefore is called "Business Excellence Review-Process". The assessment process includes Self-Assessment within the respective unit as well as assessment by assessors coming from other business units of Royal Mail. The most important aspect of the process is the site-visit by a team of assessors trying to support the people of the respective unit to assess themselves as objectively as possible. The execution of this process is done on a voluntary basis by each business unit. One assessor team consists of 6 line managers out of a pool of 200 top managers from all business units; thus, everyone can take the role of an assessor as well as being manager of the business unit to be assessed. This pool of assessors is an essential element of the process and permits an intensive exchange of experiences. The criteria model as a basis for the scoring process is oriented to the European Quality Award.

A small working group was created (Business Excellence Support Team) to manage the logistics of planning, organising and coordinating the reviews and the training of managers. This sould also lead to an improvement of the review process.

The first step in the process is an information meeting for the managers of the business unit to be assessed. The top management is informed of the different steps in the process, responsibilities are allocated and a first global assessment is carried out.

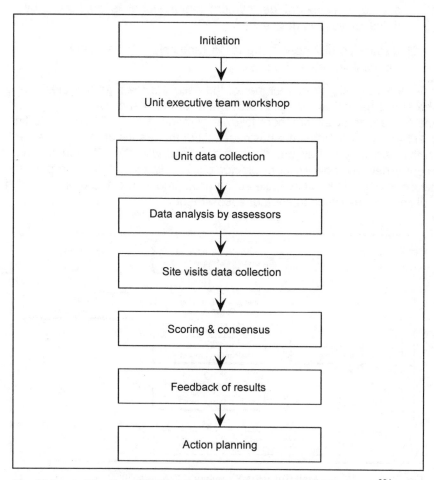

Fig. 134:   The Royal Mail Business Excellence Review-Process (I)[304]

Each unit then gathers the required data for its own area. In addition the results of a confidential questionnaire sent by the support team to a certain number of randomly invited employees is taken into consideration. An assessor team then examines this data and prepares a site-visit on the basis of it.

The on-site assessment executed within the regular review process lasts approx. 3 days and includes:

❏ an interview with the management of the business unit in order to gain an overall understanding of policies and strategies, approaches and key results (1st day),

❏ structured interviews with top and middle management in order to see to what extent deployment management is supported by those levels (2nd day) and

❏ discussion groups with up to 15 randomly selected people from the front-line staff (3rd day).

After the site-visit, every member of the assessor team judges individually the strengths and areas for improvement of the respective business unit; the consensus by all members follows (duration: approx. 2 days). The final feedback report informs the business unit of the results of the assessment. Within two weeks they are discussed on-site with the affected management. They are now responsible for converting the feedback-report into action, e.g. to work out suitable action plans, measures and projects which will again be reviewed in another assessment.

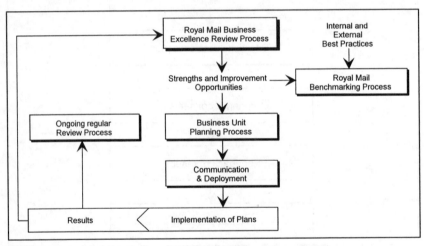

Fig. 135:   Royal Mail Business Excellence-Process (II)[305]

Here, it is also important to consider data of competitors and of other business units within Royal Mail (Royal Mail Benchmarking Process, see Figure 135).

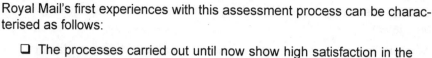

Royal Mail's first experiences with this assessment process can be characterised as follows:

❏ The processes carried out until now show high satisfaction in the affected business units.

❏ It is useful to emphasise the importance of the assessment compared to other measures within the company.

❏ It is also very important to assure the business units that results will be treated as strictly confidential.

❏ Since a complete assessment process can last up to three months, early planning and coordination of the assessment activities and other measures is necessary.

❏ The assessors have to be released from their line tasks in the scoring phase. This would not have been possible without complete support from the management of the company.

Royal Mail's (Self-)Assessment Concept clearly shows how such a process can be included in a superordinated target-finding and planning process.

The successful execution of the assessment can be guaranteed by an assessment pool and a support team. However, one can also see the problems that may arise for smaller companies. They are usually inable to provide resources to such an extent (personnel or financial) for training and release of their employees.

1.7   Summary

In order to replace "selective improvement measures" with a continuous improvement process, regular feedback is necessary - for example on the basis of Self-Assessments. Since traditional reporting does not deliver all necessary data for continuous improvement within an integrative management concept, additional assessment processes are needed. The results of these assessments serve as a basis for business planning and realisation, e.g. within improvement projects.

Combining Self-Assessment or its results with "normal" corporate planning is strictly necessary to create a management instrument.

Internal assessments can be organised in many different ways. If they aim at delivering "objective" or "objectified" data for a planning basis, Self-Assessment should be carried out as an "internal third party" assessment rather than a "self"-assessment. In any case, it is necessary to combine a

Self-Assessment with benchmarking in order to avoid emphasising inside orientation.

A more recent European study showed that the following factors are important for success:

It is important, that ...

- ❏ managers review improvements. (80 %)
- ❏ CEO is involved. (77 %)
- ❏ employees executing the Self-Assessment are trained. (76 %)
- ❏ Self-Assessment starts at the management. (76 %)
- ❏ the manner in which the results are used is determined in advance. (66 %)
- ❏ employees participating in the assessment are trained (39 %)

However, first experience in Germany reveals two problems which should not be underestimated:

- ❏ a "mechanistic" execution of the Self-Assessment without reflecting the psychological aspects and the transparency resulting from the assessment,
- ❏ the traditional quality department being responsible for the Self-Assessment; this can lead to problems because of lacking qualification and acceptance problems.

However, the rough description given here shows very clearly the limits and problems for small enterprises, companies beginning to implement TQM or companies without a future oriented corporate policy. These enterprises will only be able to start a systematic improvement process including assessments with external support.

2   Benchmarking[306]

Within the European Model for Business Excellence, the term Bench-marking is mainly used in connection with results criteria (Customer Satisfaction, People Satisfaction, Impact on Society, Business Results)[307]. The model demands the presentation of competitors' and best-in-class companies' performances and the comparison of the home company with these.[308]

However, this implies an understanding of Benchmarking which is restricted to the results criteria. If you consider the applications of winners of the European Quality Award (e.g. Rank Xerox) or the Malcolm Baldrige National Quality Award (e.g. IBM Rochester) it is obvious that Bench-marking can also mean comparing processes, activities or functions.

Moreover, it is cleary recognisable that Benchmarking activities can not only be undertaken regarding competitors and best-in-class companies. In bigger enterprises, internal Benchmarking may also have a definite use. Best-in-class companies or organisations do not have to be part of the same or a similar business. It is even more useful to identify best-in-class companies according to a special process they are undertaking (e.g. handling of a customer order) or a special result they are achieving (e.g. on-time delivery).

We will firstly deal with the definition of the word Benchmarking and then with different types of benchmarking and explanations of basic processes related to this tool. Subsequently, some examples of companies which are sucessfully undertaking Benchmarking in various ways will be discussed. Finally, the advantages and benefits of Benchmarking will be summarised.

2.1   Terms

The word benchmark literally means yardstick or reference point. Originally, bench mark was a term used in surveying as the starting point for measuring differences in altitudes.[309]

Today, the word Benchmark or the process of Benchmarking stands for a managerial tool. The original meaning is easy to remember: reference points in the sense of the best performance in a special field and mea-suring differences between these points and your own company. This method of comparing oneself with others was initially mentioned in 500 A.D. In that year, the Chinese General Sun Tzu wrote: "If you know your enemy and yourself you will not have to fear one hundred battles".[310]

Moreover, another aspect belonging to Benchmarking is the Japanese "Dantotsu": to become the best of the best.[311]

Looking at the development of the Japanese economy since the 2nd World War with the consistent execution of Dantotsu, it becomes clear how important comprehensive Benchmarking methods - practised within a conceptional frame - can be: "Copying" processes and procedures from the United States and Europe lead to Japan firstly becoming competitive against the above-mentioned competitors; the further development of the "copies", which was the next logical step, is still felt today, when we see that the Japanese companies themselves have become Benchmarks.

Thus, in general, the managerial tool of Benchmarking always means comparing oneself to, and thus learning from others.

The following figure shows some selected definitions of Benchmarking based on the statements mentioned above:[312]

Benchmarking = process / activity

❑ ... the continuous process of measuring products, services, and practices against the toughest competitors or those companies recognized as industry leaders (Rank Xerox);

❑ ... the ongoing process of comparing one's own process, practice, product or service to the "best" known similar activity. Then challenging but attainable goals can be set and a realistic course of action implemented to efficiently become and remain best of the best in a reasonable time. (IBM Rochester);

❑ ...a structured way of looking outside in order to identify, analyse and to use for oneself the best in industry or the best for a special function;

❑ ... a basis for retaining realistic performance targets by looking at how the best perform.

Benchmark = Standard

❑ Qualitative Benchmarks in the sense of "practices":

• own processes and "Benchmark" processes, with each having input and output

• better output with comparable input = better process

• to understand and implement the "Benchmark" process

❑ Quantitative Benchmarks in the sense of performance data:

• the results of processes

• conceivable for all possible targets, e.g.,

– customer and people satisfaction,

– business results,

– quality.

Alltogether, Benchmarking can be defined as follows:

> *"Benchmarking is the search for best processes, procedures or results which are relevant for a certain task within the home company. The aim is to learn from these processes, procedures and results and to use them for improving company performance."*

2.2 Types of Benchmarking

Based on this working definition, different types of Benchmarking can be singled out.[313]

Internal Benchmarking means comparing similar activities and results of the home company's different operating units. This method is not only relevant for bigger enterprises where several operating units or functions can be compared. It is even more important to see if administration processes such as invoicing can be considered as measurable processes in the same way as for example the manufacturing of a product. In this context, it may be an advantage to analyse and plan administration processes in the same systematic manner as production processes. This very simple method of Benchmarking can lead to substantial improvements. The systematic improvement of the process "collection of accounts receivable" can, for example, directly result in cost saving (e.g. interest). However, the fact that these internal investigations demand or even produce a high transparency between the operating units may possibly lead to resistance.

Competitive Benchmarking is characterised by comparing oneself to external direct market competitors - e.g. regarding special products (refrigerator A and refrigerator B) or services (car repairs in garage A and garage B).

Functional Benchmarking stands for comparisons within your own (or a similar) industry; if you take the example above, that would mean Benchmarking within the "refrigeration industry" or within the "car repair industry".

Best Practice Benchmarking means that excellent processes and proceedings from industry leaders are transferred to other industries. Here, for example, the delivery process of a building materials supplier for ready-to-use concrete may be compared to the delivery of a pizza by a Deli Service (see chapter 2.4.2). Although, at first glance, both industries appear completely different, one notices - on closer examination - that the delivery of both products shows similar quality criteria: concrete as well as pizza has to arrive punctually in a certain consistence at the customer.

Another type of Benchmarking is Award Model Benchmarking. That means benchmarking against the criteria of international quality awards. Since the criteria model of the European Quality Award is structured according to the vision of a company being successful beyond the year 2000, it may be useful for other companies to benchmark against these criteria. Here, the Benchmark is represented by the description of this fictitious company in the Self Assessment Brochure of the EQA[314]: This brochure explains how to use the award criteria. It is possible to assess how far your company is away from this ideal organisation by assessing the degree of goal accomplishment for every criterion. The Self Assessment process[315] can therefore be understood as a Benchmarking process and can, moreover, be used as a starting point for the above-mentioned types of Benchmarking (see following description).

2.3   The Benchmarking Process

The following figure shows clearly that the Benchmarking process does not start - as one might imagine - with the search for a "Benchmarking partner". It is even more important to sufficiently know and understand your own company. Without a detailled profile of strengths and weaknesses, which can for example be worked out on the basis of a Self-Assessment, it is difficult to determine target-directed action steps. This state-of-the-art method helps you to identify those processes and results which are particularly problematic or which demand improvement. These processes eventually form the framework for what is subsequently to be benchmarked.[316]

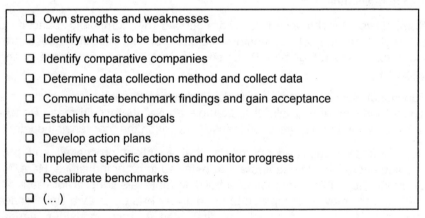

- ❑ Own strengths and weaknesses
- ❑ Identify what is to be benchmarked
- ❑ Identify comparative companies
- ❑ Determine data collection method and collect data
- ❑ Communicate benchmark findings and gain acceptance
- ❑ Establish functional goals
- ❑ Develop action plans
- ❑ Implement specific actions and monitor progress
- ❑ Recalibrate benchmarks
- ❑ (...)

Fig. 136:   The Benchmarking process[317]

Some starting points within the company could be:

❑ corporate policy and strategy

❑ business processes

❑ business results

❑ customer requirements

❑ products

❑ services

❑ other critical factors for company success

For each of these aspects, one can determine strengths and weaknesses in the sense of areas for improvement. In the end, the main issue is to get rid of weaknesses and to maintain or increase strengths.

After defining these strengths and weaknesses, the essential factors, parameters and methods should be selected. These factors, parameters and methods serve as the basis for the concrete contents of the planned Benchmarking.

The question of whether comparitive companies then have to be identified depends on the type of Benchmarking used.[318] There is no "one best way" to identify possible Benchmarking partners, but the following sources could be used to obtain helpful information:

❑ Relevant *publications* on the respective subjects

❑ *Market research institutes* which have an overall view of all companies

❑ Empirical *surveys and case studies* worked out with the help of existing companies

❑ *Plant visits* to those relevant companies which are not so well-known (e.g. competitors)

❑ *Data bases and the Internet*; this is becoming more and more important because information in international standard literature, e.g. on the subject "Who supplies what" or "Top 500's", can increasingly be found in this electronic media

❑ *Professional associations* give information on companies which are organised within the respective industry and provide professional journals with publications on leading companies

❏ *Benchmarking "clubs";* they offer - in most cases for a fee - a membership in a so-called Benchmarking partner group; however, apart from obtaining information, it is often obligatory to be available to other companies as a Benchmarking partner which means sharing information.

❏ *Consultancies;* bigger consultancies often have information networks all over the world and are therefore able to get contacts (however also not free of charge) for companies searching for a Benchmarking partner

In summary, at least bigger enterprises searching for a Benchmarking partner should look beyond the borders of Europe. On the one hand, Benchmarking requires companies which are willing to open their doors for externals; until now, this procedure has had no general acceptance in Europe. On the other hand, the above-mentioned Benchmarking clubs are not distributed all over Europe. In addition, it is a fact that many Best Practices cannot be found in Europe but rather in the USA or in Japan.

After having found the appropriate partner, the necessary data has to be collected, analysed, and compared to one's own.[319]

Communication of the   Benchmarking results within the company is especially important in order to encourage employees and give them a vision of what can be achieved in future. The results may also help to eliminate the prejudice saying "it is not possible to solve the problem in a much better way than we already have". This phenomen goes under the term of "not invented here".

The differences discovered by comparing a partner's performance to the company's own serve as a basis for setting targets and converting them into action plans.[320]

After the realisation of the determined action steps, it is nessecary to review progress by undertaking another Self-Assessment (e.g. one year later). The resulting new profile of strengths and weaknesses is the starting point for a new beginning of the Benchmarking process:

> *A rung of a ladder was never meant to be used for having a rest, but to hold a man's foot as long as to be able to put the other foot a little bit higher. (Thomas H. Huxley)*

2.4   Examples of Benchmarking[321]

2.4.1   Rank Xerox

Rank Xerox or the Xerox Corporation have been pioneers in the field of Benchmarking in the western world. They already had fixed standards for the determination of performance in the early 80s, and tried to identify methods which helped competitors to achieve world class performance.[322]

The following figure shows the more disillusioning first comparison between Rank Xerox and its Japanese competitors. But at least this "shock" caused the companies to venture in new directions. Today, Rank Xerox itself has become a Benchmark for others with many of its processes - e.g., their Benchmarking.

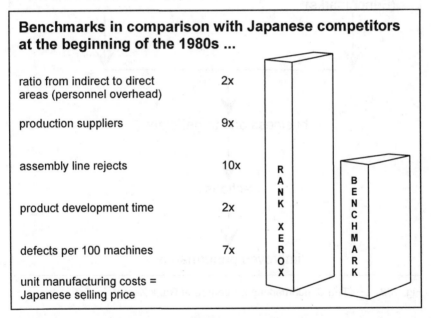

Benchmarks in comparison with Japanese competitors at the beginning of the 1980s ...

ratio from indirect to direct areas (personnel overhead)	2x
production suppliers	9x
assembly line rejects	10x
product development time	2x
defects per 100 machines	7x
unit manufacturing costs = Japanese selling price	

Fig. 137:   Rank Xerox and Japanese competitors at the beginning of the 80's[323]

Moreover, it is particularly interesting that, apart from the "usual" types of Benchmarking, Rank Xerox undertakes internal Benchmarking to a considerable extent. For example, they benchmark all Xerox and Rank Xerox data centres throughout the world.

The following figure demonstrates how general Benchmarking parameters are determined and realised: indicators (what?) and Benchmarking partners (who?).

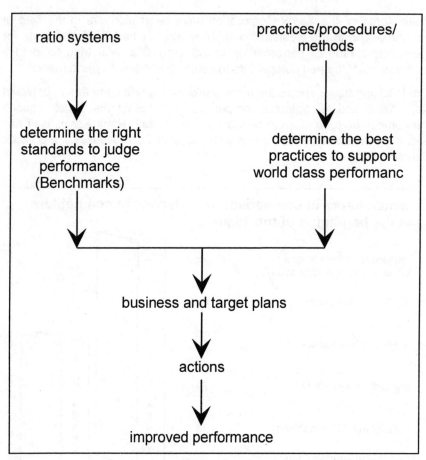

Fig. 138:   The Benchmarking procedure at Rank Xerox[324]

This performance diagnosis is transformed into action plans according to the following procedure, taking the respective priorities into consideration.

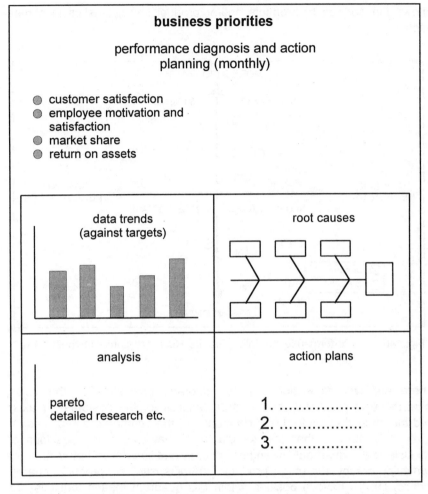

business priorities

performance diagnosis and action
planning (monthly)

- customer satisfaction
- employee motivation and
  satisfaction
- market share
- return on assets

data trends (against targets)	root causes
analysis	action plans
pareto detailed research etc.	1. .... 2. .... 3. ....

Fig. 139:   Priorities and transformation of the performance diagnosis into
             action plans[325]

2.4.2   Granite Rock[326]

This company belongs to the construction materials industry and won the
Malcolm Baldrige National Quality Award, category *Small Companies,* in
1992.

They practise a Competitive Benchmarking approach, which means that
regular customer and "not-yet-customer" surveys are executed in order to
compare the position of Granite Rock to their competitiors' position. In the
following figure, this comparison is illustrated by a performance portfolio. It

shows the position of products and/or product characteristics in competition.

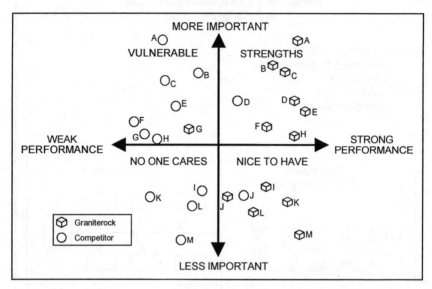

Fig. 140:   Performance portfolio: Granite Rock compared to their competitors[327]

There are two dimensions in the diagram, one showing the value/
importance of products/product characteristics for the customer (Y-axis),
and the other displaying the performance of the compared companies (X-
axis). It is obvious that one should try to have as many positions as
possible in the quadrant "strengths" and, in addition, to be better than the
particular competitor (e.g., product (characteristic) A, product (characteristic) D): To have a position within this quadrant means that this pro-
duct/product characteristic is of special importance for the customer and
here they see a company strength. Moreover, it is essential to improve the
"vunerable" positions: In this quadrant, the customer attaches special
significance to the products/product characteristics but he judges the
performance of Granite Rock as insufficient. Positions in the two quadrants
"no one cares" (not important for customer and weak performance) and
"nice to have" (not important for customer but strong performance) stand
for products/product characteristics which will not have to be at the centre
of attention of the company's interests in the future because the customers
do not attach enough value to them.

Summarising, one can say that better positions of competitors (i.e., "more
on the right side") - especially within the quadrants "vunerable" and
"strengths" - mean that there is a need to act for Granite Rock.

This tool is particularly interesting because it completely represents the customers' point of view and opinion. Even the company's own performance is assessed by the customer and not by the company itself. The customer's personal impression is more relevant than other - possibly objective - performance data. In the end, this attitude reflects a paradigm shift to true customer orientation.

Apart from Competitive Benchmarking, Granite Rock also practices Best-Practice-Benchmarking, a remarkable decision for such a small company (in total 400 employees). Here, completely different industries are considered as Benchmarks, e.g., *food service* (Domino's Pizza) for on-time delivery. This Benchmarking approach is based on the knowledge that the customer expects the same degree of on-time delivery for concrete as well as for pizza (home delivery). Concrete should neither arrive too late nor too early at the construction site. In the first case, this may cause waiting times and possible disturbances or obstructions in the work order (waste of transport capacity of the cement mixer); in the second case, this could lead to work being interrupted (waste of work capacity of the building contractor (customer)). In addition, the concrete has to arrive at the construction site "fresh", i.e. in an optimum manufacturing state. The delivery of a pizza is subject to similar rules. The customer wishes to get his pizza *neither before* his lunch break nor after his lunch break but during his lunch break (delivery window: approximately 0.25 hours) and in any case, the pizza has to be delivered *fresh and hot*.

There are other industries where Granite Rock is seeks Benchmarks, such as the *Production Sector* (production processes), *consumer durables* (e.g. refrigirators, process: securing longer keep of food) or *retrade* (small customer servicing).

2.4.3   IBM Rochester

As shown in the following figure, IBM Rochester, Malcolm Baldrige Award Winner of 1990, also performs comprehensive Benchmarking:

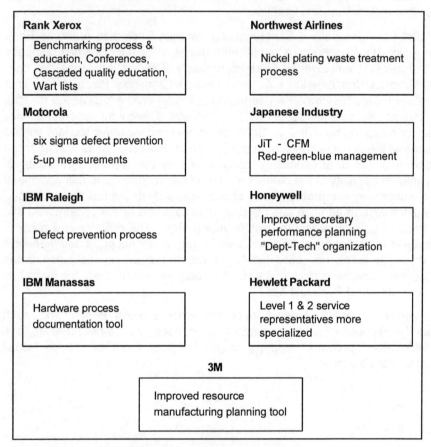

Fig. 141:   Examples of Benchmarking partners[328]

Here, something particularly interesting has occurred: after the first Award application in 1989, where the assessors identified a lack of Benchmarking as one of the main areas for improvement, IBM benchmarked the Benchmarking process itself with Xerox.[329]

Looking at the given Benchmarking partners, almost all types of Benchmarking mentioned earlier can be seen: Internal Benchmarking (IBM Raleigh, IBM Manassas), Competitive Benchmarking (Hewlett Packard), Functional Benchmarking (e.g. Honeywell) and Best Practice Benchmarking (e.g. Northwest Airlines).

For IBM Rochester, the most important reason for maintaining such a comprehensive Benchmarking program was and is the use arising out of this Benchmarking for the company:[330]

❑ to set targets based on facts

❑ to provide structures in order to generate new ideas for improvements

❑ to widen the organisational perspective

❑ to build an opposition to the "Not-Invented-Here"-syndrome

❑ to have higher expectations concerning improvements

IBM Rochester's basic Benchmarking process with the steps Self-Assessment, Benchmarking (planning, analysis) and implementation (integration, action) is shown in the following figure.

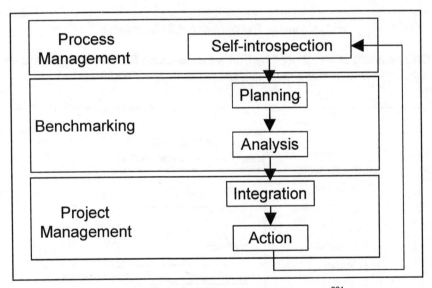

Fig. 142:   The Benchmarking process at IBM Rochester[331]

The underlying Benchmarking hierarchy reflects the different aspects already mentioned in the chapter *Benchmarking Process* (see Fig. 153).

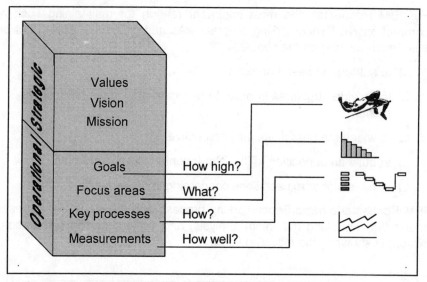

Fig. 143:   IBM Rochester: The hierarchy of Benchmarking[332]

One example of a tool used by IBM within its basic Benchmarking is the so-called process maturity gap analysis, which is described here.

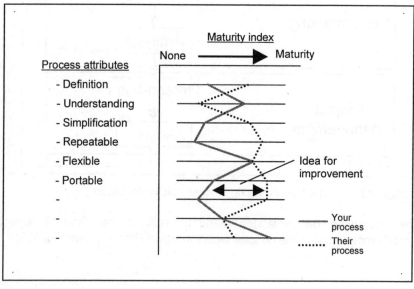

Fig. 144:   Process maturity gap analysis[333]

This tool is used for demonstrating the improvement potential of corporate processes. The idea is not to show processes as a combination of sub processes but to describe them by using key attributes. With that, one can ensure that comprehensive factors such as applicability, understanding of the process or flexibility will not be lost as comparison or improvement dimensions.

2.4.4   Texas Instruments Defense Systems and Electronics Group[334]

For the Texas Instruments Defense Systems and Electronics Group (TI DSEG), MBNQA Winner 1992 in the category *Producing companies,* Benchmarking is - in their own words - of strategic importance for their improvement process.

The so-called Network of Champions (see figure Fig. 155) is hereby used for coordinating Benchmarking activities, in particular contributing to the improvement of the following key processes:

❑ securing quality of services;

❑ production and administration processes;

❑ performance of suppliers;

❑ relations to employees.

The figure shows the variety of Benchmark information included in the Network of Champions.

Data gathering delivers real-time information and should be executed as close to the customer as possible and on all levels of the company. This can be realised by computer networks with the possibility of entering and processing data at every relevant work place.

When processing data, the network offers an opportunity to combine the gathered data with the most important quality management tools (e.g. development and production simulations, functional specific analysis tools, SPC/SQC).

Moreover, the most important quality management tools are retrievable and can therefore be applied directly by using the present data.

Quality Improvement Teams (QIT) then implement the results. The general approach for data gathering, analysis and realisation is shown in figure 156.

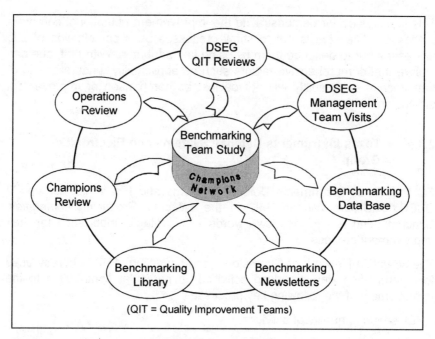

Fig. 145:   Network of Champions: Coordination of Benchmarking activities[335]

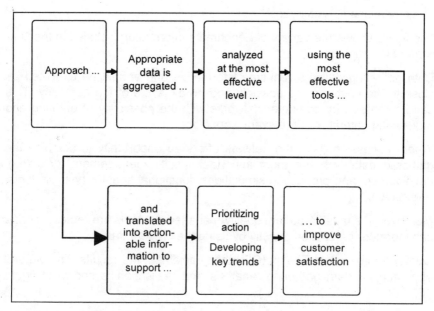

Fig. 146:   General approach to data collection, analysis and implementation[336]

2.4.5   Ritz Carlton Hotels[337]

The hotel chain Ritz Carlton was a winner of the MBNQA in 1992 in the category *Service Companies*.

This hotel chain has been involved in Benchmarking since its foundation in 1983, a fact which lead to the name "Born at Birth"-Benchmarking.

Competitive and Functional Benchmarking, which is used in the hotel business all over the world, places the emphasis on both processes and results. Worldwide, customer-oriented parameters and testing methods based on the American Automobile Association (AAA) and the Mobil Travel Guide (over 100 indicators) create the foundation for Best-Practice-Bench-marking.

Ritz Carlton took advantage of the opportunity to combine customer satisfaction with business results - this was one important conclusion they gained from Benchmarking with former MBNQA winners - and its emphasis on customer orientation also lead to a considerable increase in the internal acceptance of the Total Quality Concept.

Consistently using Benchmarking and implementing the results are the reasons for Ritz Carlton's current position, with a 10% higher total perfor-mance than the leading competitor, and a 95% higher total performance than the average competitors in this industry. Now, Ritz Carlton itself has become a Benchmark for others. This is remarkable when considering that the leading competitor had previously served as a Benchmark to Ritz Carlton.

2.5   Conclusion

The word Benchmarking stands for a managerial tool, which is once again held[338] to be increasingly important. It generally means comparing oneself to and learning from others.

Successful Benchmarking requires a profound knowledge of the company (e.g., by Self-Assessment) since, after all, thus is obligatory for determining the content of Benchmarking (processes, results) and the (best) Bench-marking-Partner.

The different types of Benchmarking are distinguished according to where the Benchmarks come from, e.g. Competitive Benchmarking with direct competitors or Best-Practice-Benchmarking with the best companies in the world.

Optimum use of this tool requires communication of the results within the company, transforming them into achievable goals and deriving appropriate action plans from them. Finally, the review of achieved targets (e.g. by carrying out another Self-Assessment) leads to a process of continuous improvement because the new Self-Assessment ideally becomes the starting point for new Benchmarking.

Worldwide, leading companies have been successfully practising Benchmarking over a long period of time, and have obviously already found the answer to the following question:

What is the use of Benchmarking?

The question is easily answered:

Benchmarking is used to become competitive and stay competitive in the long term.

This statement can be justified by the fact that Benchmarking makes it possible to analyse the competitors and thus get an impression of their strengths and weaknesses in comparison to ones' own.

Moreover, Benchmarking can provide a new horizon for unknown solutions which have already been successfully applied in other companies, thus helping to initiate changes instead of following the *Not-Invented-Here*-argument. Even if an idea for solving a problem is not yours, it may still be better than your own solution.

The Benchmarking process helps to realise customer needs. By undertaking comparisons in competition, you are confronted with market realities instead of examing your own past.

Benchmarking delivers objective data instead of opinions, and thus goes a long way to supporting the notion of a "Management by Facts", which is the basis for all modern TQM concepts.

Benchmarking helps to determine achievable targets. On the one hand, existing Benchmarks are credible and indisputable. On the other hand, they are oriented to the future, taking into account that in the sense of *Survival-of-the-Fittest,* only the most competitive and productive companies will survive in the long term: these Benchmarks single out the best companies at any one time.

3   Policy Deployment[339]

3.1   Relevance of the subject

All management concepts emphasise the importance of transforming strategic corporate goals into operational plans. Besides, the advantages of strategic and operational plans based on corresponding goals are widely recognised. The question to be addressed is, therefore, how to operationalise the goal determination and planning processes in a company from a quality-conscious point of view.

In the goal deployment process, it should be the aim of everyone involved to align the goals within each operational unit to the corporate vision and its derived policies. There is, on the one hand, the traditional approach, in which goals are communicated and deployed in a one-way process, e.g. Management by Objectives. On the other hand, more recent concepts tend to integrate horizontal components into the vertical goal deployment process. The latter approach implies that goals are established above and beyond the functional borders in a company, being more aligned to the processes which focus on customer requirements. Typically, the new concepts differ only slightly, i.e. with nuances in emphasis.

"Policy Deployment" is a widely used term to describe the intersection between vertical and horizontal goal deployment processes, but literature does not give a unified definition of the term. Moreover, the myriad of terms applied in literature makes any discussion in this field prone to misunderstanding. Traditional and modern goal deployment concepts will therefore be described and compared in the following chapters.

3.2   Demands on a Policy Deployment Concept within Total Quality Management

Total Quality Management implies a culture in which striving towards continuous improvement is given top priority. It is therefore not sufficient to lay down feasible goals based on the present situation. The systematic deployment of normative guidelines found in corporate policies and strategies, and the transformation of these into operationalised and task-oriented goals down to the executing organisational levels (Policy Deployment) constitute a significant component in a TQM concept. Accordingly, an holistic approach with regards to hierarchical levels and functions should be given serious consideration, as in the broad outlines of the following figure.

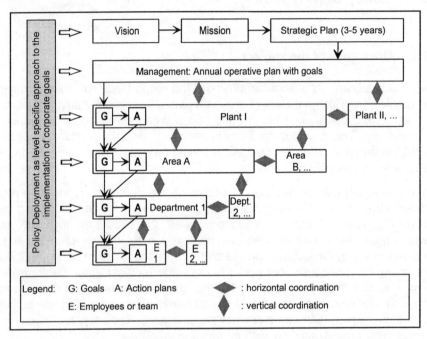

Fig. 147:   Policy Deployment as level specific approach to the implementation of corporate goals

Self assessment used by top management as a basis for decision-making could, along with other methods, serve as a sound foundation for goal deployment in a Total Quality Management concept.[340] Besides, such assessments would allow the company to develop (external and internal) quality profiles as well as identifying deviations from goals. The required information can be compiled through an assessment of the most important processes, internal and external customer surveys and an analysis of the present (Quality) Management System.[341]

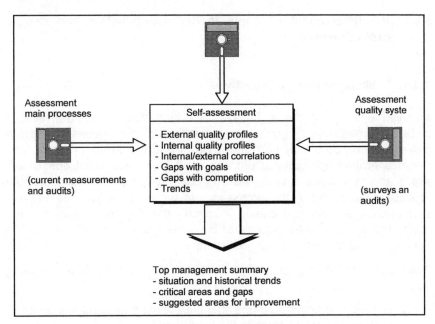

Fig. 148:   Analysis of assessment results[342]

A summary of the current corporate situation can be derived from the assessment data, and improvement goals and strategies subsequently established. Moreover, the goals indicate the directions that, from a managerial point of view, contain the biggest success potential.

Goals can either be related to a functional department or have a more cross-functional or overriding nature, in as much as this affects multiple departments and hierarchy levels. Up until now, different approaches in formulating goals have been used to react to this situation. Management by Objectives and Quality Function Deployment are one-dimensional goal identification and deployment concepts. Recently, some new and quite different alternative concepts have emerged, most significantly Hoshin Planning and Goal Deployment, which both have the multidimensional nature mentioned above in their identification and deployment of goals.

3.3   One-dimensional concepts in the determination and deployment of goals

3.3.1   Management by Objectives

Management by Objectives (MbO)[343] is a leadership model that aims to unite the organisational goals with the individual perceptions of the employees through a strictly vertical top-down and bottom-up-process. MbO revolves around a leadership process in which management consistently aligns and formulates feasible working goals (objectives). The leadership process is supported by the necessary background conditions as well as a performance assessment criteria indicating the degree of goal achievement. The specific working goals of the individual employee are thus derived from a total (hierarchical) goal system.

The process of "managing by objectives" can be structured in the following way:

- ❑ The top management formulates the overall organisational goals, and communicates them to the members.
- ❑ Each hierarchy level derives their own goals from the above level, which in turn serve as broad goals for the subordinate level.
- ❑ In discussions with every employee, individual goals are set down and agreed upon before they are returned towards the top where they can lead to goal adjustments.
- ❑ Accepted goals are used as performance assessment criteria in employee appraisal.
- ❑ The goal achievement results are communicated in scheduled employee interviews. The appraisal interview is the basis for deciding on consequences for the employee and her/his future goals.

The most essential elements and steps of the MbO process are outlined in the following figure:

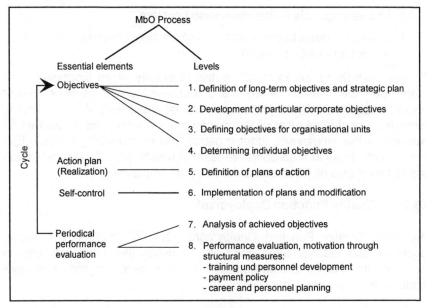

Fig. 149:   Elements and levels of MbO[344]

The following advantages have been identified:[345]

- ❑ Relief for line managers
- ❑ Improved identification with corporate goals
- ❑ More unbiased employee appraisal
- ❑ Enhancement of the employees' initiative, performance and responsibility
- ❑ An increase in planning and organisational efficiency
- ❑ Delegation of a higher degree of responsibility to the employees
- ❑ Support of developing employees' skills

Problem areas that commonly arise as a result of the MbO are, amongst others:[346]

- ❑ Maintenance of the goal commitments
- ❑ Goal conflicts
- ❑ High demand on organisational resources
- ❑ Restricted flexibility

❑ An overemphasis on the observation system

❑ Stabilising department-oriented thinking and behaviour (particularly within TQM concepts)

If these restraining forces (such as the possibility of an increased functionally-oriented division of work and increased problems at interfaces within horizontal business processes) can be dealt with, it is possible to achieve a substantial relief of the management's work load as well as an increase in the employees' independence and responsibility (People Empowerment). MbO in a co-operative fashion meets one of the most important requirements of TQM, that of involving all employees.

3.3.2 Quality Function Deployment

The term "Quality Function Deployment (QFD)"[347] embraces a cross-functional and team-oriented approach, in which the qualitative requirements of the market are systematically implemented in the company's products and services.

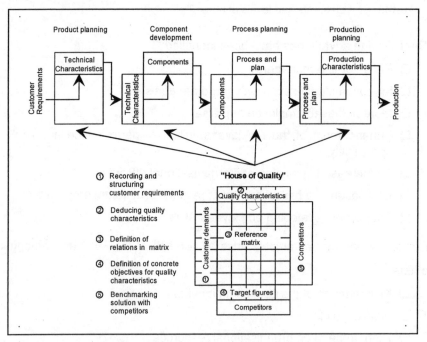

Fig. 150:   Methodology of QFD (simplified)[348]

QFD embodies a structured method for the identification and evaluation of customer requirements, the voice of the customer, in all process phases. In addition, QFD could in a broader context be applied to internal customer-supplier relationships, so that cross-functional goals for the company can be established. The methodical approach of QFD is outlined in the previous figure.

Based on a cross-functional approach, all customer requirements are determined subsequently for the different customer-supplier relationships. The customers also rank their requirements, so that the relative importance of the achievement of specific requirements is reflected. Finally, they appraise the present degree of achievement.

After this first assessment phase, the supplier, in close co-operation with the customer, determines those quality characteristics which, when altered, have a specific impact on the fulfilment of customer requirements. A comparison of the characteristics with the requirements and the degree of agreement is used to derive process targets. It is furthermore possible to determine correlation amongst the characteristics in the "Roof" of the "House of Quality".

The process-oriented cross-functional approach benefits from the fact that customer requirements that commonly affect multiple department, are considered during goal determination. Additionally, employees become increasingly aware of internal and external customer-supplier relationships.

Additional advantages mentioned are:[349]

- ❑ A more developed understanding of customer requirements amongst employees.

- ❑ Identification of internal business processes to be improved to meet customer needs in a better way.

- ❑ Swifter adaptation to changes in customer requirements.

- ❑ Development of a cross-functional understanding of quality, costs etc.

3.4   Multidimensional concepts in the determination and deployment of goals

MbO and QFD as one-dimensional methods can lead to sub-optimisation, particularly when departments develop specific functional strategies for achieving their goals. This implies that MbO and QFD, with their vertical and horizontal oriented focus, tend to loose sight of the orientation of the overall corporate goals.

In order to overcome the drawbacks of a solely vertical or horizontal goal deployment approach, concepts have evolved which aim to integrate both these goal determination dimensions. The most significant of these are the Hoshin Planning and Goal Deployment concepts.

The development of a multidimensional strategy based on the existing one-dimensional concepts is outlined in a simplified manner in the following figure. Special attention should be given to the intersection of vertical deployed goals and goals from the horizontal deployment along the process chain, since these are especially critical points.

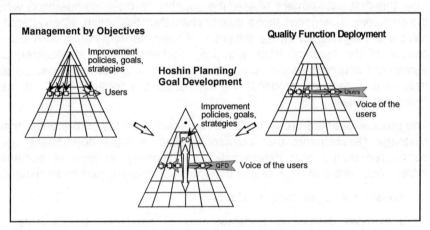

Fig. 151:   The formation of goals in a multi-dimensional concept (strongly simplified)[350]

3.4.1   Hoshin Planning (Policy Management)

The Hoshin Planning method was developed in the 60s at the Bridgestone Tire Company in Japan. Almost all Japanese winners of the Deming Award apply this goal determination method. One of the main reasons for this development is to be found in the meaning of Hoshin Kanri. Translated, "Hoshin" means objective or direction and "Kanri" means management or control. Contrary to the western Management **by** Objectives concept, Hoshin Kanri means "Management **of** Objectives" or "Policy Management".[351]

In the first phase of the planning process, the vision and strategic goals are identified or modified. Specific customer wants and needs are then compiled in the next stage through customer surveys or interviews. This phase also includes the gathering of information on the current economic situation as well as on errors in previous plans.[352]

The Hoshin Plan is developed top-down for each and every hierarchy level. It includes the following elements:[353]

- ❑ Objectives which make an aggressive or breakthrough statement about a purpose.

- ❑ Targets, broad quantifiable indicators, which measure the accomplishment of an objective.

- ❑ Strategies that show how the objectives and targets/goals are to be achieved.

- ❑ Performance measures to determine the completion of a strategy.

On a top-management level, the objectives are limited to one or two so-called breakthrough objectives, that is objectives that are crucial for the success of the company. This focus provides the biggest successfully manageable potential and, furthermore, allows subordinate management levels to add their own specific objectives to the Hoshin Plan.[354]

The objectives are operationalised in the middle and lower management levels of the organisation, which then develop specific plans though a dialogue with the level above ("catch-ball principle"). Managers of departments then develop methods for implementation and transformation of the underlying objectives. Objectives and strategies that affect multiple departments are dealt with by so-called cross-functional teams at management level.[355]

The following figure describes the relationship between the different phases of Hoshin Planning.

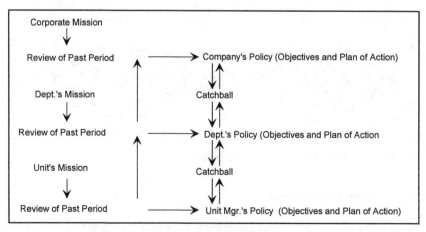

Fig. 152:   Process of Policy Management[356]

In this approach it is evident that the determination of vertical goals through the catch-ball principle is superseded by those derived from a horizontal and cross-functional orientation. The deployment of corporate goals is thus more important for Hoshin Planning than the analysis of customer requirements.

The comparative strengths of Hoshin Planning as opposed to the traditional methods can be summarised in the following four factors:[357]

- ❏ In a Hoshin Plan, the goals are determined in a systematic and structured way. Goal achievement is assured through the involvement of all hierarchical levels in the goal deployment process, as well as the commitment to achieving those goals.

- ❏ The hierarchical development of goals for the organisational units yields a ranking of the relevance and importance of the goals. For a concept like MbO this trait is only theoretically possible.

- ❏ Prior plans are systematically taken into consideration, allowing for an adjustment of the respective goal determinations.

- ❏ Cross-functional teams are established, in order to determine for example the requirements of the different process members.

The following figure shows the impact of Hoshin Planning on the co-ordination of goals. After a clear and unambiguous strategy has been formulated by top management, each and every employee can gain an understanding of the unified achievement of corporate goals. Hoshin Planning is hence commonly labelled "compass management", that is "everybody (is) managing and moving in the same direction".[358]

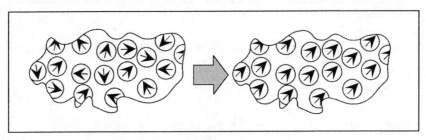

Fig. 153:   Realization of common goals[359]

3.4.2   Goal Deployment

The general aim of the "Goal Deployment" concept introduced by Conti[360] is a close intersection of vertical goal deployment over the hierarchical levels with horizontal goal deployment along the processes, as is the case with QFD. Goal Deployment enables the consideration of both customer requirements (voice of the customer) and also the voice of the company. The latter is possible through an interactive two-way process in which the corporate vision, know-how, information and data are comprehensively communicated top-down and bottom-up. However, the vertical component of Goal Deployment only works when the goals are co-ordinated with the next superior level, as with Hoshin Planning. Contrary to MbO, it is a prerequisite that feasible strategies are developed before the final goals are fixed. This is in order to avoid unrealistic goals.[361]

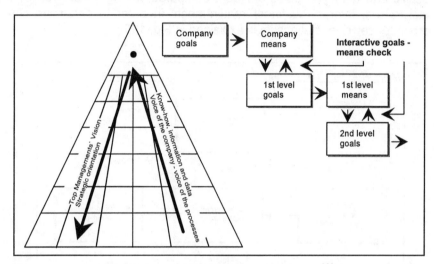

Fig. 154:   Interactive vertical strategic planning process[362]

In the goal determination process at top management level, the company's critical success factors (CSFs) should be especially monitored and considered. CSFs for a specific goal, derived from the corporate vision, include all strategies that are necessary and sufficient for the achievement of that goal.[363]

It is common to distinguish between two types of goal in Goal Deployment:[364]

❑ Function-specific goals are mainly concerned with individual functions or groups of functions, and have clearly delimited areas of responsibility, such as maintenance, personnel planning and information systems.

❑ Interfunctional goals affect different function areas and imply co-operation, for instance quality improvement, cost reduction and delivery reliability.

Function-specific goals are analysed by top management in order to reveal to what extent they can contribute to the realisation of the critical success factors. The goals are subsequently deployed to the underlying level, where the feasibility is once again analysed and synchronised with the superior level (Catch-Ball principle).[365]

This process is different at the process management level in so far as vertical deployment is swapped for horizontal deployment. The function-specific and deployed goals are here compared with goals derived from external and internal customer requirements in order to determine correspondence. This relationship is explained in Fig. 165.

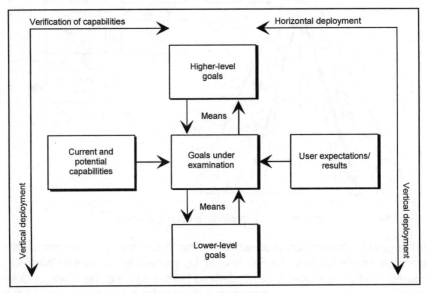

Fig. 155:   Horizontal and vertical close-up[366]

Interfunctional goals are determined and formulated by the company's top management. However, a so-called process management team is responsible for the achievement of the goals. This team identifies the affected functions and assigns interfunctional goals to the critical success factors. Those processes are chosen based on their impact on the critical success factors, commonly supported by a matrix that visualises each CSF and its correlating business processes. The set corporate goals are then assigned to these processes.

At process management level, these goals are once more compared with the horizontally deployed goals, and any necessary adjustments are made. The process goals are then deployed to the corresponding sub-processes.

The next vertical step in deployment of interfunctional goals is carried out according to the procedure for function-specific goals. A summary of the method applied in Goal Deployment related to interfunctional goals is found in Fig. 166.

Goal determination in the deployment process is strategically oriented, and aims to develop long-term corporate goals. From these strategic goals, the operational goals for the individual organisational units can be derived, being identified through the interactive "top-down and bottom-up" process including the cross-functional aspects of customer orientation. The individual departments thus strive towards an optimum achievement of set goals, contributing to a comprehensive, corporate improvement.

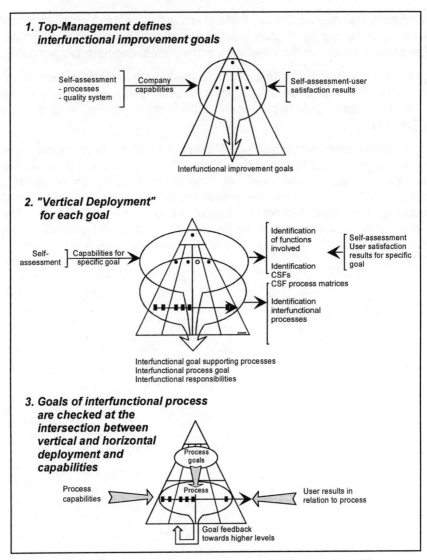

Fig. 156:   Deployment of cross-functional improvement goals[367]

The requirements for the successful application of Goal Deployment are, on the one hand, experience with teamwork in management and, on the other hand, the smooth running of the appraisal of goal achievement and strategy. The first implies involvement of employees in the decision-making process as well as in the execution of the process-oriented Quality Function Deployment method. The latter assumes that the processes in the company are transparent and adjustable. Another sound foundation for successful application is comprehensive and reliable self-assessment and the utilisation of goals as an instrument for leadership and motivation.

3.5   Conclusion

Companies currently face strong international competition that will only increase. Two of the most crucial success aspects are thus going to be short cycle times and increased flexibility. The one-dimensional methods of goal deployment are rarely a sufficient reaction to the changes in basic business conditions mentioned here.

The two multidimensional planning concepts, Hoshin Planning and Goal Deployment, distinguish themselves only slightly in emphasis on different elements. Both concepts include the determination, deployment and monitoring of goals that involve everybody and take customer requirements into consideration. Through the application of Goal Deployment, it is simultaneously possible to identify the main problem areas in the determination of function-specific and interfunctional goals. Customer requirements are therefore considered during the goal determination process through the analysis which takes place within the framework of business process management. Hoshin Planning tends to put stronger emphasis on vertical goal determination through an interactive process between corporate, divisional and departmental levels.[368] However, cross-departmental goals are also considered in the establishment of cross-functional teams.

The multidimensional concepts - regarding their horizontal and vertical methods - are superior to those which are one-dimensional in the following areas: the formulation of function-specific and interfunctional goals allows the synchronisation of cross-functional process-oriented requirements with the goals of other management levels. Notably, the different methods in the application of Hoshin Planning or Goal Deployment lead to similar outcomes, namely to uniting the advantages of the one-dimensional concepts of MbO and QFD in a multidimensional concept.

The following figure outlines some of the goal determination methods that have been covered in this chapter with respect to some relevant criteria.

	MbO	QFD	Hoshin Planning	Goal Deployment
Major Orientation	Results oriented (often - financially - oriented)	Process oriented	Process and results oriented (more strategically oriented)	Process and results oriented (more strategically oriented)
Strategic Focus	Short to medium term	Customer demands (voice of customer)	Breakthrough goals	Critical success factors (strategic goals are converted into operative goals)
Responsibility	Individually oriented	Team-oriented/ possibly with experts	Team-oriented	Team-oriented (cross-functional and function-related)
Management Style	Delegate; control is tight	Participation	Participation with checking (everybody is responsible)	Participation with checking (everybody is responsible)
Employee Participation	Top down (one direction)	Interdepartmental project teams	Stronger emphasis on "Catch-Ball"-principle, additionally interdepartmental	Equal emphasis on horizontal and vertical participation ("Catch-Ball"-principle)
Customer Orientation	Not explicitly included	The voice of the customer is decisive	Corporate goals more important than customer requirements	Equal significance of corporate goals and customer requirements

Fig. 157:   Comparison of different methods of establishing company objectives

4 People Empowerment[369]

4.1 People Empowerment - definition and distinction

People are key factors for successful Business Excellence concepts, as can be seen in the basic model for the European Quality Award (EQA):

"Better results through involvement of all employees in the continuous improvement of their processes."

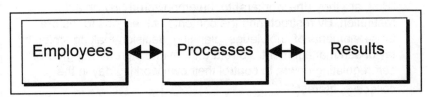

Fig. 158:   The basic EQA-Model

The importance of all people in realising extensive quality management concepts is also prominent in the "detailed" European Model for Business Excellence (especially in the criteria leadership, people management and people satisfaction). Something similar applies to the Malcolm Baldrige National Quality Award (until 1994: Category Employee Involvement, in 1997: Work Systems) and to the Australian Quality Award (Criterion Employee Involvement).[370]

The term "People Empowerment" is mainly used for practical concepts of employee motivation.

Whereas, during the 70s, participatory approaches were pursued mainly under the aspect of the quality of working life, it is the optimum use of human resources nowadays that is emphasised in People Empowerment, making it a predominantly economic target.

Two different approaches to People Empowerment can therefore be distinguished with regard to Business Excellence:[371]

❑ Business-related explanations

These apply primarily to the efficiency of the company. Alongside the more classical advantages of employee participation, such as improvement in quality and acceptance of decisions as well as the levels of qualification, the aspects of customer orientation are especially relevant in TQ. Customer orientation (both internal and external) is ultimately only possible if customers as well as suppliers have the necessary skills required for working together.

❑ Employee-Related Definition:

This includes the changes in employees' demands concerning their work and the many positive effects of employee participation on work satisfaction and motivation.[372]

As with many modern catchwords, People Empowerment also has no standardised, self-contained definition. The following figure shows various examples:

"How are they (the workers) to be empowered? By an act of restitution. By restructuring the contents of their jobs to restore those elements of knowledge, planning, decision-making stolen by taylorised management. To return them into a greater degree of self-regulating power to control their own working day in the collective interest."[373]

"Empowerment simply means encouraging people to make decisions and initiate actions with less control and direction from their manager."[374]

"Empowerment - giving people the authority and autonomy to do their jobs."[375]

Empowerment is defined as "being given a job to do and being given the tools with which to carry out that job."[376]

Fig. 159:   Exemplary Definitions of People Empowerment

When distinguishing the different tools for People Empowerment, it is useful to differentiate between two fundamental terms:[377]

❑ Empowerment of individual employees:

The focus of interest is on the ability of employees to completely fulfil their tasks, i.e., to make the necessary decisions in order to meet customers' demands without or with less supervision/consultation. Employees are able to work effectively when they possess the abilities, possibilities and authority to solve emerging problems on their own, thus contributing to continuous improvement.

❑ Empowerment of teams:

Teams (e.g., semi-autonomous work teams) usually have a higher degree of empowerment. Not only do they accomplish their "regular" tasks, but they also deal with all processes concerning their unit. This means that they integrate organisational, planning, supervision and improvement tasks, which were traditionally performed by supervisors or special departments. The whole team takes on the responsibility for achieving the unit's goal.

A second dimension of classifying the tools of People Empowerment is the degree of participation. According to Lawler[378], three areas can be distinguished (see Fig. 170):

❑ Suggestion Involvement

The first level is made up by the employees' "right to make suggestions". They are given the chance to voice their own suggestions and ideas, but they have no influence on the organisation and adaptation of their suggestions. Theoretically, at least, every employee possesses this form of People Empowerment, and institutionalisation is carried out by methods such as suggestion schemes.

❑ Problem-Solving Involvement

Employees are, for example, involved in the planning of concepts, the preparation of decisions, the analysis of problems and in problem-solving, and are able to actively influence their work life. However, the decision to adapt their ideas is still made at management level.

❑ Job Involvement

Employees have the capacity to make and adapt their own decisions in an earlier-defined task area, within an agreed upon scope. Accordingly, employees are totally responsible for their actions, whereby the supervisors' roles are more co-ordinating than advisory. When transferring decision-making capacities, codetermination is also transferred to the "bottom", unlike suggestions and problem-solving involvement.

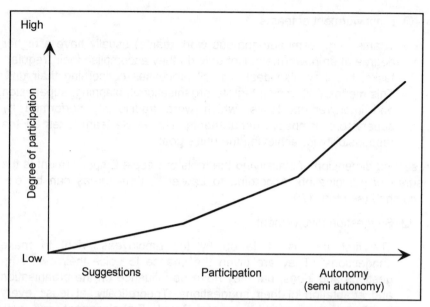

Fig. 160:   Different Levels of People Empowerment according to Law-
              ler[379]

People Empowerment cannot fully come into effect until decision-making capacities have been transferred. The restriction to suggestions and problem solving involvement - and thereby often management's rejection and ignoring of employees' ideas - result in employee frustration and refusal in the long run. This was the main reason for the failure of many Quality Circle Introductions at the end of the 80s. [380]

On one hand, empowerment can be differentiated according to the significance of participation and to the involvement of individuals or teams. On the other, one has to distinguish between empowerment intended only for a restricted area (partial tasks, projects, regular meetings etc., which is therefore more limited in its contents and time) and permanent empowerment that covers all elements of work.

Before taking a closer look at the different tools, we shall outline some fundamental requirements for the successful expansion of People Empowerment.

4.2   Requirements of People Empowerment

The fundamental requirements are clearly visible when putting the suggestion schemes - as one form of People Empowerment - into action (see also part II, section 2.3). One can distinguish between four different barriers hindering many employees from participating:[381]

- ❑ Ability Barriers (not being able to)
  Lack of criticism, unimaginativeness, difficulties in articulating their criticism

- ❑ Information Barriers (not knowing)
  Insufficient knowledge of internal operations and structures

- ❑ Risk Barriers (not daring)
  Fear of substantial ("self-rationalism") and idealistic disadvantages ("loss of status", disgrace), fear of taking on responsibilities

- ❑ Will Barriers (not wanting)
  Indifference towards the business, aversion to the company's organisation, resistance to change

The fundamental requirements of People Empowerment - and thereby any form of employee participation - can be derived from these barriers:

- ❑ Qualification of employees, i.e., support of their professional, methodical and social abilities

- ❑ Adequate information and communication systems (i.e., each employee has to have the necessary information and resources to complete his work at all times)

- ❑ A trusting atmosphere in the company - i.e., it is possible to make mistakes and to admit these (freedom to fail) - as a basis for supporting the awareness of responsibility (entrepreneurship) of employees.

- ❑ Support and promotion by management and the senior staff on all levels.

At the same time, People Empowerment needs to be integrated into a structured, holistic concept such as Business Excellence. The following prerequisites, although only indirectly connected to People Empowerment, are also necessary:

❑ Quality and performance-oriented reward systems with material and other forms of recognition

❑ Transparent and controlled processes (both technical and administrative)

❑ Constant deployment and regular review of objectives to guarantee a uniform alignment of activities

❑ Constant customer orientation (internal and external)

❑ Process-oriented structure of the organisation

The tools of People Empowerment can only be successfully implemented when the above prerequisites are fulfilled.

4.3   Tools of People Empowerment

4.3.1   Empowerment of individual employees depending on management style and task

Alongside the organisational requirements outlined above, empowerment depends very much on the type of leadership of the respective supervisor. The levels of empowerment of individual employees (and also of teams) are made visible in the classification of different leadership styles by Tannenbaum and Schmidt (see Fig. 171).

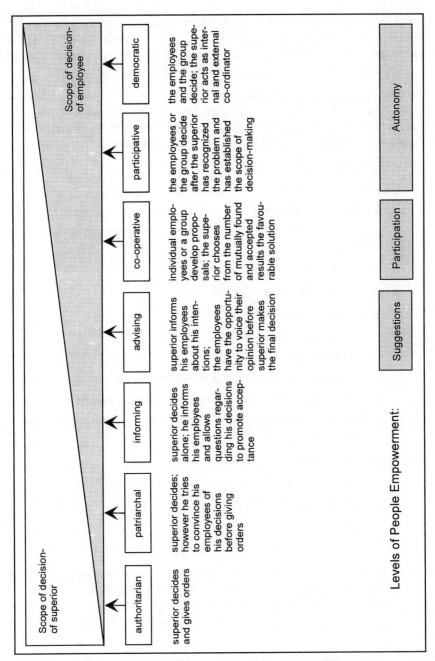

Figure 161:   People Empowerment and management style[382]

This shows that a participative and - from case to case - "democratic" leadership style creates possibilities for empowerment for subordinate employees. The supervisor does not intervene directly in the execution of his employee's tasks, but rather acts as consultant and coordinator.

The classification by Tannenbaum and Schmidt is, however, an idealisation, which only takes one type of leadership into consideration (continuum theory). Therefore, Tannenbaum and Schmidt always refer to considering the interaction of leadership style, employees and situation.[383]

❑ Scope of supervisor's influence

- Value system
- Trust in employees
- Understanding of his/her role as leader/personal inclinations
- Self-confidence in insecure situations

❑ Scope of employee influence

- need for independence
- willingness to take on responsibility
- interest in the type of tasks
- knowledge and experience in solving problems
- practical experience in the decision-making process
- tolerance of the superior's leadership attitude, depending on the situation

❑ Influence of the situation

- corporate structure and culture of the organisation
- composition and effectiveness of the team
- type of problem
- external basic conditions (e.g., time pressure)

As leadership attitude has to be oriented towards these aspects, it may be necessary for a superior with a participative leadership style to make decisions without including his employees. These will, however, be accepted and supported, if there is mutual trust between the employees and their superior.[384]

Management by objectives[385] is the direct consequence of the practical transfer of a participative leadership style. According to Business Excellence, one has to ensure that the goals fit vertically (hierarchical overlapping) as well as horizontally (cross-functional). [386]

A corresponding restructuring of the employees' work tasks is closely linked to People Empowerment through a leadership attitude, delegating competence and responsibility. Reacting to Taylor's[387] observations, Hellpach demanded as early as 1922 that the following points should be taken into consideration:

- personal planning of task accomplishment
- freedom to make decisions regarding the type of task accomplishment
- personal work planning and
- personal assessment or supervision of the results. [388]

Consequently, the work content supporting People Empowerment has to fulfil the following requirements: [389]

- Completeness (a comprehensive task with visible significance for the total process)
- Variety of requirements (avoidance of monotonous demands, use of different abilities)
- Possibility of social interactions
- Autonomy
- Learning and development opportunities

For most of the work tasks - at least on the lower hierarchical levels - these demands can only be met by transferring competencies to teams.

4.3.2   Suggestion schemes

Suggestion schemes describe an institution for the support, assessment, recognition and implementation of improvement suggestions. Their goals can be divided into business-related (rationalisation, quality improvement etc.) and employee-related (participation in business operations, motivation, improvement of work conditions and occupational safety). All employees of a company are eligible, as well as external persons (retirees, suppliers, customers, etc.), whereby suggestions of individual persons and teams (submission teams, suggestion circles) can be included. In order for a suggestion to be recognised as an "official improvement suggestion", various requirements have to be met:[390]

❑ The suggestion has to show a satisfactory solution or a clearly recognisable improvement of an (unsatisfactory) situation.

❑ The suggestion has to be an up-to-date and useful innovation in the area of application for which it is intended.

❑ A bonus may- in some systems - only be given if the suggestion goes beyond the employee's actual task (professional duty).

❑ Without the applicant's idea, the measure would not be realised at this point.

❑ In principle, these suggestions may concern all areas of the respective company and its relations to the environment.

The assessment of suggestions, i.e., the decision to accept or refuse them, is mostly carried out by a committee consisting of one representative of the suggestion scheme, one member of the works council, and various other managers. If there is a measurable benefit to be gained by implementing a recognised suggestion, a bonus is given in accordance with the net savings of the first year after implementation. A scoring system is used to agree on the bonus if it cannot be determined quantitatively. In some companies, the amount of the bonus depends on the hierarchical level of the applicant; supervisors therefore receive a lower bonus since they have an advantage in finding ideas due to their qualification and position.

The suggestion scheme has met with little enthusiasm in Germany and the USA compared to Japan (see Fig. 172), the reason being found mainly in the following problem areas:

❑ No appreciation of suggestions concerning one's own working area

❑ Often a long period of time between the submission of a suggestion and the evaluation (sometimes more than a year)

❑ Poor quality of the evaluation or justification of the refusal

❑ Bonuses are established primarily according to quantitative benefits

❑ Frustration instead of motivation due to low implementation rates

	Japan (1993)	Germany (1994)	USA (1993)
Suggestions for improvement per 100 employees	2 540	17.5	15
Average bonus per suggestion (DM)	5.6	907	742
Total amount of bonuses per employee (DM/year)	142.2	158.73	111.13
Realised suggestions	87 %	44 %	38 %
Realised suggestions per 100 employees	2 210	7.8	5.7
Net cost reduction per realised suggestion (DM)	209	3 800	11 500
Net cost reduction per employee (DM)	4 619	296.4	655.5

Fig. 162:   Suggestion schemes in Japan, Germany and the USA[391]

The following measures are necessary to enable the use of suggestion schemes as a tool of People Empowerment:

❑ Participation of direct superiors, who are able to decide on acceptance, implementation, and bonuses; starting points are, e.g., "minor suggestions". The superior himself can decide on these within an agreed bonus-scale (e.g., $ 100)

❑ Fast processing including feedback of the present situation to the applicant(s)

❑ Enhanced use of other forms of awards (appreciation)

❑ Integration of suggestions from one's own working area

❑ Bonuses for good suggestions, even when they are not carried out

4.3.3   Team Concepts with Suggestion Involvement

Traditional approaches are submission teams or the above-mentioned suggestion circles, who develop suggestions in a team. These teams rarely take part in the decision-making or problem-solving transfer. Something similar is true for the experience-interchange teams on different levels.

Their authority is usually also in the field of suggestion schemes. More possibilities are only within the already existing area of responsibility of individual members and not in the team as a whole.

Learning teams have an equal right to suggest improvements, should the need arise. But in Germany, for example, they primarily aim at qualifying aspects in the form of conveying professional, methodical and social competencies. A classic example of learning teams is the so-called "Lernstatt" (learning at the shopfloor level),[392] which was introduced at BMW and Bosch, among others, in the beginning of the 80s.

The original concept of the "Lernstatt" as a starting-point for conveying information and integration of new employees, especially from foreign countries, has been modified and extended in the meantime regarding the circle of participants and goals, by also picking up specific problem situations of one's own work area. These modified learning teams should therefore be assigned more to team concepts with participatory rights. This also applies to specific small team concepts such as so-called "starting-up circles", where qualifying aspects in the launching period of a new product series are linked to problem-solving tasks.[393]

4.3.4   Team Concepts with Problem-Solving Involvement

Two forms of team should be particularly distinguished on this level of People Empowerment: Quality Circles and Project Teams (Task Forces). Both exist alongside the "regular" organisation of the business, their members meeting only temporarily.

❑   **Quality Circles**[394]

Quality Circles (QC), originated in Japan shortly after WW II, when the quality concept became an important philosophy of industry there. The goal linked with quality circles was the - initially predominantly product-oriented - improvement of quality standards by including as many employees from the shopfloor level as possible to solve problems related to their own work. Contrary to most forms of realisation in the western world, quality circles in Japan were only one element of a more comprehensive system of promoting quality.

The basic idea of the QC concept is to solve problems where they arise. Its main characteristics are as follows:

❑ Voluntary participation for an unlimited time frame

❑ 7-10 participants in one work area

- ❑ Regular meetings (e.g., every fortnight) with a duration of about one hour during worktime

- ❑ Leadership by an adequately trained facilitator (usually the immediate supervisor of the employees)

- ❑ Structured process by applying different problem-analysing and problem-solving techniques

- ❑ Solving problems within one's own work area; if necessary experts of that area may be invited to participate as guests

- ❑ Independent choice of topics by the team, suggestions may also be proposed by superiors of other areas

- ❑ Holistic approach to solving problems and participation in transferring the problem-solving process

- ❑ Participation in the implementation process

An adequate organisation as part of the overall Business Excellence concept is necessary to ensure meaningful use and implementation of quality circles as a permanent concept. Quality circle concepts can be applied practically in all problem areas. They have been implemented in different models in the western world - especially regarding structure, voluntary participation and autonomy (e.g., choice of topic).

❑   Project Teams (Task Force Teams)

A project team is often referred to as a task force and includes employees of different hierarchical levels and areas. The team is formed in order to solve a defined problem, and its participants are usually appointed. The duration of the teamwork is therefore limited to dealing with a specific problem.

The authority of project teams is quite different. In most cases, the teams are responsible for solving the problem and occasionally afterwards for its implementation. But the decision to implement the solution is often made by management.

Project teams with comprehensive decision rights are scarce, and should therefore be assigned to the highest level of People Empowerment. They are usually hierarchically top-level teams, managing a multi-level project organisation (e.g., steering committee when implementing teamwork) with sometimes unlimited duration.

4.3.5   Permanent Teams

Forms of permanent teamwork were originally limited to semi-autonomous teams in the manufacturing sector. In the meantime, they have also been introduced in the development -, sales- and administrative areas, as well as on various other levels of the organisation.

❏   Semi-Autonomous Teams

It was in the beginning of the 1920s that Lang first described the idea of a team-oriented manufacturing process - based on the increasing problems of shop-floor production of large quantities - by suggesting team manu-facturing.[395] A wider distribution of this type of work organisation in the following period did not, however, take place. It was not until the beginning of the 60s that semi-autonomous teams were tried in Scandinavia as a possibility for employee participation.[396]

The original idea of teamwork is that a team decides to a large extent how expected output will be produced. The regulations made by the team fit the global performance targets of the company.[397] According to Lattmann, a team is "therefore a small team, to whom the responsibilities are given to accomplish a task, making regulations, with all activities and interactions put under the control of their own established standards".[398] It is obvious that alongside job performance, the extended tasks of disposition, mana-ging and controlling of one's own work as well as the continuous improve-ment of the process are assigned to the team as a permanent task.

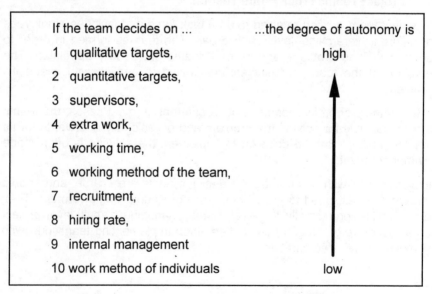

If the team decides on ...	...the degree of autonomy is
1 qualitative targets,	high
2 quantitative targets,	
3 supervisors,	
4 extra work,	
5 working time,	
6 working method of the team,	
7 recruitment,	
8 hiring rate,	
9 internal management	
10 work method of individuals	low

Fig. 163:   Degree of autonomy according to Gulowsen[399]

Semi-autonomous teams can be distinguished according to the degree of their self-autonomy (see Fig. 173), whereas there is no uniform definition of "semi-autonomous". These teams are one type of People Empowerment whereby a high degree of self-management can be achieved, where work structuring measures (especially of work enrichment and work expansion)[400] may also be carried out to a large extent. However, employees must therefore be appropriately informed and qualified (professionally, methodically and socially). Qualification measures have to be implemented at the same time, either "on-the-job" according to contents and targets, or in the form of workshops, seminars etc.[401]

Using Gulowsen's ideas as a basis, SIEMENS differentiates between seven types of teams, where, at the most, only types 3, 4, and 6 fulfil the requirements for semi-autonomous teams. Only these have an internal task assignment and they are not closely related to the following areas (see Fig. 174).

Type of Team / Team characteristics		Type 1	Type 2	Type 3	Type 4	Type 5	Type 6	Type 7
Leadership/	external	●	●					
Task assignments	by team			●	●	●	●	●
Qualification	only semi-skilled	●						
	semi-skilled and skilled workers			●	●	●		●
	only skilled workers		●				●	
horizontal scope of work								
	everyone masters everything		●			●		
	some know more than the others	●		●	●		●	●
vertical scope of work								
	some know everything	●	●	●		●	●	
	everyone knows at least one				●			●
link to	loose		●	●	●		●	
following areas	tight	●				●		●
25 % of the 566 teams cannot be classified		28 %	3 %	17 %	2 %	14 %	14 %	5 %

Fig. 164: Differentiation of various types of teams at SIEMENS[402]

Here, it is obvious that the concept of semi-autonomous teams - as well as other small-team-concepts - comes up against limiting factors, where there are no appropriate prerequisites, such as technology, organisational struc-

ture, or compensation forms. This shows the significance of the requirements mentioned earlier to all forms of People Empowerment.

The basic concept of semi-autonomous teams is increasingly being transferred to other areas of the business as well as to different hierarchical
levels. By doing so, universal, team-oriented organisational structures can
be developed in which these teams often have a leader with the professional and disciplinary position of a supervisor.[403] Therefore, People
Empowerment depends - once more - on the type of leadership.

4.4   Possibilities and limits of People Empowerment

People Empowerment - as previously shown - offers numerous possibilities
for involving employees on all levels, a process which is absolutely necessary for the continuous improvement of all processes within Business
Excellence.[404] Different prerequisites for the transfer of decision-making
authorities have to be met in order to accomplish possible advantages. It is
not only the appropriate qualifications and information, but also, and in
particular, the identification with the organisation (goal: "corporate identity")
and the good will and support of management that are critical success
factors.[405]

This requires a long-term development process. Empowerment measures
remain ineffective or can even be counterproductive without appropriate
management behaviour. Middle and lower management in particular
belong to the team within the corporation that has to change the most
regarding their behaviour, without - at least for a short time - seeing a direct
benefit (e.g., in form of a relief of controlling tasks).[406] However, as the
downsizing of hierarchical levels in many organisations has shown, this
target team fears for their positions or even their jobs. Therefore,
comprehensive measures are necessary until management has inter-
nalised the necessity for People Empowerment. Most of all, aside from
qualification measures, comprehensive information is necessary concerning management's new tasks.

As the prearranged implementation of People Empowerment is a "social
innovation"[407], a step-by-step introduction seems advisable (see Fig. 175),
beginning with an analysis of the current situation.[408] A simultaneous
development of participation possibilities for employees, which is essential
for success should follow thereafter.[409] Otherwise problems will arise when
employees are over- or underchallenged. In particular, the different "implementation speed" of new structures (e.g., teamwork) on one hand, and the
necessary hiring and behavioural changes on the other, create difficulties

for many organisations, especially as, at the time, there is external pressure to restructure rapidly and radically.

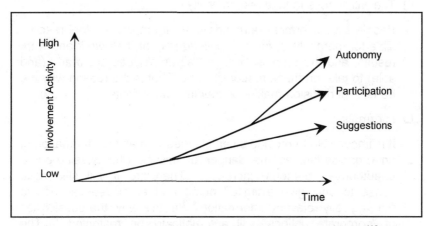

Fig. 165:   Step-by-step implementation of People Empowerment[410]

Opinions differ regarding the question of whether measures for People Empowerment should be carried out by individual employees or by team concepts.[411] Empowerment should always start with one's own work; "corporate" thinking and action cannot be expected if employees do not even have the possibility to remedy mismanagement of their own job tasks.[412]

However, one has to take into consideration that People Empowerment has "natural" limits at all levels of employee involvement, and especially in the transfer of decision-making rights:

❏ Task Structure

Many jobs, especially on the shopfloor level, have a high degree of determination and therefore only a limited potential for transferring structure - and decision-making authority - at least in the practical transfer, where economic aspects are often more important. This is, in fact, where team concepts are occasionally implemented, but one can rarely refer to them as "semi-autonomous" teams.

❏ Qualification

The qualification potential of employees is limited - depending on their willingness and on individual skills. It is therefore unwise, even in the sense of Business Excellence, to give employees responsibilities when they are not sufficiently qualified to take these on.

❑ The willingness to take responsibility

People Empowerment demands that all employees feel respon-sible for themselves, for their colleagues, for their work and work results, and the organisation. Not all employees are ready (and able) to take on these responsibilities. That is the reason why the transfer of decision-making authorities has it limits.

❑ Information:

It is impossible to provide all employees with all the information of an organisation, as the danger of misuse (the passing-on to unauthorized persons) increases. Therefore it will still make sense to only give a limited number of employees access to "strategically relevant" information.[413] In this way, the possibilities of "corporate actions" will automatically be restricted.[414] The selective availability of information may also lead to having to revise decisions.

❑ Co-ordination

As with all forms of delegation, People Empowerment requires a specific amount of co-ordination and qualified employees to avoid a sub-optimisation.

❑ Resources

Diverse qualification measures for employees and supervisors require permanent availability of information and other (personnel and financial) resources.

These limitations show that People Empowerment can never be regarded as "accomplished", but that the limiting factors can be widened by increasing infiltration.

In order to exploit the advantages of comprehensive People Empowerment in the long run without faltering at the hurdles described above, it is of utmost importance that the different tools are not used separately, but rather as components of an holistic concept.

Comments and References

1   see Arbeitsgemeinschaft Industrieller Forschungsvereinigungen e.V. (AIF) (Ed.): Initiative Qualitätssicherung, Colone 1988, p. 22

2   Ford, General Motors and Chrysler

3   see e.g. Staehle W.: Management, 4. ed., Munich 1989, Part 1, pp. 3-87

4   see Bleicher, K.: Das Konzept Integriertes Management, 4. ed., Frankfurt/ Main 1996

5   see ibid, pp. 34-35

6   see Ulrich, P. and Fluri, E.: Management, Eine konzentrierte Einführung, 6. revised and supplied ed., Bern, Stuttgart 1992, p. 19

7   see Bleicher, K., loc. cit., p. 59

8   in Bleicher designated as "Vorgaben"

9   in Bleicher designated as "Programme"

10   figure from Bleicher, K., loc. cit., p. 72

11   see ibid, p. 415 and following pages

12   figure modified according to ibid, p. 416

13   The term "integrative" is used here because it has a more process-related character than the term "integrated".

14   see Womack, J.P.; Jones, D.T. and Roos, D.: The Machine That Changed The World: Based on the Massachusetts Institute of Technology 5-million-Dollar 5-year study on the future of the automobile, New York 1990, pp. 71-103

15   Traditional forms of production organisation are characterised as robust / buffered, i.e. robustness is targeted against disruptions using extensive (material) buffers. A reminder of the word "fragile" may be useful for later discussions.

16   see Daum, M. and Piepel, U.: Lean Production - Philosophie und Realität, in: io Management Zeitschrift, Vol. 61 (1992), Issue 1, pp. 40-42

17   see Shingo, S.: Das Erfolgsgeheimnis der Toyota Produktion, Landsberg/Lech 1992, p. 37 and following pages

18   see ibid, p. 259 and following pages

19   see Womack, J.P. et al., loc. cit., p. 188

20   see ibid

21   see Curtius, B.; Riedmaier, U. and Zink, K.J.: Result Questionaire Simul-
        taneous Engineering and Quality Function Deployment, Internal working
        paper Nr. 45 of the chair for Industrial Management and Human Factors,
        University of Kaiserslautern, Kaiserslautern 1992

22   see Curtius, B.: Quality Function Deployment in der westdeutschen
        Automobil- und Zulievererindustrie: Versuch einer Darstellung fördernder
        und hemmender Faktoren, doctoral thesis at the University of Kaisers-
        lautern 1994, pp. 197-198 and pp. 200-202

23   see Wildemann, H.: Das Just-In-Time-Konzept, Produktion und Be-
        schaffung auf Abruf, 2. ed., Frankfurt 1990

24   see Babson, S.: Lean or Mean - The MIT Model and Lean Production at
        Mazda. Wayne State University / Labor Studies Center, Detroit 1992,
        shown in: MacShane, D.: Ausbeutung wächst, in: Der Gewerkschafter,
        Vol. 41 (1993), Issue 2, pp. 36-37

25   Figure from Imai, M.: KAIZEN - The Key to Japan´s Success, 1984 New
        York, p. 4

26   Figure from ibid, p. 18

27   see Zink, K.J.: Quality Circles - noch ein Thema? in: Personalführung,
        Vol. 23 (1990) 3, pp. 147-153

28   see ibid

29   figure from Imai, M., loc. cit., pp. 26-27

30   figure from ibid, pp. 81-82

31   see also Ishikawa, K.: What is Total Quality Control, New York 1985, p.
        91 and following pages

32   see e.g. TPM (Total Productive Maintenance)

33   see Part I, Chapter 4.3

34   see Zink, K.J.: Quality Circles ..., loc. cit.

35   see Hammer, H. and Champy, J.: Reengineering the Cooperation - A
        Manifesto for Business Revolution, New York 1994

36   ibid, p. 32

37   see ibid, p. 33

38   Parallels can be seen here to the "lean consultants" who promise double
        output for the same input.

39   see ibid, p. 49

40   see ibid, pp. 50-54

41   see e.g. Rühl, G.: Untersuchungen zur Arbeitsstrukturierung, in: Industrial
        Engineering, Vol. 3 (1973), Issue 3, pp. 147-197

42   see e.g. Scheer, A.-W.: EDV-orientierte Betriebswirtschaftslehre, 3. ed.,
        Berlin, Heidelberg 1987, p. 16 and following pages

43   see e.g. Höhn, R.: Führungsbrevier der Wirtschaft, 7. ed., Bad Harzburg
        1970

44   see Hammer, M. and Champy, J., loc. cit., pp. 83-101

45   see ibid, p. 75

46   see ibid., pp. 200-213. This becomes particularly clear in the second book
        by the same authors (Champy, J.: Reengineering Management: The
        Mandate for New Leadership, New York 1995).

47   see Hammer, M. and Champy, J., loc. cit., p. 49

48   Compare with the presentation of this topic in the publications of Juran,
        Deming or Feigenbaum and the appropriate criteria for international
        quality awards which demand the definition of key processes and
        corresponding organisational consequences.

49   see e.g. Matsuda, T.: "Organizational Intelligence" als Prozeß und als
        Produkt, in: Technologie & Management, Vol. 42 (1993), Issue 1, pp. 12-
        17; Momm, C.: Organizational Intelligence. Das japanische Management-
        konzept der Zukunft?, in: Technologie & Management, Vol. 42 (1993),
        Issue 1, pp. 45-46

50   e.g. the multinational companies with subsidiaries in Japan, such as
        Hewlett Packard. see Legat, D.: Hewlett Packard Europe: TQM and the
        quality of management, in: Zink, K.J. (Ed.): Successful TQM: inside
        stories from European quality award winners, Hampshire 1997, pp. 23-35

51   see Zink, K.J.: Traditionelle und neuere Ansätze der Organisations-
        entwicklung, in: Zink, K.J. et al. (Ed.): Industrial Engineering und Orga-
        nisationsentwicklung im kommenden Dezennium, Munich 1979, pp. 61-75

52   see Zink, K.J.: Selbststeuerung im Rahmen differentieller und dyna-
        mischer Ausbildungskonzepte, in: Arnold, R. (Ed.): Taschenbuch der
        betrieblichen Bildungsarbeit, Hohengehren 1991, p. 193

53   ibid, p. 195-196, as well as Zink, K.J.; Blickle, G. and Ritter, A.: Lernen als
        kooperative Problembewältigung vor Ort - Arbeitsstrukturierung, quali-
        fizierende Arbeitsgestaltung, Problemlösungsgruppen, in: Arnold, R.
        (Ed.): Taschenbuch der betrieblichen Bildungsarbeit, Hohengehren 1991,
        pp. 179-190

54   see Hammer, M. and Champy, J., loc. cit., pp. 65-82

55   figure according to Tavolato, P. and Vicena, K.: Prototyping Methodology
        and its Tool, in: Budde, R. et al. (Ed.): Approaches to Prototyping,
        Heidelberg, New York 1984, p. 425

56   figure from Whiteley, R.C.: The Customer Driven Company, Moving from
        Talk to Action, The Forum Corporation, Reading (Mass.) 1992, p. 10

57   figure from ibid, p. 14

58   see Berwick, D.M.; Godfrey, A.B. and Roessner, J.: Curing Health Care,
        San Francisco 1990, p. 55

59   see Ford (Ed.): Q 101 - Qualitätssystemrichtlinie, Colone 1990, p. 40 and
        following pages; Ford (Ed.): Systemüberprüfung und -bewertung - Leit-
        faden, Colone 1990

60   see Ford (Ed.): Q 101, loc. cit., e.g. p. 1

61   see N.N. (automobil): Was Automobilhersteller von ihren Zulieferanten
        zukünftig erwarten, in: VDI-Nachrichten, Vol. 47 (1993), No 28, p. 8

62   figure from Legat, D.: Total Quality im Management Prozeß, Genf 1994
        (unpublished manuscript), w/o page

63   see Deutsches Institut für Normung e.V. (Ed.): DIN 55 350: Begriffe der
        Qualitätssicherung und Statistik, Teil 11, Berlin 1987, p. 6; Figure from
        Eggs, I. and Rosemann, K.: Informationstechnik als Instrument der Quali-
        tätssicherung, in: CIM Management, Vol. 3 (1987), Issue 2, p. 27

64   figure from Willenbacher, K.: Qualitätsmanagement in der Praxis, in: Zink,
        K.J. (Ed.): Qualität als Mangementaufgabe, 3. ed., Landsberg 1994, p. 64

65   see Brunner, F.J.: Einflüsse der Qualität auf die Betriebswirtschaft im
        Unternehmen, in: CIM Management, Vol. 3 (1987), Issue 2, p. 16

66   figure from Sullivan, L.P.: Quality Function Deployment, in: Quality Pro-
        gress, w/o Vol. (1986), June, p. 50

67   see Tavaloto, P. and Vicena, K., loc.cit.

68   see § 93 Abs. 2 BSHG

69   The clear emphasis placed on customer satisfaction in recent years was
        dropped in 1995 in favour of an evenly balanced evaluation of "Business
        Results" and "Customer Focus and Satisfaction". Furthermore, "quality-
        related" elements such as "Strategic Quality Planning" were applied to all
        company activities (now: "Strategic Planning"). See United States Depart-
        ment of Commerce (Ed.): Malcolm Baldrige National Quality Award - 1995
        Award Criteria, Gaithersburg (Mass.) 1994, p. 20

70   see ibid, p. 13

71   see European Foundation for Quality Management (Ed.): Self-Assessment based on The European Model for Business Excellence 1997 - Guidelines for Companies, Brussels 1996, pp. 15-32

72   see Deutsches Institut für Normung (Ed.): Vision 2000 - eine Strategie zur Entwicklung Internationaler Normen zu Qualitätsmanagement und Qualitätssicherung für die '90er Jahre, in: DIN Mitteilungen, Vol. 70 (1991), Issue 6, pp. 344-351 and explanation, in: Geiger, W.: Qualitätslehre - Einführung, Systematik, Terminologie, 2. ed., Braunschweig 1994, pp. 69-70.

73   compare also in this context the (legally liable) significance of quality assurance agreements; Ensthaler, J.: Haftungsrechtliche Bedeutung von Qualitätssicherungsvereinbarungen, in: Neue Juristische Wochenschrift, Vol. 47 (1994), issue 13, pp. 817-821

74   figure from Zink, K.J. and Schmidt, A.: Quality Assessments als zukunftsorientierte Instrumentarien zur Unternehmensbewertung und -entwicklung, in: Nedeß, C. (Ed.): Produktion im Umbruch - Herausforderungen an das Management, Hochschulgruppe Arbeits- und Betriebsorganisation HAB e.V., Forschungsbericht 5, Munich 1993, p. 345

75   see Feigenbaum, A.V.: Total Quality Developments into the 1990's - An International Perspective, in: EOQC (Ed.): Qualität - Herausforderung und Chance, Munich 1987, p. 64

76   Deutsches Institut für Normung e.V. (Ed.): DIN ISO 8402 - Qualitätsmanagement und Qualitätssicherung - Begriffe, Berlin 1992, p. 25

77   figure from Zink, K.J.: Qualität als europäische Herausforderung, in: Zink, K.J. (Ed.): Business Excellence durch TQM, loc. cit., p. 16; The criticism is based on the European Model for comprehensive Quality Management, which is characterized in Part II.

78   see United States Department of Commerce, National Institute of Standards and Technology (Ed.): Malcom Baldrige National Quality Award: 1989 (respectively 1997) Award Criteria, Gaithersburg (MS) 1988 (respectively 1996)

79   figure from United States Department of Commerce (Ed.): Malcolm Baldrige National Quality Award - 1997: Criteria for Performance Excellence, Gaithersburg (Mass.) 1996, p. 42

80   see ibid

81   this model is described in detail in Part II.

82   see Part I, chapter 2.1

83   see Pall, G.A.: Quality Process Management, Englewood Cliffs, New Jersey 1987

84   Bleicher, K., loc. cit., p. 83

85   e.g. as a member of a control circle, see Part I, chapter 4.3

86   see the detailed description of this in Part III, chapter 2

87   figure modified after Bleicher, K., loc. cit., p. 72

88   see Zink, K.J.: Traditionelle und neuere Ansätze der Organisations-
        entwicklung, loc. cit., p. 64

89   Figure following Gebert, D.: Organisationsentwicklung, Stuttgart 1974,
        p. 25

90   see also Part I, chapter 4.3, pp. 82-83

91   Quality Function Deployment

92   Failure Mode and Effects Analysis

93   Statistical Process Control

94   thus, e.g., the opportunity to hand in suggestions for improvement to the
        company suggestion book system, or to include one's own ideas in the
        problem-solving process

95   see also Part II, chapter 2.5, criterion 5b

96   figure from Striening, H.-D.: Prozeß-Management - Versuch eines inte-
        grierten Konzeptes situationsadäquater Gestaltung von Verwaltungspro-
        zessen, Frankfurt / Main 1988, p. 109

97   figure from Conti, T.: Building Total Quality, London 1993, p. 165 and p.
        166

98   figure borrowed from ibid, p. 166

99   figure from Gaitanides, M., Scholz, R. and Vrohlings, A.: Prozeßmanage-
        ment - Grundlagen und Zielsetzungen, in: Gaitanides, M. et al. (Ed.):
        Prozeßmanagement: Konzepte, Umsetzungen und Erfahrungen des Re-
        engineering. Munich, Vienna 1994, p. 12

100   figure from Sommerlatte, T.; Wedekind, E.: Leistungsprozesse und
        Organisationsstruktur, in: Little, A.D. (Ed.): Management der Hoch-
        leistungsorganisation, Wiesbaden 1990, p. 30

101   see Simon, H.: Neue Konzepte für die Managementstrukturen der Zu-
        kunft, in: Zink, K.J. (Ed.): Wettbewerbsfähigkeit durch innovative Struk-
        turen und Konzepte, Munich 1994, pp. 323-336

102   ibid, p. 327

103   ibid

104   ibid, p. 326

105   figure from ibid

106   figure from ibid, p. 330

107   figure from Striening, H.-D., loc. cit., p. 164

108   see also the detailed presentation of this in Part III, chapter 4

109   compare this with the statements made earlier relating to the Toyota Production System (TPS)

110   figure from Zink, K.J. and Schick, G.: Quality Circles - 1 (Grundlagen), 2. revised ed. Munich, Vienna 1987, p. 25

111   see Part I, Chapter 2.2.3

112   Source: internal working paper IBM

113   figure borrowed from Schöler, H.R.: QFD - eine Methode zur qualitätsgerechten Produktgestaltung, in: VDI-Z, Vol. 132 (1990), Issue 11, p. 50

114   figure from Striening, H.D.: Prozeß-Management, loc. cit., p. 168

115   figure from ibid, p. 206

116   figure from Scholz, R. and Vrohlings, A.: Realisierung von Prozeßmanagement, in: Gaitanides, M. et al. (Ed.): Prozeßmanagement: Konzepte, Umsetzungen und Erfahrungen des Reengineering, Munich, Vienna 1994, p. 34

117   Of course, the modifications to the organisation of processes discussed up until this point are interdependent on the changes to structural organisation presented here. We are therefore merely talking about accentuated disassociation or accentuating definition.

118   figure borrowed from Leyde, J.: Prozeßorientierte Gruppenorganisation durch JIT, in: Wildemann, H. (Ed.): Lean Management - Der Weg zur schlanken Fabrik, Munich 1992, p. 382

119   figure from Warnecke, H.-J.: Die Fraktale Fabrik - Revolution der Unternehmenskultur, Berlin, Heidelberg, 1992, p. 182

120   see also the more detailed description of the cooperation plans in Part III, chapter 5

121   see Zink, K.J. (Ed.): Erfolgreiche Konzepte zur Gruppenarbeit - Aus Erfahrungen lernen, Neuwied 1995

122   figure from Ritter, A. and Zink K.J.: Differenzierte Kleingruppenkonzepte als wesentlicher Bestandteil eines umfassenden, integrierenden Qualitätsmanagements, in: Zink, K.J. (Ed.) Qualität als Managementaufgabe, 3. ed., Landsberg / Lech 1994, p. 255

123   see Johnson, H.T.; Kaplan, R.S.: Relevance Lost - The Rise and Fall of Management Accounting, 2. ed., Boston (Mass.) 1991

124   see Mackrodt, D.: TQM - Total Quality Management im Vertrieb - dargestellt am Beispiel Hewlett Packard GmbH, in: Zink, K.J. (Ed.): Qualität

als Managementaufgabe, 3. ed., Landsberg / Lech 1994, p. 191 and following pages

125   amongst these, Self-Assessment, Policy Deployment and Benchmarking are particularly important

126   Project team "approaches to dissiminate quality related knowledge" supported by the German Federal Ministry of Research and Technology within the scope of the programme Quality Assurance, 1992-1996, promotion index 02QF8001 and 02QF0048. See also Zink, K.J. et al.: Qualitätsmanagement in der innerbetrieblichen Umsetzung: Schlüssel-faktoren und Erfahrungen, 2. ed. Karlsruhe 1995

127   Background data for the empirical investigation:

        Type of investigation: written, structured questionnaire (the questionnaire was tested in October 1992 and subsequently modified accordingly.)

        Target group: 3382 companies in the original federal states; all sizes; 28 types of industry

        Feedback quota: Total: 33 % (n = 1121); of these 9 % "non-assessable" (n = 307), 12 % "reasons given for declining" (n = 409) and 12 % "assessable questionnaires" (n = 405)

        Contact person: Management (the way in which management deals with these questions has long been recognised as a decisive indicator for the extent of implementation.)

        Period of investigation: First quarter of 1993

        The model for the standard series DIN EN ISO 9000 and the criteria model for the European Quality Award of the EFQM/EOQ were also taken into consideration alongside the questionnaire.(vgl. Zink, K.J.; Hauer, R. and Schmidt, A.: Quality Assessment, Teil 1, Instrumentarien zur Analyse von Qualitäts-Konzepten auf der Basis von EN 29000, Malcolm Baldrige Award und European Quality Award, in QZ - Qualität und Zuverlässigkeit, Vol. 37 (1992), Issue 10, pp. 585-590). In this way, firstly, the quality assurance / quality management knowledge of the participants in the context of a certification of QA/QM systems can be examined, and secondly, the understanding of quality in the context of Total Quality Management.

        Concerning the safeguard regarding data and results collected in this empirical investigation, it is to be noted that the general results have been detailed and verified within the context of fifteen comprehensive state of the art case studies in selected companies.

128   e.g. through the definition of key processes and the deployment of these into evaluable sub-processes or process elements, the naming of process owners, increased process orientation of the organisation including the clarification of interfaces; see Zink, K.J.: Prozeßorientierung - ein Bau-

stein umfassender Veränderungskonzepte, in: Zülch, G. (Ed.) Vereinfachen und Verkleinern - die neuen Strategien in der Produktion, Stuttgart 1994, pp. 53-83

129 "Lernstatt" is a German term introduced by BMW in 1972 in order to provide language training for foreign employees. From these beginnings, training workshops have been developed which are available to all company employees.

130 figure from Develin + Partners (Ed.): The Effectiveness of Quality Improvement Programmes in British Business, London 1989, w/o page

131 N.B. Statements concerning the European Quality Award, its creation and its individual elements are based on material from the European Foundation for Quality Management.

132 see Conti, T.: Company Quality Assessments (Part 1), in: The TQM Magazine, Vol. 3 (1991), Issue 3, pp. 111-115

133 see Part III, chapter 1

134 see European Foundation for Quality Management (Ed.): Self-Assessment based on The European Model for Business Excellence 1997 - Guidelines for Companies, Brussels 1996, pp. 15-32

135 The case studies used in this part mostly come from the following firms: BMW, BOC Special Gases, Ciba Geigy, Granite Rock, Hewlett Packard, IBM, Milliken European Division, Royal Mail, Ritz Carlton, Texas Instruments, Toyota, Ubisa, Xerox

136 European Foundation for Quality Management (Ed.): Self-Assessment based on The European Model for Business Excellence 1997 - Guidelines for Companies, loc. cit., p. 7

137 see Ritz-Carlton Hotel Company (Ed.): Application Summary, National Quality Award, 1992 Winner, Atlanta (Georgia), p. 3

138 see Granite Rock Company (Ed.): Application Summary - Quality By Design, National Quality Award, 1992 Winner, Watsonville (Cal.), pp. 2-3

139 see Waldron, S.; Hurdle, T.: BOC Special Gases: Führung und Mitarbeiterorientierung, in: Zink, K.J. (Ed..): Businesse Excellence durch TQM, Munich, Vienna 1994, pp. 95-96

140 see Texas Instruments - Defense Systems & Electronics Group (Ed.): Malcolm Baldrige Application Summary, Plano (Texas), p. 2

141 see Part III, chapter 1

142 see Part I, chapter 4.3

143   see Ritz-Carlton Hotel Company (Ed.), loc.cit., pp. 3-4

144   see Granite rock Company (Ed.), loc. cit., pp. 4-5

145   see Waldron, S.; Hurdle, T.: BOC Special Gases: Führung durch
        Mitarbeiterorientierung, loc. cit., p. 98

146   see Texas Instruments - Defense Systems & Electronics Group (Ed.), loc.
        cit., p. 1

147   see Waldron, S.; Hurdle, T.: BOC Special Gases: Führung durch
        Mitarbeiterorientierung, loc. cit., pp. 100-101

148   see Granite Rock Company (Ed.), loc. cit., pp. 6-7

149   see ibid, pp. 12-13

150   see Stone, S.; Ashworth, S.: Milliken Carpet - customer and staff satis-
        faction, in: Zink, K.J. (Ed.): Successful TQM: inside stories from European
        quality award winners, Hampshire 1997, pp.139-149

151   see also Part II, chapter 2.5

152   see the appropriate announcements of events of the EFQM

153   see Texas Instruments - Defense Systems & Electronics Group (Ed.): loc.
        cit., p. 3

154   see the appropriate announcements of events of the EFQM

155   see the appropriate announcements of events of the EFQM

156   see Rückle, H.: Feedback, in: Management Enzyklopädie, Band 3, 2. ed.,
        Munich 1982, p. 487-488

157   see ibid., p. 485

158   see e.g. Neuberger, O.: Das Mitarbeitergespräch, Munich 1973 (in
        particular, chapter 5: Das Mitarbeitergespräch bei Anerkennung und
        Kritik)

159   see Stone, S.; Ashworth, S.: Milliken Carpet - customer and staff satisfac-
        tion, loc. cit.

160   see de Sousa, B.: CIBA-GEIGY: Die Einführung von TQM - Erfahrungen
        aus unterschiedlichen europäischen Werken, in: Zink, K.J. (Ed.): Busi-
        ness Excellence durch TQM: Erfahrungen europäischer Unternehmen,
        Munich, Vienna 1994, p. 41

161   see IBM Rochester (Ed.): The Quality Showcase, loc. cit., p. 18

162   figure from Turner, L.; Droege, W.: Rank Xerox Ltd.: Ressourcen, Auswirkungen auf die Gesellschaft und Geschäftsergebnisse, in: Zink, K.J. (Ed.): Business Excellence durch TQM: Erfahrungen europäischer Unternehmen, Munich, Vienna 1994, p. 157

163   see Granite Rock Company (Ed.), loc. cit., p. 2

164   see IBM Rochester (Ed.): The Quality Showcase, Presentation Visuals and Note Pages, Rochester 1993, p. 11

165   see Hewlett Packard (Ed.): Internal documents provided by HP

166   see also Appendix to Part III, chapter 3

167   figure from Conti, T.: Building Total Quality, loc. cit., p. 157

168   see IBM Rochester (Ed.): The Quality Journey Continues, 2. ed., Rochester 1991, p. 7

169   PDCA = Plan, Do, Check, Act

170   see also e.g. Soin, S.S.: Total Quality Control Essentials, New York 1992 (in particular. chapter 3)

171   see IBM Rochester (Ed.): The Quality Showcase, loc. cit., p. 17

172   figure based on Crew, T.: Business Excellence Self-Assessment within Royal Mail, in: European Foundation for Quality Management (Ed.): Total Quality: The Learning Edge, Proceedings of the 5th conference on Education, Training and Research, Universidad de Navarra, Barcelona 1994, w/o page; see also the detailed presentation of the assessment process in Part III, chapter 1

173   see Toyota Motor Corporation (Ed.): The Customer Fight - TQC at Toyota, 1992, p. 15

174   see Schartner, H.: Eine neue Rolle des Personalwesens bei BMW?, in: Personalführung, Vol. 23 (1990), Issue 1, pp. 32 - 37

175   figure from ibid, p. 36

176   figure from ibid, p. 37

177   figure from Laukamm, T.: Strategisches Management von Human-Ressourcen, in: Cisek, G. et al. (Ed.): Personalstrategien der Zukunft - Wie Unternehmen den technisch-kulturellen Wandel bewältigen, Hamburg 1988, p. 48

178   see Ishikawa, K.: What is Total Quality Control?, New York 1985

179   see Waldron, S.; Hurdle, T.: BOC Special Gases: Führung durch
       Mitarbeiterorientierung, loc. cit., pp. 102-107

180   see Hewlett Packard (Ed.): internal documents (w/o page)

181   see Granite Rock Company (Ed.), loc. cit., p. 6

182   figure from Neumann, T.: Integrierte Personalarbeit durch Projektmanage-
       ment - Die Rolle der Personalabteilung, in: Ackermann, K.-F. (Ed.): Reor-
       ganisation der Personalabteilung, Stuttgart 1994, p. 80

183   CIBA-Geigy (Ed.): Internal documents (provided by CIBA)

184   see IBM, taken from the study "Framework for the Future" by Electronic
       Business and Ernst & Young 1991, w/o page

185   BMW AG (Ed.): BMW Lernstatt, Munich 1983, p. 5

186   see Ritz-Carlton Hotel Company (Ed.), loc. cit., p. 6 and p. 8

187   The basis for this figure was provided by Bosch.

188   see IBM Rochester (Ed.) : The Quality Journey Continues, loc. cit., p. 10

189   European Foundation for Quality Management (Ed.): The European
       Quality Award 1997, Information brochure, Brussels 1996, p. 24

190   European Foundation for Quality Management (Ed.): European Foun-
       dation for Quality Management (Ed.): Self-Assessment based on The
       European Model for Business Excellence 1997 - Guidelines for Com-
       panies, loc. cit., p. 20

191   N.N. (Brisa): On the road to excellence, in: European Quality, 1996,
       special edition: 1996 European Quality Award, p. 17

192   In this context, it is possible to use a differentiation suggested by
       Wildemann in costs of correspondence (Kosten der Übereinstimmung)
       (contributing to company success) and costs of deviation (Kosten der
       Abweichung) (Waste of resources). See Wildemann, H.: Kosten- und
       Leistungsbeurteilung von Qualitätssicherungssystemen, in: Zeitschrift für
       Betriebswirtschaft, Vol. 62 (1992), Issue 7, pp. 761-782

193   figure based on Cervellini, U.: Prozeßkostenrechnung für das Manage-
       ment indirekter Kosten - das Beispiel der Porsche AG, in: Witt, F.J. (Ed.):
       Aktivitätscontrolling und Prozeßkostenmanagement, Stuttgart 1991, p.
       203

194   figure based on ibid.p. 201

195   Conrad, J.: Compagnie de Saint-Gobain: Qualité Totale - Anspruch und
        Wirklichkeit nach mehrjähriger Erfahrung, in: Zink, K.J. (Ed.): Business
        Excellence durch TQM: Erfahrungen europäischer Unternehmen, Munich,
        Vienna 1994, p. 59

196   figure from Rommel, R. et. al.: Einfach überlegen - Das Unternehmens-
        konzept, das die Schlanken schlank und die Schnellen schnell macht,
        Stuttgart 1993, p. 136. In this long-term study carried out by McKinsey
        and the Technical University of Darmstadt, successful companies were
        assessed according to the result amounts of capital return, growth,
        liquidity and operative performance in the areas of cost, time and quality.
        See ibid. pp. 1-8

197   figure based on IBM Rochester (Ed.): The Quality Journey Continues, loc.
        cit., p. 13

198   see Texas Instruments - Defense Systems & Electronics Group (Ed.), loc.
        cit., pp. 4-5

199   see IBM Rochester (Ed.): The Quality Journey Continues, loc. cit., p. 17

200   figure based on ibid, p. 17

201   figure based on Womack, J.P.; Jones, D.T.; Roos, D, loc. cit., pp. 97-99
        and p. 155

202   Ford Motor Company, Corporate Quality Office (Ed.): Leitfaden - Welt-
        weites Qualitätsbewertungssystem, w/o location 1990, pp. 1-2

203   Ford Motor Company (Ed.): Leitfaden - Q1-Qualitätsauszeichnung, w/o
        location 1990, p. 3

204   see Turner, L.; Dröge, W., loc. cit., p. 164

205   see Granite Rock Company (Ed.), loc. cit., p. 10

206   see Ritz-Carlton Hotel Company (Ed.), loc. cit., p. 12

207   see Texas Instruments - Defense Systems & Electronics Group (Ed.):
        Malcolm Baldrige Application Summary, loc. cit., pp. 10-12

208   European Foundation for Quality Management (Ed.): The European
        Quality Award 1997, Information brochure, Brussels 1996, p. 24

209   European Foundation for Quality Management (Ed.): Self-Assessment
        based on The European Model for Business Excellence 1997 - Guide-
        lines for Companies, loc. cit., p. 22

210   see Nakajima, S.: Introduction to TPM, Cambridge 1988, pp. 10-11

211   see Jacobi, H.: Unterschiedliche Ansätze zur Realisierung von Total
       Productive Maintenance (TPM), in: Biedermann, H. (Ed.): Instand-
       haltungsmanagement im Wandel, Cologne 1993, pp. 112-116

212   figure from ibid, p. 116

213   figure from Wolfrum, B.: Grundgedanke, Formen und Aussagewert von
       Technologieportfolios (I), in: Wirtschaftstudium, w/o Vol. (1992), Issue 4,
       p. 319 based on: Pfeiffer, W.; Dögl, R.; Schneider, W.: Das Technologie-
       Portfolio-Konzept als Tool zur strategischen Vorsteuerung von
       Innovationsaktivitäten, in: Wirtschaftsstudium, w/o Vol. (1989), Issue 8/9,
       p. 486

214   see Hammer, M.; Champy, J., loc. cit., pp. 122-133

215   European Foundation for Quality Management (Ed.): Self-Assessment
       based on The European Model for Business Excellence 1997 - Guide-
       lines for Companies, loc. cit., p. 22

216   figure according to IBM Rochester (Ed.): The Quality Showcase, loc. cit.,
       p. 11

217   figure according to ibid

218   see Badenwerke AG (Ed.): Badenwerk mit Zukunft - Im Team zum Pro-
       jekterfolg, Karlsruhe 1994, pp. 10-11

219   figure according to Martinéz, J.L.:Industrias del Ubierna SA (UBISA) -
       processes, policy and strategy, in: Zink, K.J. (Ed.): Successful TQM:
       inside stories from European quality award winners, Hampshire 1997, p.
       123

220   figure from Texas Instruments (Ed.): Semiconductor Group Total Quality,
       Dallas 1994, p. 5

221   figure according to Scholz, R.; Vrohlings A.: Prozeß-Leistungs-Trans-
       parenz, in: Gaitanides, M. et al. (Ed.): Prozeßmanagement - Konzepte,
       Umsetzungen und Erfahrungen des Reengineering, Munich, Vienna
       1994, p. 63

222   figure from Jung, M: Business Process Management: Ein vielseitiges
       Werkzeug, in: Mehdorn, H.; Töpfer, A. (Ed.): Besser - schneller -
       schlanker: TQM-Konzepte in der Praxis, Neuwied, Kriftel, Berlin 1994, p.
       157

223   figure according to IBM Rochester (Ed.) : The Quality Journey Continues,
       loc. cit., p. 15

224   figure according to Legat, D.: Hewlett Packard Europe: TQM and the
       quality of management, in: Zink, K.J. (Ed.): Successful TQM: inside

stories from European quality award winners, Hampshire 1997, loc. cit., pp. 28-29

225 figure according to Scholz, R.; Vrohlings A.: Prozeß-Leistungs-Transparenz, loc. cit., p. 72

226 see IBM Rochester (Ed.): The Quality Showcase, loc. cit., p. 40; IBM Rochester (Ed.): The Quality Journey Continues, loc. cit., pp. 14-15

227 see Zink, K.J.; Braig, D.: Mitarbeiterbeteiligung bei Innovations- und kontinuierlichen Verbesserungsprozessen, in: Wildemann, H. (Ed.): Kreative Unternehmen, Spitzenleistungen durch Produkt- und Prozeßinnovationen, Stuttgart 1995, S. 286-298

228 see Wagenstaller, H.: Modularbeit bei BMW, in: Zink K.J. (Ed.): Erfolgreiche Konzepte zur Gruppenarbeit - aus Erfahrungen lernen, Neuwied 1995, pp. 237-252

229 figure from ibid, p. 249

230 see IBM Rochester (Ed.): The Quality Journey Continues, loc. cit., p. 11

231 figure according to ibid, p. 11

232 see ABB Sweden (Ed.): Customer Focus Program, w/o location 1994, w/o page

233 figure from ibid

234 see United States Department of Commerce: Malcolm Baldrige National Quality Award - 1995 Award Criteria, loc. cit., pp. 36-39 and United States Department of Commerce: Malcolm Baldrige National Quality Award - 1997 Award Criteria, loc. cit., pp. 39-41

235 see Granite Rock Company (Ed.), loc. cit, p. 13

236 Sommerlatte, T.; Wedeking, E., loc. cit., p. 30

237 Case-Study for the presentation of the Malcom Baldrige National Quality Awar; see Steeples, M.M.: The corporate guide to the Malcolm Baldrige National Quality Award, 2. ed., Milwaukee (Wisc.) 1993, p. 200

238 see IBM Rochester (Ed.): The Quality Journey Continues, loc. cit., p. 17

239 see ibid

240 see Stone, S.; Ashworth, S.: Milliken Carpet - customer and staff satisfaction, in: Zink, K.J. (Ed.): Successful TQM: inside stories from European quality award winners, loc. cit., p. 143

241 according to IBM Rochester (Ed.): Center for Excellence - Customer Satisfaction Workshop, Rochester 1992, pp. 14-17

242   see Conti, T.: Building total quality, loc. cit., p. 125

243   see ibid, p. 126

244   compare The Ritz-Carlton Hotel Company (Ed.), loc. cit., pp. 14-15. The
        customer satisfaction data has been gathered through surveys which
        could be found in every hotel room.

245   see Granite Rock Company (Ed.): Quality by Design Application Sum-
        mary, Watsonville (Cal.) 1993, pp. 12-14

246   see IBM Rochester (Ed.): Center for Excellence, loc. cit., p. 8. The
        number "multiplier" facilitates statements about how often observed
        persons tell third persons about their experience with regard to failure
        elimination.

247   see IBM Rochester (Ed.): The Quality Journey Continues, loc. cit., pp. 16-
        17

248   see United States Department of Commerce: Malcolm Baldrige National
        Quality Award - 1995 Award Criteria, loc. cit., pp. 36-39 and United States
        Department of Commerce: Malcolm Baldrige National Quality Award -
        1997 Award Criteria, loc. cit., pp. 39-41

249   The documents on employee satisfaction were provided by Hewlett
        Packard.

250   figure from Martin, C.; Weber, A.: Was wissen die Mitarbeiter?, in:
        Personalführung, Vol. 27 (1994), Issue 5, p. 246

251   see Hewlett Packard (Ed.): Internal Paper

252   see Striening, H.-D., loc. cit., p. 218-219

253   see Domsch, M.: Mitarbeiterbefragungen - ein Instrument zeitgemäßer
        Personalführung, in: io-Management-Zeitschrift, Vol. 60 (1991), Issue 5,
        pp. 56-58

254   see. Ford, D.J.: Benchmarking HRD, in: Training & Development, Vol. 47
        (1993), Issue 6, p. 39; Schulte, C.: Personal-Controlling mit Kennzahlen,
        Munich 1989, pp. 51-52

255   see ibid

256   see decree (EWG) Nr. 1836/93 of the Council of the European Union, in:
        The European Union Gazette, No L 168/1 of 10 July 1993

257   see Article 1, paragraph 2 of the EU decree

258   see Kunert AG (Ed.): Ökobericht der Kunert AG, Immenstadt 1993;
        Kunert AG (Ed.): Geschäftsbericht der Kunert AG, Immenstadt 1993

259   figure based on Kunert AG (Ed.): Ökobericht der Kunert AG, loc. cit, pp. 16-17

260   ibid

261   see Zink, K.J.: Total Quality Management, in: Zink, K.J. (Ed.): Qualität als Managementaufgabe, 3. ed., Landsberg / Lech 1994, pp. 18-20

262   see Schöberl, O.: Latzhosen oder Nadelstreifen: Umweltschutz als Personalführungsaufgabe, in: Personalführung, Vol. 26 (1993), Issue 10, pp. 832-838

263   see Texas Instruments - Defense Systems & Electronics Group (Ed.), loc. cit., p. 13

264   see Kunert AG (Ed.): Ökobericht der Kunert AG, loc. cit.; Kunert AG (Ed.): Geschäftsbericht der Kunert AG, loc. cit.

265   see ibid, pp. 25-26

266   see Pies, W.: Effiziente Unfallverhütung durch basisnahe Sicherheitsarbeit unter Einbeziehung der Mitarbeiter, in: Ritter, A.; Zink, K.J. (Ed.): Gruppenorientierte Ansätze zur Förderung der Arbeitssicherheit, Berlin 1992, pp. 91-98

267   see IBM (Ed.): IBM - Partnerschaft mit behinderten Menschen, Stuttgart 1992, pp. 35-40

268   see ibid

269   Case-Study for the presentation of the Malcom Baldrige National Quality Award. Figure from United States Department of Commerce: Malcolm Baldrige National Quality Award - 1994 Award Criteria, loc. cit., p. 38

270   figure from Turner, L.; Dröge W., loc. cit., p. 166

271   figure from IBM Rochester (Ed.): Center for Excellence, loc. cit., p. 2

272   figure from IBM Rochester (Ed.): The Quality Showcase, loc. cit., p. 6

273   figure from IBM Rochester (Ed.): Center for Excellence, loc. cit., p. 2

274   figure according to Texas Instruments - Defense Systems & Electronics Group, loc. cit., p. 12

275   figure from Turner L.; Dröge W., loc. cit., p. 165

276   figure according to IBM Rochester (Ed.): The Quality Showcase, loc. cit., p. 5

277   figure from ibid, p. 28

278   figure from Stone, S.; Ashworth, S.: Milliken Carpet - customer and staff
        satisfaction, in: Zink, K.J. (Ed.): Successful TQM: inside stories from
        European quality award winners, loc. cit., p. 142

279   see Turner, L.; Dröge W., loc. cit., pp. 164-165

280   see The Ritz-Carlton Hotel Company (Ed.), loc. cit, pp. 12-13

281   see Texas Instruments - Defense Systems & Electronics Group (Ed), loc.
        cit., p. 12

282   see ibid

283   figure from ibid

284   Together with the implementation of Management by Objectives (MbO) at
        IBM and General Motors (GM) systematic and regular assessments of the
        management were already known as an important approach in the 1930s.
        Peter Drucker mentioned - based on his examinations of the GM
        management system - already in 1954 in his publication "The Practice of
        Management" the terms MbO and Self Control (see Odiorne, G.S.:
        Management by Objectives: Führungssysteme für die achtziger Jahre,
        Moderne Industrie, Munich 1980, pp. 14-18).

285   see Deutsches Institut für Normung: DIN EN ISO 9001 - QM-Systeme:
        Modell zur Darlegung des QM-Systems in Design/Entwicklung, Produk-
        tion, Montage und Kundendienst, Beuth, Berlin 1992 and Deutsches
        Institut dür Normung: DIN ISO 8402/E03.92: Qualitätsmanagement und
        Darlegung des QM-Systems - Begriffe, Beuth, Berlin 1992

286   see Blackburn, R.; Rosen, B.: Total Quality Management - Lessons
        learned from Baldrige Award-winning companies, in: Executive, Vol. 7
        (1993), No 3, p. 59

287   figure according to Turner, L.; Dröge, W.: Rank Xerox Ltd.: Ressourcen,
        Auswirkungen auf die Gesellschaft und Geschäftergebnisse, in: Zink, K.J.
        (Ed.): Business Excellence durch TQM: Erfahrungen europäischer Unter-
        nehmen, Munich, Vienna 1994, p. 157

288   see Bleicher, K.: Das Konzept integriertes Management, 2nd revised and
        extended edition, Frankfurt/Main, New York 1992 and Frese, E.: Ziele als
        Führungsinstrument: Kritische Anmerkungen zum Management by
        Objectives, in: Zeitschrift für Organisation, Vol. 40 (1971), No 5, p. 227
        and Staehle, W.H.: Management: Eine verhaltenswissenschaftliche Per-
        spektive, 7th edition, revised by Conrad, P. and Sydow, J., Munich 1994,
        p. 633

289   see figure 126 and Conti, T.: Building Total Quality: A Guide for
        Mangement, London 1993, p. 120

290   see Conti, T.: Company Quality Assessments (part 1), in: The TQM
        Magazine, Vol. 3 (1991), No 3, p. 112

291   see Davis, V.S.: Self-audits: First Step in TQM, in: Human Resource
        Magazine, Vol. 37 (1992), No 9, p. 39

292   see Conti, T., Building Total Quality, loc. cit., p. 120

293   see Zink, K.J.; Hauer, R.; Schmidt, A.: Quality Assessment: Instrument
        zur Analyse von Qualitätskonzepten auf der Basis von EN 29000,
        Malcom Baldrige National Quality Award und European Quality Award
        (part 2), in: Qualität und Zuverlässigkeit, Vol. 37 (1992), No 11, pp. 657-
        658 and Ritter, D.: A tool for improvement using the Baldrige Criteria, in:
        National Productivity Review, Vol. 12 (1993), No. 2, pp. 167-182

294   see. Sayle, A.J.: Managment Audits: The assessment of quality systems,
        London 1988, pp. 11-1 - 11-5

295   Especially big enterprises with several business units have the possibility
        to send manangers or assessors to an assessment of other units. Smaller
        companies should cooperate with companies of a different branch using
        similar assessment instruments. In addition an application for an
        international quality award - even if you have no ambitions of winning it -
        may be useful since the feedback-report does in any case show
        opportunities for improvements.

296   see Zink, K.J.; Hauer, R.; Schmidt, A., loc. cit., pp. 657-658

297   see Striening, H.D.: Prozeßmanagement, Frankfurt 1988, pp. 159-163

298   see Conti, T., Building Total Quality, loc. cit., pp. 121-122

299   figure modified according to ibid, p. 29
        The Self-Assessment process of the EFQM does not discuss the criteria
        itself since they are already included in that form in the assessment
        scheme of the European Quality Award. The EFQM emphasises that the
        self assessment cycle shall include - after execution of several cycles - all
        levels and units of the whole company.

300   figure from European Foundation for Quality Management (Ed.): Self-
        Assessment based on The European Model for Business Excellence
        1997 - Guidelines for Companies, loc. cit., p. 43

301   The intention is to repeat the Business Excellence Process in each
        business unit every two years.

302   see Heller, R.: How the Royal Mail rode out its shame and found a
        culture, in: Management Today, 1993, No 4, pp. 30-34

303   see Crew, T.: Business Excellence Self-Assessment within Royal Mail, in:
        European Foundation for Quality Management (Ed.): Total Quality: The
        Learning Edge, Proceedings of the 5th conference on Education, Training
        and Research, Barcelona 1994

304   figure similar to ibid

305   figure modified according to ibid

306   I would like to thank Dipl.-Wirtsch.-Ing. A. Schmidt for compiling and
        reworking the material for this chapter.

307   see chapter 4.2.6 - 4.2.9

308   see European Foundation for Quality Management (Ed.): Self-
        Assessment based on The European Model for Business Excellence
        1997 - Guidelines for Companies, loc. cit., p. 14; for the positioning of
        Benchmarking within the Malcolm Baldrige National Quality Award see
        e.g.: Mills Steeples, loc. cit., pp. 104-106

309   see e.g. Terrell, P. (Ed.): Pons Großwörterbuch deutsch-englisch,
        englisch-deutsch, Teil II: englisch-deutsch, Stuttgart 1991, p. 57

310   cited according to Clavel, J.E.: Sun Tzu - The Art of War, New York 1983

311   see Camp, R.C.: Learning from the Best - Leaders to Superior Perfor-
        mance, in: The Journal of Business Strategie, Vol. 13 (1992), No 3, p. 3

312   figure according to Camp, R.C., loc. cit., pp. 10-15; see also IBM
        Rochester (Ed.): The Quality Showcase, loc. cit., p. 37; for further
        definitions see the cited literature in this chapter

313   see also Camp, R.C., loc. cit., pp. 60-65 as well as Watson, G.H.:
        Benchmarking - vom Besten lernen, Landsberg/Lech 1993, pp. 106-109

314   see European Foundation for Quality Management (Ed.): Self-Assess-
        ment based on The European Model for Business Excellence 1997 -
        Guidelines for Companies, loc. cit.

315   see part III, chapter 1

316   see Karlöf, B.: Das Benchmarking-Konzept: Wegweiser zur Spitzen-
        leistung in Qualität und Produktivität, Munich 1994, pp. 91-117

317   see Camp, R.C., loc. cit., p. 17

318   see ibid, pp. 119-135

319   for the development of questionnaires which can be used for data
        collection and for a target-directed analysis of Benchmarking data see
        Leibfried, K.H.J.: Benchmarking - Von der Konkurrenz lernen, die Konkur-
        renz überholen, Freiburg 1993, pp. 336-366

320   see Camp, R.C., loc. cit., pp. 173 -181

321   for further examples as Hewlett Packard, General Motors see Watson,
        G.H., loc. cit., pp. 111-163

322 see Turner L.; Dröge W.: Rank Xerox Europe Ltd - resources, impact on society and business results, in: Zink, K.J. (Ed.): Successful TQM: inside stories from European quality award winners, Hampshire 1997, pp. 69

323 figure from ibid, p. 150

324 ibid, p. 153

325 figure from ibid, p. 155

326 see also Granite Rock: Malcolm Baldrige Application Summary, Watson-ville, California

327 see Granite Rock, loc. cit., p. 13

328 figure from IBM Rochester (Ed.), loc. cit., p. 40

329 see Mills Steeples, M., loc. cit., pp. 282-283

330 see IBM Rochester (Ed.), loc. cit., p. 38

331 see ibid., p. 39

332 figure from ibid, p. 38

333 figure from ibid, p. 40

334 see Texas Instruments - Defense Systems & Electronics Group, loc. cit.

335 figure from ibid, p. 4

336 figure from ibid, p. 5

337 see The Ritz-Carlton Hotel Company, loc. cit.

338 The approach of undertaking comparisons between companies is not a new one.

339 I would like to thank Dipl.-Wirtsch.-Ing. U. Klein for compiling and rewor-king the material for this chapter.

340 see Part III, chapter 1

341 see Conti,T.: Building Total Quality, loc. cit., p. 146

342 figure from ibid, p. 147

343 This expression was used the first time by Drucker in 1954. See Drucker, P., loc. cit., p. 62

344 figure from Heinen, E. (Ed.): Industriebetriebslehre. Entscheidungen im Industriebetrieb, 8. ed., Wiesbaden 1985, p. 106

345 see Six, B.; Kleinbeck, U.: Arbeitsmotivation und Arbeitszufriedenheit, in: Roth, E. (Ed.): Organisationspsychologie, Enzyklopädie der Psychologie, Serie III, Band 3, Göttingen, Toronto, Zürich 1989, pp. 350-351

346 see ibid

347   The methodology of QFD has been formalized and used by Yoji Akao in
        the 60s and 70s in Japan. See therefore Akao, Y.: Quality Function De-
        ployment, Landsberg/Lech 1992

348   figure according to Schöler, H.R.: QFD - eine Methode zur qualitäts-
        gerechten Produktgestaltung, loc. cit., p. 50

349   see Soin, S.S.: Total Quality Control Essentials, New York 1992, pp. 137-
        138

350   figure according to Conti, T.: Building Total Quality, loc. cit., pp. 151-152

351   see, Soin, S.S., loc. cit., pp. 53-54

352   see ibid, p. 54

353   see ibid, p. 59

354   see ibid, pp. 59-60

355   see ibid, p. 70

356   figure according to Suzkai, K.: Die ungenutzten Potentiale - Neues
        Management im Produktionsbetrieb, Munich, Vienna 1994, p. 246

357   see Soin, S.S., loc. cit., p. 57

358   ibid, p. 57

359   figure according to Suzaki, K., loc. cit., p. 245

360   see Conti, T.: Building Total Quality, loc. cit., p. 293

361   see ibid, p. 150

362   figure according to ibid, pp. 152-153

363   see ibid, p. 154

364   see ibid

365   see ibid, pp. 154-155

366   figure according to ibid, p. 157

367   figure according to ibid, p. 161

368   see Soin, S.S., loc. cit., p. 56

369   I thank Mr. Dipl.-Wirtsch.-Ing. Walter Steinmetz for putting together and
        preparing the material for this chapter.

370   see United States Department of Commerce (Ed.): Malcolm Baldrige
        National Quality Award - 1997: Criteria for Performance Excellence,
        Gaithersburg (Mass.) 1996, p. 40; see also Australian Awards Fundation
        (Ed.): Australian Quality Awards 1994 - Assessement Criteria & Applica-
        tion Guidelines, St. Leonards 1994, p. 15

371   according to Zink, K.J.: paritzipative Konzepte in der Fabrik, in: Milling, P.;
        Zäpfel, G. (Ed.): Betriebswirtschaftliche Grundlagen moderner Produk-
        tionsstrukturen, Herne, Berlin 1993, p. 271

372   see Nölle-Neumann, E.; Strümpel, B.: Macht Arbeit krank? Macht Arbeit
        glücklich?, Munich, Zürich 1984

373   Price, F.: Perspectives - Educated power, in: The TQM Magazine, Vol. 5
        (1993), No 3, p. 10

374   Hand, M.: Freeing the Victims, in: The TQM Magazine, Vol. 5 (1993), No
        3, p. 11

375   European Foundation for Quality Management (Ed.): EFQM Viewpoint -
        Power up the people, in: The TQM Magazine, Vol. 5 (1993), No 3, p. 9

376   Ashworth, S.: Milliken, in: The TQM Magazine, Vol. 5 (1993), No 3, p. 10

377   compare with Donovan, M.: The „Empowerment" Plan, in: Journal for
        Quality and Participation, Vol. 17 (1994), no 4, p. 12

378   see Lawler, E.E.: Choosing an Involvement strategy, in: Academy of
        Management Executive, Vol. 2 (1988), pp. 197-204; Lawler distinguishes
        between the levels Suggestion Involvement, Job Involvement and High
        Involvement

379   figure with reference to Lathin, D.: Overcoming fear of self-directed
        teams, in: Journal for Quality and Participation, Vol. 17 (1994), No 4, p.
        17

380   see Ackermann, M.: Quality Circles in der Bundesrepublik Deutschland -
        Hemmende und fördernde Faktoren einer erfolgreichen Realisierung,
        Frankfurt/Main 1989, pp. 332-333; Besides the unsufficient competence
        of the teams, the reason for fail or the „silt up" of many projects was
        mainly the lacking integration of the Quality-Circle-Concept in
        comprehensive Quality Improvement Approaches

381   compare with Ganz, D.: Verbesserungsvorschläge im Betrieb, Mannheim
        1962, pp. 11-12

382   figure according to Tannenbaum, R.; Schmidt, W.H., loc. cit., p. 96 (pp.
        95-101)

383   see Tannenbaum R.; Schmidt, W.H.: How to choose a leadership pattern,
        in: Havard Business Review, 1958 No 2, pp. 173-174

384   see ibid, p. 178

385   see Drucker, P.: The Practice of Management, New York 1954. Two
        forms of characteristics were developed in the practical application of
        Management by Objectives „management by defined goals and objec-
        tives" and „management by agreement on targets".

386   see therefore Part III, Chapter 3

387   Taylor, F.W.: Grundsätze wissenschaftlicher Betriebsführung, Munich,
        Oldenburg 1913 (German translation of: Taylor, F.W.: The Principles of
        Scientific Management, New York 1911)

388   see Hellpach, W.: Sozialpsychologische Analyse des betriebstechnischen
        Tatbestandes Gruppenfabrikation, in: Lang, R.; Hellpach, W. (Ed.): Grup-
        penfabrikation, Berlin 1922, p. 27

389   see Ulich E.; Conrad-Betschart, H.; Baitsch, C.: Arbeitsform mit Zukunft:
        ganzheitlich-flexibel statt arbeitsteilig, Bern 1989, p. 27

390   see Brinkmann, E.; Heidack, C.: Unternehmenssicherung durch Ideen-
        management, Bd. 1: Mehr Innovationen durch Verbesserungsvorschläge,
        2. ed., Freiburg 1987, p. 22; Bumann, A.: Das Vorschlagswesen als
        Instrument innovationsorientierter Unternehmensführung, Freiburg 1991,
        p. 15

391   German Institute for Business Management 1993

392   see BMW AG (Ed.): BMW Lernstatt, Munich 1983

393   see Zink, K.J. Braig, D.: Mitarbeiterbeteiligung bei Innovations- und
        kontinuierlichen Verbesserungsprozessen, loc. cit.

394   see also Zink, K.J.; Schick, G.: Quality Circles 1 - Grundlagen, 2nd ed.,
        Munich, Vienna 1987; Zink, K.J.: Qualitätszirkel und Lernstatt, in: Frese,
        E. (Ed.): Handwörterbuch der Organisation, 3. ed., Stuttgart 1992, p.
        2133-2140; Zink, K.J.: Qualitätszirkel, in: Strunz, H. (Ed.): Handbuch
        Personalmarketing, Wiesbaden 1989, p. 542-554 and the literature
        mentioned there; Zink, K.J.; Ritter, A.: Quality Circles - ein Instrumen-
        tarium partizipativer Gestaltung und Einführung neuer Informationstech-
        nologien, in: Computer & Recht, Vol. 6 (1990), Issue 2, p. 147-152

395   see Lang, R.: Gruppenfabrikation, in: Lang, R.; Hellpach, W. (Ed.) loc cit.,
        p. 12

396   see Lattmann, C.: Das norwegische Modell der selbstgesteuerten
        Arbeitsgruppe, Bern 1982; Thorsrud, E.: Demokratisierung der Arbeits-
        organisation - einige konkrete Methoden zur Neustrukturierung des Ar-
        beitsplatzes, in: Vilmar, F. (Ed.): Menschenwürde im Betrieb, Hamburg
        1973, pp. 117-132

397   see Lattmann, C., loc. cit., p. 26

398   see ibid, p. 27

399   see Gulowsen, J.: A measure of work group autonomy, in: Davis, L.;
        Taylor, J. (Ed.): Job design, Harmondsworth 1972, p. 374-390

400   see Rühl, G.: Untersuchungen zur Arbeitsstrukturierung, in: Industrial
        Engineering, Vol. 3 (1973), Issue 3, p. 147 and p. 152

401   see Gollnick, R.; Hohmann, R.: Gestaltungsprinzipien ganzheitlicher
        Gruppenarbeit, in: Personalführung, 1993, No 2, pp. 106-115

402   figure from Grob, R.: Teilautnome Arbeitsgruppen - Bilanz der Er-
        fahrungen in der Siemens AG, in: Angewandte Arbeitswissenschaft, w/o
        Vol. (1992), No 134, p. 6

403   Concepts as for example the system of overlapping teams of Likert have
        their origins in the 60s (see Likert, R.: New patterns of management, New
        York 1961); an universal team structure was implemented, e.g., at
        Wiggins Connectors in the USA (see Wernick, S.: Self-directed Work
        Teams and Empowerment, in: Journal for Quality and Participation, Vol.
        17 (1994), Issue 4, p. 34-36)

404   see Fournier, P.: The European Foundation for Quality Management -
        Self-Assessment based on the European Model for TQM, in: Technologie
        & Management, Vol. 43 (1994), Issue 4, p. 178; Reich, R.; Copening, L.:
        „Empowerment" without the rhetoric, in: Quality Progress, w/o Vol. (1994),
        Issue 6, p. 35

405   Both factors are prerequisites for a „culture of trust" in the corporation. A
        description of different methods for the support of a „culture of trust" are
        defined, among others, by Ray (see Ray, D.W.: The missing in
        TQM...trust, in: Journal for Quality and Participation, Vol. 17 (1994), Issue
        3, pp. 64-67)

406   see inter alia Letize, L.; Donovan, M.: The Supervisor's Changing Role in
        High Involvement Organisations, in: Journal for Quality and Participation,
        Vol. 13 (1990), Issue 3, pp. 62-63

407   see Thom, N.: Grundlagen des betrieblichen Innovationsmanagements,
        2nd. ed., Bern 1980, p. 37

408   see Wallace, G.W.: Empowerment is work, not magic, in: Journal for
        Quality and Participation, Vol. 16 (1993), Issue 5, p. 13; exemplary
        questions are: relation of management and employees, present decision-
        making processes and involvement of the employees, present culture of
        the organisation, state-of-the-art of TQM implementation; Dawson
        developed a questionnaire regarding the behavior of the respective
        supervisor, which makes a continuous review possible for the
        development of the „empowerment"-behaviour (see Dawson, G.: Is
        Empowerment increasing in your organisation?, in: Journal for Quality
        and Participation, Vol. 15 (1992), Issue 5, pp. 26-27; Seath developed an
        „Empowerment-Audit" on the basis of hierarchical needs according to
        Maslow (see Seath, I.: Turning theory into practice, in: Managing Service
        Quality, w/o Vol. (1993), Issue 6, pp. 35-37).

409   see Barner, R.: Designing human scale continuous improvement, in:
        Journal for Quality and Participation, Vol. 17 (1994), Issue 3, p. 62

410   Fig. following on Eccles, T.: The Deceptive Allure of „Empowerment", in:
       Long Range Planning, Vol. 26 (1993), Issue 6, p. 19

411   see Donovan, M., loc. cit., p. 14; unlike Dawson (see Dawson, G., loc.
       cit., p. 25) there is a call for the setting-up of teams as the first necessary
       step of „Empowerment".

412   see Eccles, T., loc. cit., p. 19

413   Ray proposes giving every employee access to information that he and
       his immediate supervisor need in order to take care of their tasks. Thus,
       all employees have the possibility to look at their own work from a higher
       perspective and to make decisions against this background.

414   see Wallace, G.W., loc. cit., p. 11

Bibliography

ABB Sweden (Ed.):
Customer Focus Program, w/o location 1994, w/o page

Ackermann, M.:
Quality Circles in der Bundesrepublik Deutschland - Hemmende und fördernde Faktoren einer erfolgreichen Realisierung, Frankfurt / Main 1989

Akao, Y.:
Quality Function Deployment - Integrating Customer Requirements into Product Design, Cambridge (Mass.) 1990

Akao, Y.:
Quality Function Deployment, Landsberg / Lech 1992

Arbeitsgemeinschaft Industrieller Forschungsvereinigungen e.V. (AIF) (Ed.):
Initiative Qualitätssicherung, Colone 1988

Ashworth, S.:
Milliken, in The TQM Magazine, Vol. 5 (1993), No 3, p. 10

Australian Quality Awards Foundation (Ed.):
Australian Quality Awards 1994 - Assessment Criteria & Application Guidelines, St. Leonards 1994

Badenwerke AG (Ed.):
Badenwerk mit Zukunft - Im Team zum Projekterfolg, Karlsruhe 1994

Babson, S.:
Lean or Mean - The MIT Model and Lean Production at Mazda. Wayne State University / Labor Studies Center, Detroit 1992, shown in: Mac Shane, D.: Ausbeutung wächst, in: Der Gewerkschafter, Vol. 41 (1993), Issue 2, pp. 36-37

Barner, R.:
Designing human scale continuous improvement, in: Journal for Quality and Participation, Vol. 17 (1994), Issue 3, pp. 60-63

Bergman, B.; Klefsjö, B.:
Quality, From Customer Needs to Customer Satisfaction, London 1994

Berwick, D.M.; Godfrey, A.B.; Roessner, J.:
Curing Health Care, San Francisco 1990

Blackburn, R.; Rosen, B.:
Total Quality and Human Resources Management - Lessons learned
from Baldrige Award-winning companies, in: Executive, Vol. 7 (1993),
Issue 3, pp. 46-66

Bleicher, K.:
Das Konzept Integriertes Management, 2. ed., Frankfurt 1992

BMW AG (Ed.):
BMW Lernstatt, Munich 1983

Boehling, W.; Joksch, H.:
Strategies for the 1992 and beyond, in: The TQM Magazine, Vol. 2
(1990), Issue 1, pp. 21-23

Brinkmann, E.; Heidack, C.:
Unternehmenssicherung durch Ideenmanagement, Band. 1: Mehr Inno-
vationen durch Verbesserungsvorschläge, 2. ed., Freiburg 1987

Bumann, A.:
Das Vorschlagswesen als Instrument innovationsorientierter Unternehmensführung, Freiburg 1991

Brunner, F.J.:
Einflüsse der Qualität auf die Betriebswirtschaft im Unternehmen, in:
CIM Management, Vol. 3 (1987), Issue 2, p. 16

Camp, R.C.:
Benchmarking - the search for industry best practices that lead to
superior performance, Milwaukee (Wisc.) 1989

Camp, R.C.:
Benchmarking, Munich, Vienna 1994

Camp, R.C.:
Learning from the Best Leaders to Superior Performance, in: Journal of
Business Strategy, Vol. 13 (1992), Issue 3, pp. 3-6

CIBA-Geigy (Ed.):
Internal documents (provided by CIBA)

Cervellini, U.:
Prozeßkostenrechnung für das Management indirekter Kosten - das Beispiel der Porsche AG, in: Witt, F.J. (Ed.): Aktivitätscontrolling und Prozeßkostenmanagement, Stuttgart 1991, pp. 191-212

Champy, J.:
Reengineering Management: The Mandate for New Leadership, New York 1995

Clavel, J.E.:
Sun Tzu - The Art of War, New York 1983

Claybaker, C.:
Quality Enhancement Projects Improve Health Care, in: Quality Progress, Vol. 25 (1992), Issue 4, pp. 103-106

Conrad, J.:
Compagnie de Saint-Gobain: Qualité Totale - Anspruch und Wirklichkeit nach mehrjähriger Erfahrung, in: Zink, K.J. (Ed.): Business Excellence durch TQM: Erfahrungen europäischer Unternehmen, Munich, Vienna 1994, pp. 49-64

Conti, T.:
Company Quality Assessments (Part 1), in: The TQM Magazine, Vol. 3 (1991), Issue 3, pp. 111-115

Conti, T.:
Building Total Quality, London 1993

Cooper, R.G.:
Perspective: Third-Generation New Product Process, in: Journal of Product Innovation Management, Vol. 11 (1994), Number 1, pp. 3-14

Crew, T.:
Business Excellence Self-Assessment within Royal Mail, in: European Foundation for Quality Management (Ed.): Total Quality: The Learning Edge, Proceedings of the 5th conference on Education, Training and Research, Universidad de Navarra, Barcelona 1994

Cullen, J.; Hollingum, J.:
Implementing Total Quality, Bedford (UK) 1987

Curtius, B.:
Quality Function Deployment in der westdeutschen Automobil- und Zulifererindustrie: Versuch einer Darstellung fördernder und hemmender Faktoren, Dissertation an der Universität Kaiserslautern, Kaiserslautern 1994

Curtius, B.; Riedmaier, U.; Zink, K.J.:
Result Questionaire Simultaneous Engineering and Quality Function Deployment, Internal working paper Nr. 45 of the chair for Industrial Management and Human Factors, University of Kaiserslautern, Kaiserslautern 1992

Dahlgaard, J. J.; Kristensen, K.; Kanji, G. K.:
Total Quality Journey, (Kanji, G. (Ed.): Advances in Total Quality Management, Series, No. 2), Abingdon 1994

Daum, M.; Piepel, U.:
Lean Production - Philosophie und Realität, in: io Management Zeitschrift, Vol. 61 (1992), Issue 1, pp. 40-42

Davis, L.E., Cherns, A.B. (Ed.):
The Quality of Working Life, New York 1975

Davis, V.S.:
Self-audits: First Step in TQM, in: Human Resources Magazine, Vol. 37 (1992), Issue 9, pp. 39-41

Dawson, G.:
Is Empowerment increasing in your organization?, in: Journal for Quality and Participation, Vol. 15 (1992), Issue 5, pp. 24-28

de Sousa, B.:
CIBA-GEIGY: Die Einführung von TQM - Erfahrungen aus unterschiedlichen europäischen Werken, in: Zink, K.J. (Ed.): Business Excellence durch TQM: Erfahrungen europäischer Unternehmen, Munich, Vienna 1994, pp. 31-48

Deming, W.E.:
Out of the Crisis, Cambridge (Mass.)1986

Deutsches Institut für Normung e.V. (Ed.):
DIN 55 350: Begriffe der Qualitätsregelung und Statistik, Teil 11, Berlin 1987

Deutsches Institut für Normung e.V. (Ed.):
Vision 2000 - eine Strategie zur Entwicklung Internationaler Normen zu
Qualitätsmanagement und Qualitätssicherung für die '90er-Jahre, in:
DIN-Mitteilungen, Vol. 70 (1991), Issue 6, pp. 344-351

Deutsches Institut für Normung e.V. (Ed.):
DIN ISO 8402/E03.92: Qualitätsmanagement und Darlegung des QM-
Systems - Begriffe, Berlin 1992

Deutsches Institut für Normung e.V. (Ed.):
DIN ISO 8402: Qualitätsmanagement und Qualitätssicherung - Begriffe,
Berlin 1992

Deutsches Institut für Normung e.V. (Ed.):
DIN EN ISO 9001: QM-Systeme: Modell zur Darlegung des QM-
Systems in Design/Entwicklung, Produktion, Montage und Kunden-
dienst, Berlin 1994

Develin + Partners (Ed.):
The Effectiveness of Quality Improvement Programmes in British Business, London 1989

Domsch, M.:
Mitarbeiterbefragungen - ein Instrument zeitgemäßer Personalführung,
in: io-Management-Zeitschrift, Vol. 60 (1991), Issue 5, pp. 56-58

Donovan, M.:
The „Empowerment" Plan, in: Journal for Quality and Participation, Vol.
17 (1994), Issue 4, pp. 12-14

Drucker, P.:
The Practice of Management, New York 1954

Eccles, T.:
The Deceptive Allure of „Empowerment", in: Long Range Planning, Vol.
26 (1993), Issue 6, pp. 13-21

Eggs, I.; Rosemann, K.:
Informationstechnik als Instrument der Qualitätssicherung, in: CIM
Management, Vol. 3 (1987), Issue 2, p. 27

Electronic Business; Ernest & Young:
Framework for the Future, w/o location 1991

Ensthaler, J.:
Haftungsrechtliche Bedeutung von Qualitätssicherungsvereinbarungen, in: Neue Juristische Wochenschrift, Vol. 47 (1994), Issue 13, pp. 817-821

European Foundation for Quality Management (Ed.):
EFQM Viewpoint - Power up the people, in: The TQM Magazine, Vol. 5 (1993), Issue 3, pp. 9-10

European Foundation for Quality Management (Ed.):
Self-Assessment based on the European Model for Business Excellence 1997 - Guidelines for Companies, Brussels 1996

European Foundation for Quality Management (Ed.):
The European Quality Award 1997, Information Brochure, Brussels 1996

Feigenbaum, A. V.:
Total Quality Control, Engineering and Management, New York 1961

Feigenbaum, A.V.:
Total Quality Developments into the 1990's - An International Perspective, in: EOQC (Ed.): Qualität - Herausforderung und Chance, Munich 1987, pp. 59-70

Foley, E.C.:
Winning the European Quality Award - Interpreting the requirements for the European Quality Award, European Foundation for Quality Management, Brussels 1994

Ford (Ed.):
Q 101 - Worldwide Quality System Standards, Detroit 1990

Ford Motor Company (Ed.):
Leitfaden - Q1-Qualitätsauszeichnung, w/o location 1990

Ford Motor Company, Corporate Quality Office (Ed.):
Leitfaden - Weltweites Qualitätsbewertungssystem, w/o location 1990

Ford, D.J.:
Benchmarking HRD, in: Training & Development, Vol. 47 (1993), Issue 6, p. 39

Fournier, P.:
The European Foundation for Quality Management - Self-Assessment based on the European Model for TQM, in: Technologie & Management, Vol. 43 (1994), Issue 4, p. 178

Frehr, H.-M.:
Total Quality Management: unternehmensweite Qualitätsverbesserung; ein Praxis-Leitfaden für Führungskräfte, Munich, Vienna, 1993

Frese, E.:
Ziele als Führungsinstrument. Kritische Anmerkungen zum Management by Objectives, in: Zeitschrift für Organisation, Vol. 40 (1971), No 5, pp. 227-238

Gaitanides, M., Scholz, R., Vrohlings, A.:
Prozeßmanagement - Grundlagen und Zielsetzungen, in: Gaitanides, M. et al. (Ed.): Prozeßmanagement: Konzepte, Umsetzungen und Erfahrungen des Reengineering. Munich, Vienna 1994, S. 1-19

Ganz, D.:
Verbesserungsvorschläge im Betrieb, Mannheim 1962

Garvin, D. A.:
Managing Quality, New York 1988

Gebert, D.:
Organisationsentwicklung, Stuttgart 1974

Geiger, W.:
Qualitätslehre - Einführung, Systematik, Terminologie, 2. ed., Braunschweig 1994

Geschka, H.:
Wettbewerbsfaktor Zeit, Landsberg / Lech 1993

Gollnick, R.; Hohmann, R.:
Gestaltungsprinzipien ganzheitlicher Gruppenarbeit, in: Personalführung, Vol. 26 (1993), Issue 2, pp. 106-115

Granite Rock Company (Ed.):
Malcolm Baldrige Application Summary, Watsonville (Cal.) 1992

Granite Rock Company (Ed.):
Quality by Design Application Summary, Watsonville (Cal.) 1993

Grob, R.:
Teilautonome Arbeitsgruppen - Bilanz der Erfahrungen in der Siemens AG, in: Angewandte Arbeitswissenschaft, w/o Vol. (1992), No 134, pp. 1-31

Gulowsen, J.:
A measure of work group autonomy, in: Davis, L.; Taylor, J. (Ed.): Job design, Harmondsworth 1972, pp. 374-390

Haist, F.; Fromm, H.:
Qualität im Unterrnehmen, 2. ed., Munich 1991

Hammer, M.; Champy, J.:
Reengineering the Cooperation - A Manifesto for Business Revolution, New York 1994

Hand, M.:
Freeing the Victims, in: The TQM Magazine, Vol. 5 (1993), No 3, p. 11

Heinen, E. (Ed.):
Industriebetriebslehre. Entscheidungen im Industriebetrieb, 8. ed., Wiesbaden 1985

Heller, R.:
TQM - The Quality Makers, St. Gallen 1993

Hellpach, W.:
Sozialpsychologische Analyse des betriebstechnischen Tatbestandes Gruppenfabrikation, in: Lang, R.; Hellpach, W. (Ed.): Gruppenfabrikation, Berlin 1922, pp. 5- 186

Hewlett Packard (Ed.):
Internal documents (provided by HP)

Höhn, R.:
Führungsbrevier der Wirtschaft, 7. ed., Bad Harzburg 1970

IBM (Ed.):
IBM - Partnerschaft mit behinderten Menschen, Stuttgart 1992

IBM Rochester (Ed.):
The Quality Journey Continues, 2. ed., Rochester 1991

IBM Rochester (Ed.):
Center for Excellence - Customer Satisfaction Workshop, Rochester 1992

IBM Rochester (Ed.):
The Quality Showcase, Rochester 1993

Imai, M.:
KAIZEN - The Key to Japan`s Success, New York 1984

Ishikawa, K.:
What is Total Quality Control?, New York 1985

Jacobi, H.:
Unterschiedliche Ansätze zur Realisierung von Total Productive Maintenance (TPM), in: Biedermann, H. (Ed.): Instandhaltungsmanagement im Wandel. Kaizen, Lean Maintenance, TPM, Outsourcing. Colone 1993, pp. 99-120

Japanese Union of Scientists and Engineers (JUSE) (Ed.):
The DEMING PRIZE Guide for Overseas Companies, Tokyo 1986

Johnson, H.T.; Kaplan, R.S.:
Relevance Lost - The Rise and Fall of Management Accounting, 2. ed., Boston (Mass.) 1991

Jung, M:
Business Process Management: Ein vielseitiges Werkzeug, in: Mehdorn, H.; Töpfer, A. (Ed.): Besser - schneller - schlanker: TQM-Konzepte in der Praxis, Neuwied, Kriftel, Berlin 1994, pp. 137-164

Juran, J. M.:
Universal in management planning and controlling, in: The Management Review, November 1954

Juran, J. M.:
Management of Quality, New York 1982

Juran, J. M.:
Juran on Planning for Quality, New York 1988

Kanji, G. K.; Asher, M.:
Total Quality Management Process: A Systematic Approach, (Kanji, G. (Ed.): Advances in Total Quality Management Series, No. 1), Abingdon 1993

Karlöf, B.:
Das Benchmarking-Konzept: Wegweiser zur Spitzenleistung in Qualität und Produktivität, Munich 1994

King, B.:
Hoshin Planning - The Development Approach, Methuen (Mass.) 1989

Kunert AG (Ed.):
Ökobericht der Kunert AG, Immenstadt 1993

Kunert AG (Ed.):
Geschäftsbericht der Kunert AG, Immenstadt 1993

Lang, R.; Hellpach, W. (Ed.):
Gruppenfabrikation, Berlin 1922

Lathin, D.:
Overcoming fear of self-directed teams, in: Journal for Quality and Participation, Vol. 17 (1994), Issue 4, pp. 16-20

Lattmann, C.:
Das norwegische Modell der selbstgesteuerten Arbeitsgruppe, Bern 1972

Laukamm, T.:
Strategisches Management von Human-Ressourcen, in: Cisek, G. et al. (Ed.): Personalstrategien der Zukunft - Wie Unternehmen den technisch-kulturellen Wandel bewältigen, Hamburg 1988, pp. 39-88

Lawler, E.E.:
Choosing an Involvement Strategy, in: Academy of Management Executive, 2. ed. (1988), pp. 197-204

Legat, D.:
Hewlett Packard Europe - TQM and the quality of management, in: Zink, K.J.: Successful TQM: inside stories from European Quality Award winners, Hampshire 1997, pp. 23-35

Legat, D.:
Total Quality im Management Prozeß, Genf 1994 (unpublished manuscript), w/o page

Leibfried, K.H.J.:
Benchmarking - Von der Konkurrenz lernen, die Konkurrenz überholen, Freiburg 1993

Letize, L.; Donovan, M.:
The Supervisor's Changing Role in High Involvement Organizations, in: Journal for Quality and Participation, Vol. 13 (1990), Issue 3, pp. 62-65

Leyde, J.:
Prozeßorientierte Gruppenorganisation durch JIT, in: Wildemann, H. (Ed.): Lean Management - Der Weg zur schlanken Fabrik, München 1992, pp. 341-382

Likert, R.:
New patterns of management, New York 1961

Mackrodt, D.:
TQM - Total Quality Management im Vertrieb - dargestellt am Beispiel Hewlett Packard GmbH, in: Zink, K.J. (Ed.): Qualität als Managementaufgabe, 3. ed., Landsberg / Lech 1994, pp. 185-202

Martin, C.; Weber, A.:
Was wissen die Mitarbeiter?, in: Personalführung, Vol. 27 (1994), Issue 5, p. 246

Martinéz, J.L.:
Industrias del Ubierna SA - Ubisa: Prozesse, Politik und Strategie, in: Zink, K.J. (Ed.): Business Excellence durch TQM: Erfahrungen europäischer Unternehmen, Munich, Vienna 1994, pp. 118-120

Masing, W. (Ed.):
Handbuch Qualitätsmanagement, 3. completely reworked and extended ed., Munich 1994

Matsuda, T.:
„Organizational Intelligence" als Prozeß und als Produkt, in: Technologie & Management, Vol. 42 (1993), Issue 1, pp. 12-17

Momm, C.:
Organizational Intelligence. Das japanische Managementkonzept der Zukunft?, in: Technologie & Management, Vol. 42 (1993), Issue 1, pp. 45-46

Nakajiama, S.:
Introduction to TPM, Cambridge 1988

Neuberger, O.:
Das Mitarbeitergespräch, Munich 1973

Neumann, T.:
Integrierte Personalarbeit durch Projektmanagement - Die Rolle der Personalabteilung, in: Ackermann, K.-F. (Ed.): Reorganisation der Personalabteilung, Stuttgart 1994

N.N. (Brisa):
On the road to excellence, in: European Quality, w/o Vol. (1996), Sonderheft: 1996 European Quality Award, pp. 17-20

N.N. (automobil):
Was Automobilhersteller von ihren Zulieferantenzukünftig erwarten, in: VDI-Nachrichten, Vol. 47 (1993), No 28, p. 8

N.N. (quality):
Quality through Customer Care at Rank Xerox, in: Industrial Relations Review & Report, w/o Vol. (1993), No 544, p. 3

Nölle-Neumann, E.; Strümpel, B.:
Macht Arbeit krank? Macht Arbeit glücklich?, Munich, Zürich 1984

Odiorne, G.S.:
Management by Objectives: Führungssysteme für die achtziger Jahre, Munich 1980

Pall, G. A.:
Quality Process Management, Englewood Cliffs (New Jersey) 1987

Pfeifer, T.:
Qualitätsmanagement: Strategien, Methoden, Techniken, Munich, Vienna 1993

Pfeiffer, W.; Dögl, R.; Schneider, W.:
Das Technologie-Portfolio-Konzept als Tool zur strategischen Vorsteuerung von Innovationsaktivitäten, in: Wirtschaftsstudium, w/o Vol. (1989), Issue 8/9, p. 486

Pies, W.:
Effiziente Unfallverhütung durch basisnahe Sicherheitsarbeit unter Einbeziehung der Mitarbeiter, in: Ritter, A.; Zink, K.J. (Ed.): Gruppenorientierte Ansätze zur Förderung der Arbeitssicherheit, Berlin 1992

Porter, M.E.:
Wettbewerbsvorteile, Frankfurt 1986

Price, F.:
Perspectives - Educated power, in: The TQM Magazine, Vol. 5 (1993), No 3, p. 10

Ray, D.W.:
The missing in TQM ... trust, in: Journal for Quality and Participation, Vol. 17 (1994), Issue 3, pp. 64-67

Reich, R.; Copening, L.:
„Empowerment" without the rhetoric, in: Quality Progress, w/o Vol. (1994), Issue 6, pp. 35-37

Reichwald, R.; Schmelzer H.J.:
Durchlaufzeiten in der Entwicklung, Munich, Vienna 1990

Ritter, A.; Zink, K.J.:
Differenzierte Kleingruppenkonzepte als wesentlicher Bestandteil eines umfassenden, integrierenden Qualitätsmanagements, in: Zink, K.J. (Ed.): Qualität als Managementaufgabe, 3. ed., Landsberg / Lech 1994

Ritter, D.:
A tool for improvement using the Baldrige Criteria, in: National Productivity Review, Vol. 12 (1993), Issue 2, pp. 167-182

Ritz-Carlton Hotel Company (Ed.):
Application Summary, Atlanta 1992

Ritz-Carlton Hotel Company (Ed.):
Application Summary, Atlanta 1993

Rommel, R. et al.:
Einfach überlegen - Das Unternehmenskonzept, das die Schlanken schlank und die Schnellen schnell macht, Stuttgart 1993

Rückle, H.:
Feedback, in: Management Enzyklopädie, Band 3, 2. ed., Munich 1982

Rühl, G.:
Untersuchungen zur Arbeitsstrukturierung, in Industrial Engineering, Vol. 3 (1973), Issue 3, pp. 147-197

Runge, J.H.:
ISO 9000 - Ausgangsbasis auf dem Weg zum Qualitätsunternehmen, in: Bläsing, J.P. (Ed.): 10. Qualitätsleiterforum. Quality Based Management - Qualitätsbewußte Unternehmensführung, Munich 1992, pp. 119-166

Runge, J.H.:
Schlank durch Total Quality Management - Strategien für den Standort Deutschland, Frankfurt / Main, New York 1994

Sayle, A.J.:
Management Audits: The assessment of quality systems, London 1988, pp. 11-1 - 11-5

Schartner, H.:
Eine neue Rolle des Personalwesens bei BMW?, in: Personalführung, Vol. 23 (1990), Issue 1, pp. 32-37

Scheer, A.-W. :
EDV-orientierte Betriebswirtschaftslehre, 3. ed., Berlin, Heidelberg 1987

Scheer, A.-W. (Ed.):
Simultane Produktentwicklung, Munich 1992

Schöberl, O.:
Latzhosen oder Nadelstreifen: Umweltschutz als Personalführungs- aufgabe, in: Personalführung, Vol. 26 (1993), Issue 10, pp. 832-838

Schöler, H.R.:
QFD - eine Methode zur qualitätsgerechten Produktgestaltung, in: VDI-Z, Vol. 132 (1990), Issue 11, pp. 49-51

Scholz, R.; Vrohlings, A.:
Realisierung von Prozeßmanagement, in: Gaitanides, M. et al. (Ed.):
Prozeßmanagement - Konzepte, Umsetzungen und Erfahrungen des
Reengineering, Munich, Vienna 1994, pp. 21-36

Scholz, R.; Vrohlings A.:
Prozeß-Leistungs-Transparenz, in: Gaitanides, M. et al. (Ed.):
Prozeßmanagement - Konzepte, Umsetzungen und Erfahrungen des
Reengineering, Munich, Vienna 1994, pp. 57-98

Schulte, C.:
Personal-Controlling mit Kennzahlen, Munich 1989

Seath, I.:
Turning theory into practice, in: Managing Service Quality, w/o Vol.
(1993), Issue 6, pp. 35-37

Seghezzi, H.D., Hansen, J.R. (Ed.):
Qualitätsstrategien: Anforderungen an das Management der Zukunft,
Munich 1993

Shingo, S.:
Study of 'Toyota' Production System from Industrial Engineering Viewpoint, Cambridge 1989

Simon, H.:
Neue Konzepte für die Managementstrukturen der Zukunft, in: Zink, K.J.
(Ed.): Wettbewerbsfähigkeit durch innovative Strukturen und Konzepte,
Munich 1994, pp. 323-336

Six, B.; Kleinbeck, U.:
Arbeitsmotivation und Zufriedenheit, in: Roth, E. (Ed.): Organisationspsychologie, Enzyklopädie der Psychologie, Serie III, Band 3, Göttingen, Toronto, Zürich 1989

Smith, P.G.; Reinertsen, D.G.:
Developing Products in Half the Time, New York 1991

Soin, S.S.:
Total Quality Control Essentials: Key elements, methodologies and
managing for success, New York 1992

Sommerlatte, T.; Wedekind, E.:
Leistungsprozesse und Organisationsstruktur, in: Little, A.D. (Ed.): Management der Hochleistungsorganisation, Wiesbaden 1990, pp. 23-41

Specht, G.; Schmelzer, H.J.:
Instrumente des Qualitätsmanagements in der Produktentwicklung, in: Zeitschrift für betriebswirtschaftliche Forschung, Vol. 44 (1992), Issue 6, pp. 531-547

Staehle, W.H.:
Management. Eine verhaltenswissenschaftliche Perspektive, 7. ed., reworked by Conrad, P.; Sydow, J., Munich 1994

Steeples, M.M.:
The corporate guide to the Malcolm Baldrige National Quality Award - proven strategies for building quality into your organisation, 2. ed., Milwaukee (Wisc.) 1993

Striening, H.-D.:
Prozeß-Management - Versuch eines integrierten Konzeptes situationsadäquater Gestaltung von Verwaltungsprozessen, Frankfurt / Main 1988

Stone, S.; Ashworth, S.:
Milliken Carpet - customer and staff satisfaction, in: Zink, K.J.: Successful TQM: inside stories from European Quality Award winners, Hampshire 1997, pp. 139-149

Sullivan, L.P.:
Quality Function Deployment, in: Quality Progress, w/o Vol. (1986), June, p. 50

Suzaki, K.:
Die ungenutzten Potentiale - Neues Management im Produktionsbetrieb, Munich, Vienna 1994

Takeuchi, H.; Nonaka, I.:
The new product development game, in: Harvard Business Review, without Volume (1986), January-February, pp. 137-146

Tannenbaum, R.; Schmidt, W.H.:
How to choose a leadership pattern, in: Havard Business Review, w/o Vol. (1958), No 2, pp. 95-101

Tavolato, P; Vicena, K.:
Prototyping Methodology and its Tool, in: Budde, R. et al. (Ed.):
Approaches to Prototyping, Heidelberg, New York 1984

Taylor, F.W.:
The Principles of Scientific Management, New York 1911

Terrell, P. (Ed.):
Pons Großwörterbuch Deutsch-Englisch, Englisch-Deutsch, Teil II:
Englisch-Deutsch, Stuttgart 1991

Texas Instruments (Ed.):
Semiconductor Group Total Quality, Dallas 1994

Texas Instruments - Defense Systems & Electronics Group (Ed.):
Malcolm Baldrige Application Summary, Dallas 1992

Thom, N.:
Grundlagen des betrieblichen Innovationsmanagements, 2. ed., Bern
1980

Thorsud, E.:
Demokratisierung der Arbeitsorganisation - einige konkrete Methoden
zur Neustrukturierung des Arbeitsplatzes, in: Vilmar, F. (Ed.): Men-
schenwürde im Betrieb, Hamburg 1973, pp. 117-132

Töpfer, A., Mehdorn, H. (Ed.):
Total Quality Management: Anforderungen und Umsetzung im Unternehmen, 3. ed., Neuwied, Kriftel, Berlin 1994

Toyota Motor Corporation (Ed.):
The Customer Fight - TQC at Toyota, w/o location 1992

Turner, L.; Dröge, W.:
Rank Xerox Europe Ltd - resources, impact on society and business
results, in: Zink, K.J.: Successful TQM: inside stories from European
Quality Award winners, Hampshire 1997, pp.65-81

Turner, L.; Droege, W.:
Rank Xerox Ltd.: Ressourcen, Auswirkungen auf die Gesellschaft und
Geschäftsergebnisse, in: Zink, K.J. (Ed.): Business Excellence durch
TQM: Erfahrungen europäischer Unternehmen, Munich, Vienna 1994,
pp. 147-168

Ulich, E.; Conrad-Betschart, H.; Baitsch, C.:
Arbeitsform mit Zukunft: ganzheitlich-flexibel statt arbeitsteilig, Bern 1989

Ulrich, P.; Fluri, E.:
Management , Eine konzentrierte Einführung, 6. revised and expanded ed., Bern, Stuttgart 1992

United States Department of Commerce (Ed.):
The Malcolm Baldrige National Quality Award - 1994 Award Criteria, Gaithersburg (Mass.) 1993

United States Department of Commerce (Ed.):
The Malcolm Baldrige National Quality Award - 1995 Award Criteria, Gaithersburg (Mass.) 1994

Wagenstaller, H.:
Modularbeit bei BMW, in: Zink, K.J. (Ed.): Erfolgreiche Konzepte zur Gruppenarbeit - Aus Erfahrungen lernen, Neuwied 1995, pp. 237-252

Waldron, S.; Hurdle, T.:
BOC Special Gases: Führung durch Mitarbeiterorientierung, in: Zink, K.J. (Ed.): Business Excellence durch TQM: Erfahrungen europäischer Unternehmen, Munich, Vienna 1994, pp. 102-107

Wallace, G.W.:
Empowerment is work, not magic, in: Journal for Quality and Participation, Vol. 16 (1993), Issue 5, pp. 10-14

Warnecke, H.J.:
Revolution der Unternehmenskultur - Die Fraktale Fabrik, 2. ed., Berlin 1994

Watson, G.H.:
Benchmarking - vom Besten lernen, Landsberg / Lech 1993

Wellins, R.S.; Byham, W.C.; Wilson, J.M.:
Empowered Teams, San Francisco 1991

Wernick, S.:
Self-directed Work Teams and Empowerment, in: Journal for Quality and Participation, Vol. 17 (1994), Issue 4, pp. 34-36

Wheelwright, S.C.; Clark, K.B.:
Revolution der Produktentwicklung, Frankfurt / Main, New York 1994

Whiteley, R.C.:
The Customer Driven Company, Moving from Talk to Action, The Forum Corporation, Reading (Mass.) 1992

Wildemann, H.:
Das Just-In-Time-Konzept, Produktion und Beschaffung auf Abruf, 2. ed., Frankfurt 1990

Wildemann, H.:
Kosten- und Leistungsbeurteilung von Qualitätssicherungssystemen, in: Zeitschrift für Betriebswirtschaft, Vol. 62 (1992), Issue 7, pp. 761-782

Wildemann, H.:
Zeit als Wettbewerbsinstrument in der Informations- und Wertschöpfungskette, in: Wildemann, H. (Ed.): Zeitmanagement, Frankfurt / Main 1992, pp. 15-24

Willenbacher, K.:
Qualitätsmanagement in der Praxis, in: Zink, K.J. (Ed.): Qualität als Mangementaufgabe, 3. ed., Landsberg 1994

Wolfrum, B.:
Grundgedanke, Formen und Aussagewert von Technologieportfolios (I), in: Wirtschaftsstudium, w/o Vol. (1992), Issue 4, p. 319

Womack, J.P.; Jones, D.T.; Roos, D.:
The Machine That Changed The World: Based on the Massachusetts Institute of Technology 5-million-Dollar 5-year study on the future of the automobile, New York 1990

Zahn, E.; Braun, F.; Dogan, D.; Weidler, A.:
Ganzheitliche Produktentwicklung als Schlüssel zur Reduzierung von Entwicklungszeiten, in: Scheer, A.-W. (Ed.): Simultane Produktentwicklung, Munich 1992, pp. 429-484

Zink, K.J.:
Traditionelle und neuere Ansätze der Organisationsentwicklung, in: Zink, K.J. et al. (Ed.): Industrial Engineering und Organisationsentwicklung im kommenden Dezennium, Munich 1979, pp. 61-75

Zink, K.J.:
Qualitätszirkel, in: Strunz, H. (Ed.): Handbuch Personalmarketing, Wiesbaden 1989, pp. 542-554

Zink, K.J.:
Quality Circles - noch ein Thema? in: Personalführung, Vol. 23 (1990), Issue 3, pp. 147-153

Zink, K.J.:
Selbststeuerung im Rahmen differentieller und dynamischer Aus-bildungskonzepte, in: Arnold, R. (Ed.): Taschenbuch der betrieblichen Bildungsarbeit, Hohengehren 1991, pp. 190-199

Zink, K.J.:
Simultaneous Engineering und Total Quality Management, in: Scheer, A.-W. (Ed.): Simultane Produktentwicklung, Munich 1992, pp. 485-515

Zink, K.J.:
Qualitätszirkel und Lernstatt, in: Frese, E. (Ed.): Handwörterbuch der Organisation, 3. ed., Stuttgart 1992, column 2133-2140

Zink, K.J.:
Partizipative Konzepte in der Fabrik der Zukunft, in: Milling, P.; Zäpfel, G. (Ed.): Betriebswirtschaftliche Grundlagen moderner Produktions-strukturen, Herne, Berlin 1993, pp. 267-280

Zink, K.J. (Ed.):
Business Excellence durch TQM - Erfahrungen europäischer Unter-nehmen, Munich, Vienna 1994

Zink, K.J. (Ed.):
Qualität als Managementaufgabe - Total Quality Management, 3. ed., Landsberg / Lech 1994

Zink, K.J.:
Prozeßorientierung - ein Baustein umfassender Veränderungskonzepte, in: Zülch, G. (Ed.): Vereinfachen und verkleinern - die neue Strategie in der Produktion, Stuttgart 1994, pp. 53-84

Zink, K.J.:
Qualität als europäische Herausforderung, in: Zink, K.J. (Ed.): Business Excellence durch TQM: Erfahrungen europäischer Unternehmen, Munich, Vienna 1994, pp. 9-52

Zink, K.J.:
Total Quality Management, in: Zink, K.J. (Ed.): Qualität als Managementaufgabe, 3. ed., Landsberg / Lech 1994

Zink, K.J. et al.:
Qualitätsmanagement in der innerbetrieblichen Umsetzung: Schlüsselfaktoren und Erfahrungen, 2. ed., Karlsruhe 1995

Zink, K.J.:
Erfolgreiche Konzepte zur Gruppenarbeit - Aus Erfahrungen lernen, Neuwied 1995

Zink, K.J.; Blickle, G.; Ritter, A.:
Lernen als kooperative Problembewältigung vor Ort - Arbeitsstrukturierung, qualifizierende Arbeitsgestaltung, Problemlösungsgruppen, in: Arnold, R. (Ed.): Taschenbuch der betrieblichen Bildungsarbeit, Hohengehren 1991, pp. 179-190

Zink, K.J.; Braig, D.:
Mitarbeiterbeteiligung bei Innovations- und kontinuierlichen Verbesserungsprozessen, in: Reichwald, R., Wildemann, H. (Ed.): Kreative Unternehmen - Spitzenqualität durch Produkt- und Prozeßinnovationen, Suttgart 1995, pp. 286-298

Zink, K.J.; Hauer, R.; Schmidt, A.:
Quality Assessment: Instrument zur Analyse von Qualitätskonzepten auf der Basis von EN 29000, Malcolm Baldrige Award und European Quality Award, in: Qualität und Zuverlässigkeit, Vol. 37 (1992), Issue 10, pp. 585-590 and Issue 11, pp. 651-658

Zink, K.J.; Ritter, A.:
Quality Circles - ein Instrumentarium partizipativer Gestaltung und Einführung neuer Informationstechnologien, in: Computer & Recht, Vol. 6 (1990), Issue 2, pp. 147-152

Zink, K.J.; Ritter, A.; Thul, M.:
Kleingruppenunterstützte Prozeßinnovationen, Bonn 1993

Zink, K.J.; Schick, G.:
Quality Circles 1 - Grundlagen, 2. reworked ed., Munich, Vienna 1987

Zink, K.J.; Schmidt, A.:
Quality Assessments als zukunftsorientierte Instrumentarien zur Unternehmensbewertung und -entwicklung, in: Nedeß, C. (Ed.): Produktion im Umbruch - Herausforderungen an das Management, Hochschulgruppe Arbeits- und Betriebsorganisation HAB e.V. Forschungsbericht 5, Munich 1993, pp. 339-386

Zülch, G. (Hrsg.):
Vereinfachen und verkleinern - die neue Strategie in der Produktion, Stuttgart 1994

List of Abbreviations

AEE   Association of Energy Engineers

AIF   Arbeitsgemeinschaft Industrieller Forschungsvereinigungen (Industrial Research Organization)

ASU   Abgassonderuntersuchung (compulsory annual test of car`s emission level)

BSHG Bundessozialhilfegesetz (German Federal Social Welfare Law)

CAD   Computer-Aided Design

CAQ   Computer-Aided Quality Assuranc

CBT   Computer-Based Training

CEO   Chief Executive Officer

CIB   Computer-Integrated Business

CIM   Computer-Integrated Manufacturing

CIP   Continous Improvement Process

DFA   Design for Assembly

DFM   Design for Manufacturability

DIN   Deutsches Institut für Normung e.V. (German Standardization Organization)

DM   Divison Manager

EC   European Community

EDP   Electronic Data Processing

EFQM European Foundation for Quality

EN   European Norm

EOQ   European Organization for Quality

EQA   European Quality Award

EU   European Union

FMEA Failure Mode and Effect Analysis

GL   Group Leader

HDP   Head of Department

HSS   High-shelved Storage

IPDB   Individual Professional Development Plan

ISO   International Standardization Organization

JIT   Just-in-Time

MBA   Master of Business Administration

MbO   Management by Objectives

MBNQA   Malcolm Baldrige National Quality Award

MIT   Massachusetts Institute of Technology

MITI   Ministry of International Trade and Industry

MTBF Mean Time Between Failures

OA   Output Assigned

O.D.   Organizational Development

O.I.   Organizational Intelligence

ON   Output Neutral   SQC   Statistical Quality Control

PCM   Part Count Methode   TQ   Total Quality

PDCA Plan, Do, Check, Act   TOP   Team-oriented Production

QC   Quality Circle   TPM   Total Productive Maintenance

QFD   Quality Function Deployment   TPS   Toyota Production System

QIT   Quality Improvement Team   TQC   Total Quality Control

QM   Quality Management   TQM   Total Quality Management

SPC   Statistical Process Control   VDI   Verein Deutscher Ingenieure e.V.
                                             (German Organization of
SPS   Small Parts Storage   Engineers)

Index

S

Segmentation
  customer-oriented 72
Self-appraisal 56
Self-Assessment 146; 221
  Achievement Matrix 236
  Award Simulation 239
  Consensus 240; 244
  Data Gathering 233
  Frame Conditions 224
  Improvement Actions 233
  Information 225
  On-Site-Visit 243
  Pilot-Assessment 226
  Process 227
  Questionaires 236
  Review Cycles 225
  Submission 237
  Teams 226
  Training 232
  Workshop 232
Self-managing Work Group 13; 20; 294
Shareholder Value 206
Simultaneous Engineering 2
Single Sourcing 28
Solving problems 1
Success Factors
  critical 155; 156
Suggestion Scheme
  Company 130
  decentralized 131
Supplier
  Assessment 148
  Information System 149
  Partnership 149
  Reduction 149
  Relationships 147; 148
Surrounding Area 101
Survey 189
Survey- and feedback methods 21
System Supplier 147

T

Taylorism 13
Teams 124
  cross-functional 148; 164; 166; 167
  cross-funtional 163
  global-oriented 129
  industry-wide 148
  Module Teams 169
  process-oriented 170
Teamwork
  Training 54
Technology
  Improvement 155
Technology-Portfolio 153
Top-down Training Concept 53
Total Productive Maintenance 149;
  150
Total Quality Control 2
Total Quality Culture 97
Total Quality Management 38
  Co-ordinator 77
  Evaluation Concept 39
  Introduction
    Communication 83
    Misunderstandings 85
    Release of Resources 84
    Staff Turnover 84
    Philosophy 41
    Works Council 84
  Steering Committee 77
  Support 98
  Tools 80
Toyota Production System 11; 19
TPS *see Toyota Production System*
TQM *see Total Quality Management*
Training 56
Train-the-Trainer 54
Transfer of Technology 168

Druck: Strauss Offsetdruck, Mörlenbach
Verarbeitung: Schäffer, Grünstadt